SUPPORT YOUR LOCAL LEAGUE

A SOUTH EAST ASIAN FOOTBALL ODYSSEY

SUPPORT YOUR LOCAL LEAGUE

A SOUTH EAST ASIAN FOOTBALL ODYSSEY

ANTONY SUTTON

First published in 2018 by Fair Play Publishing
PO Box 4101, Balgowlah Heights NSW 2093 Australia
www.fairplaypublishing.com.au
sales@fairplaypublishing.com.au

ISBN: 978-0-6481333-2-2

ISBN: 978-0-6484073-1-7 (ePub)

© Antony Sutton 2018

The moral rights of the author have been asserted.

All rights reserved. Except as permitted under the Australian Copyright Act 1968 (for example, a fair dealing for the purposes of study, research, criticism or review), no part of this book may be reproduced, stored in a retrieval system, communicated or transmitted in any form or by any means without prior written permission from the Publisher.

Design and typesetting by Retta Laraway, Looksee Design.

All photographs supplied by the author

All inquiries should be made to the Publisher via sales@fairplaypublishing.com.au

 A catalogue record for this book is available from the National Library of Australia

Disclaimer

To the maximum extent permitted by law, the authors and publisher disclaim all responsibility and liability to any person, arising directly or indirectly from any person taking or not taking action based on the information in this publication.

CONTENTS

Introduction 1

Part 1: Singapore

1. The SLeague Experience 4
2. Where Have All The Heroes Gone? 14
3. A Japanese Experience In Singapore 20
4. The Lions' First Roar 29

Part 2: Malaysia

5. Malaysia's First Super Club 40
6. The Failed Groundhopper 54
7. The Story Of Super Mokh 67
8. Football's Uniform Fetish 75

Part 3: Thailand

9. Just A Football Fan Hanging Out On Pattaya Beach ... 89
10. Chonburi & The Rise Of Representative Football Clubs ... 101
11. Bangkok's Football Mile 113

Part 4: Indonesia

12. A Lesson In Geography 119
13. Double Trouble 128
14. Football On The Big Screen 145
15. Jakarta, The Football Crazy City Of Malls 151

16.	Indonesian Clubs Take To Asia	160
17.	The World Cup Star Who Made Indonesia Home	167
18.	Bandung Is Blue	175
19.	Persib, A Way Of Life	185
20.	Give Youth A Chance	200
21.	The Good, The Bad, & The Ugly	207
22.	May The Green Force Be With You	223
23.	Choirul Huda - 100% Lamongan	240
	Acknowledgements	250
	About Me	251

Who'd be a linesman?

INTRODUCTION

I am often asked why I follow South East Asian football, and unfortunately my answer seems to leave people somewhat underwhelmed. 'Because I live here.' I'm not sure what people were expecting but the answer is as mundane as they come.

As I look back though it dawns on me. I started my blog, Jakarta Casual, in 2006, around about the time my frustrations with Arsenal, and their French manager Arsene Wenger, came to the fore. Was I looking for a surrogate Arsenal until we woke up to the reality, our French legend who had thrilled us so much for the first ten years of his time at the Arsenal had lost his mojo and it was unlikely to return? Or was I just continuing where I had left off in Australia, where I had spent my weekends following St George in the old National Soccer League, and Germany, where I divided my time between 1FC Koln and Bayer Leverkusen, before heading to the Alps and watching FC Bayern Munich home games?

Jakarta Casual started in Indonesia, expanded to Singapore and spread out to Malaysia and Thailand. Long weekends would be spent flying Asia's friendly skies courtesy of the budget airlines that were springing up at the time. Watching football would take me to places I never thought I would ever visit; Samarinda, Madura, Chonburi, Palembang. Along the way I would be treated with massive friendliness... usually. Curiosity occasionally. Why, local thinking would go, would this big white guy be watching our local team? So, they would ask me, 'Are you a coach?' 'Are you a scout?' 'Are you lost?' Even, once or twice 'Are you a player?'

Whatever the reason, something that I had started almost as a time killer to keep me out of the pub before getting married went on to become a massive part of my life and through it I met heaps of bloody good football fans who shared my passion for football, south east Asia, and yes, the odd beer or seven.

South East Asian football has been good to me, but as I have aged my priorities have changed. In recent years I have focused less on Singapore, Malaysia, and Thailand but that is due less to apathy and more to wanting to see my son grow up. I can no longer justify weekends in Bangkok watching Thai Port, when my lad is out playing football himself.

I have tried through the pages of this book to capture some of the atmosphere of football in the region that keeps me coming back for more. The places, the flavours, and most of all the people.

They say football is the world language and it truly is. I am typing this foreword in Cairo, where the name Mohamed Salah, the Liverpool striker, will start conversations in the same way that Atep does in Bandung, Fandi Ahmad does in Singapore, Bambang Pamumgkas does in Jakarta, and Liam Brady in the red part of North London.

In my mind I can see the heaving terraces of PSS, Persib, Persebaya et al, witnessing the passion, the colour of the faithful.

The football terrace anywhere in the world is a window on the local culture you won't find in any guidebook. A living, heaving cauldron of chaos, and beauty on stone steps chanting with one voice. What player cannot help but be inspired to go out and play for those supporters week in, week out. What well-travelled football fan doesn't want to witness it, at least once.

Antony Sutton

October 2018

PART 1: SINGAPORE

Singapore's National Stadium, home of the Kallang Roar

1.
THE SLEAGUE EXPERIENCE

I've been lucky. Over the years I've seen games in England, Germany, Italy, as well as Australia, Indonesia, and Singapore. One thing I learnt early on was to never compare. The game of football is the same, a bunch of people kick a ball around and blame the ref when they lose, and that for me is a major part of the appeal of football.

The war on the terraces of 1980s England has been replaced by rubber necking tourists, synchronised rah rahs, and slick marketing. In Germany, the match day experience was defined by the drinking of beer then claiming a refund from the empty plastic glass! Indonesia's fans are young, passionate, and enthusiastic, and it's a major factor behind the sheer unbridled enthusiasm that flows down from the terraces each game.

Football is the world-wide game with unified rules, but football also mirrors its host society. Fans brought up on a diet of the English Premier League on TV shouldn't go to a SLeague match expecting to see thousands of fans singing, *You'll Never Walk Alone* with arms held aloft because that just isn't going to happen. Instead, sit back and enjoy the football, Singapore style.

The fans, like the country, are disciplined, and squeaky clean. The Eastern Derby between Tampines Rovers and Geylang United isn't going to be accompanied by brawling fans disrupting passengers on the MRT. The people are too 'nice.' The, at times, deafening tannoy even welcomes visiting supporters and hopes they enjoy their short stay between the best of chipmunk rock.

That's not to say there isn't any abuse. We are, after all, talking about football. But this is Singapore and yelling at the match officials is usually prefixed with an 'excuse me.'

In such an orderly society it is perhaps surprising to see regulation breaking going on inside the stadiums. Match tickets specifically state, '... banners, flags, poles, airhorns, whistles, drums, musical instruments,' are prohibited but fan club members, it seems, are exempted!

What atmosphere there is in the SLeague comes from these fan clubs, often with cheerleaders, who make the most of the percussion instruments they managed to smuggle past unsuspecting stewards, singing songs that vary little from club to club. Go, go, go (insert team name here) go; fight, fight, fight (insert team name here) fight; win, win, win (insert team name here) win; we are the (insert team name here) fans.

The anonymity of the players in the SLeague keeps football real to a degree many other countries have forgotten. Tell me another league where you will see the leading goal scorer queuing up for a bus after the game with his wife and children? While the media concentrates on players in the west holding their clubs ransom or boasting about spending big cash on a Bentley, it is refreshing and indeed 'real' to see said striker standing patiently at the stop, ignored by all but a blogger, a football journalist, and a fan.

Singapore, of course, is a go-ahead kind of place and it is fitting that the league used to have its very own official convergence communication partner and fair play to those fine people for supporting the game. Now, if only we knew what they actually did!

But for me, what defines the SLeague experience as uniquely Singaporean comes at half time when older spectators nip outside for a quick cigarette, while younger fan club members and cheerleaders settle down on the stone terrace and dig into a packed lunch that has been provided for them. Food, the very essence of Singapore! Indeed, so concentrated on their food are the fans that many times the second half kicks off in absolute silence as spectators negotiate that last piece of fried chicken and rice.

It's easy to have a pop at Singapore football. I know, I have been doing it for years! Dwindling crowds, apathetic media, and a crowded fixture list that can see teams potentially play each other in five competitive games over the course of a single season, are just fodder for the cynics.

If I was a visitor-obsessed blogger, I would have given up covering Singapore football years ago. The interviews attract the fewest visitors to my YouTube channel, Jakarta Casual TV, while my posts generally attract no response unless I am having a good old fashioned whine... then check the stats! But despite the sarcasm and irony I sometimes direct towards football here, I do have a soft spot for it. A massive soft spot. It annoys the crap out of me that a country that can go from being a bunch of kampungs (semi-rural villages) to a world class nation boasting an airport that is a destination in itself in half a century, does so little for its football.

It bugs me that everywhere you go you see people wearing Liverpool, Manchester United, or Arsenal shirts, yet SLeague replica shirts are like hens' teeth. In all my visits to catch football here, I have seen the odd Geylang shirt on the bus or the train but that is about it. In fact, I have seen more Kelantan shirts in Singapore than I have seen Home United, Tampines Rovers, or Young Lions shirts.

A sad indictment of the attitude to the local game here and a sadder indictment that I should even notice that kind of thing!

The SLeague began back in 1996, and since then only Singapore Armed Forces (eight times), Tampines Rovers (five), Geylang United, Home United (twice each), and Etoile with a single title, have won the title. Etoile were a short-lived French-backed team who won the league in 2010 at their first attempt.

Short-lived is a phrase often used in Singapore football. No fewer than seven teams have only spent one season in the league (Dalian Shide, Liaoning Guangyuan, Beijing Guoan (all from China), Paya Lebar Punggol (well, under that particular name at least), Sporting Afrique, Harimau Muda

A and Harimau Muda B (the latter two from Malaysia), while just six of the current 12 team set up have been involved since the first season in 1996.

Other clubs seem to come and go. And come back again. Tanjong Pagar United, for example, came back for a second spell, while Gombak United also had two spells but are currently taking a hiatus! In all, 25 teams have played a part in the SLeague, including 10 foreign teams. When I began researching this chapter in 2014, Malaysia's Harimau Muda B were joined by Albirex Niigata from Japan (there is also a team with the same name playing in Cambodia's CLeague), and DPMM from Brunei in a 10 team league. By 2018, the SLeague was down to nine teams with two foreign sides, Albirex and DPMM.

Against the backdrop of falling attendances, clubs, and the Singapore Football Association have been wracking their brains to try and arrest the slide. A couple years ago, the SLeague came under fire for releasing crowd figures that clearly bore no relation to the reality in the stadium. The official attendance would include members of the media, VIPs, and the number of free tickets distributed by the clubs and sponsors, as well as the number of tickets actually sold, a familiar scenario to Arsenal fans but even more noticeable in a small, near empty stadium It was obvious though that not all issued tickets were being used, and after some media complaints the authorities just stopped announcing crowds. An odd decision for sure, as it just gives the perception that the people who run the game are not too keen on transparency.

There does seem to be some kind of league marketing policy in play, but it is low key and seems to revolve around giving things away. For example, fans turning up for a top of the table clash between Tampines Rovers v DPMM I attended, needed a wheelbarrow to carry all the freebies home. There were tubes of potato crisps, ice cream, those little handheld fan things, and a clapper that doubled as the match day programme. Or is it a match day programme that doubles as a clapper?

An aside. As I approached the ticket office to buy my ticket for the game, the staff behind the window were busy packing away the potato crisps. A fan approached me and without a word, handed me a match ticket and in I strolled, free, the ticket office staff just smiling!

- What do all these freebies say about football in general, and Singapore football in particular?
- Consumers, of course, love something for nothing!
- An article in Time magazine once suggested there were five ways that companies win by offering freebies to consumers:
- Customers feel obligated to buy more.
- When given something for free, customers are more likely to pay more for it later.
- Getting more is seen as superior to getting discounts.
- People buy more when there is an element of mystery.
- People talk more about free gifts.

This is all well and good, but the SLeague is actually giving nothing away. It is the sponsors. The company that makes the potato crisps is getting a higher profile, not the football clubs. The fan who got the free crisps may be in a mini mart, see the same crisps and buy them because they are familiar with them. But what is in it for the football club?

In all my 40-odd years of watching football, I have never felt the offer of a free iced lolly was sufficient to get me to make the effort to go to a football match.

It would be interesting to know the rationale behind this spate of freebie giving and what would define success, or the key performance indicators in Singaporean business school speak, but in a country where attendances are a secret I guess we will never know.

So, while the FA tries to attract fans to a healthy activity by giving them food packed with sugar and fat, some supporters, those at Hougang United and Geylang International spring to mind, have been doing their own thing when it comes to creating their own terrace culture. And that, after all, is the way football support and culture has developed in other countries, from the bottom up. But, who knows. Singapore is a country used to initiatives coming from up high, individuality is discouraged. For now, empirical evidence suggests attendances are levelling or to quote the cynics, flatlining — much like the game.

Back to the Tampines game, beyond the free food on offer at the main gate, there didn't seem to be much going on in the way of marketing. Plenty of Tampines fans — I use the word plenty, but a good description would be about a dozen or so — were wearing replica shirts but there didn't seem to be anywhere you could buy them. Tampines, the champions in the previous three seasons, came from behind to win 2-1 against the team who were top of the table in what was a very good game of football.

After the game, Tampines' veteran striker, the 43-year-old, Aleksander Duric, was kept busy by young fans who wanted their picture taken with him or to have him sign their shirts. Duric obliged, patiently standing in the steady drizzle, making the kids and their parents very happy indeed.

Steve Kean, the DPMM coach who was widely loathed during his stint with Blackburn Rovers recently, was ignored. For the faithful, Alex was the man.

Forget the likes of Wayne Rooney and Ashley Cole with their 'celebrity' lifestyles and their WAGS in tow, if Aleksander Duric ever wants a book written about him, I would volunteer to do it for him. Born in Yugoslavia, competed for Bosnia in the 1992 Olympics, took out Australian nationality in a bid to play for the Socceroos, made his Singapore debut in 2007, and now lives in Malaysia, Duric is globalisation wrapped up in one neat, professional package, and an absolute gentleman to boot. Just ask those kids at Clementi Stadium, standing in the rain to get close to their hero.

As Duric was catering to the next generation of Singapore football fans, I was standing alongside Chris Harvey. An English expat who has spent bloody yonks in Lion City, Chris lives and breathes football, a passion he is passing on to his son. With a bit of time on his hands, the Torquay United fan has teamed up with a Singaporean friend to resurrect Players, a football magazine devoted to the beautiful game in the city state.

Chris probably has the largest collection of Torquay United programmes not just in Singapore but probably throughout South East Asia. For him, football is more than just 11 people kicking a ball with Germany winning on penalties. He sees football as the ultimate community builder, which needs to offer fans something tangible.

He has a point. Until the introduction of the clapper come programme, there was nothing for fans to identify who was who on the field. The team sheets were for the media while the MC ran through the line ups, 'wearing jersey number 12...' quickly ahead of kick off. That was it. There was nothing a fan could hang their hat on; nothing to help them identify with the players of the teams because they didn't know who they were. And websites aren't much cop.

For a country so enthralled by business school speak — you are never far from a hub or being leveraged in Singapore — the fact that the game has done nothing to develop the SLeague and the teams as brands is one of those things that mystify me about the country.

Chris loves football, loves Singapore, and wants to create a game with names a new generation of fans can identify with. 'I want to see kids... put the pictures of the players on their bedroom walls in the same way you (he means me) and I did when we were young. I want them to feel that they are part of football and football is part of them. That it is a community.'

Our conversation went on long into the night. Long after the punk-looking waitress had served up our last beer and the food court had been shuttered up and the staff gone home. Our conversation went on as we climbed into a taxi to begin our trans island ride home.

As we paused for breath, another voice joined our conversation. It was the taxi driver! He remembered the good old days of 1994 when Singapore had last won the Malaysia Cup, defeating Pahang 4-0 up in Kuala Lumpur. It's the Lion City's equivalent of catching the Sex Pistols at the 100 Club back in 1976. Everyone was there, if not in person then stashed away with the other sperm in their father's ball bag awaiting the thrill of ejaculation.

And yet. Instead of building on that triumph, in the eyes of many, the opportunity was fritted away. Singapore withdrew from the historic trophy to concentrate on developing the SLeague, which commenced two years later. The fans, bemused, started to lose interest. The players were not as good, the coaches were not as good, are still common refrains. Our taxi driver was singing from the same song sheet.

He liked football. He wanted to see a team, but he felt alienated by the SLeague. Teams like Tampines Rovers and Woodlands Wellington failed to find common cause with people in their backyards yet stick a footballer in a red Singapore shirt and everyone was a fan.

Which in one respect is odd. Around the world people mostly associate themselves with their local side be it West Ham United, St Pauli, or Persipura Jayapura. Yet the Singaporeans seem reluctant to support the team that plays round the corner from their flat or their favourite food court.

The idea that the old days were better is nothing new of course. Today, there are Arsenal fans unfavourably comparing Olivier Giroud with Thierry Henry for example. We are all guilty of sepia tinged nostalgia. Hell, my old man recently told me the last decent prime minister the UK had was Margaret Thatcher! You should have heard the vitriol he would spew at the TV screen when she was in power but now, with the benefit of hindsight, he was viewing her in a different light. 'Anyway,' he added, 'she had balls.'

The Class of '94 was before my time unfortunately. Then, I was a poverty-stricken, drunken English teacher in Bangkok. Jakarta Casual and an interest in South East Asian football was 12 years further down the line. But 1994 remains very real for a great many Singaporeans, people like our taxi driver. For years, the game has done nothing to stop the fan haemorrhage and now its efforts, with free ice cream for goodness sake, feel like the captain of the Titanic asking the violinist to use his case to scoop water off the deck.

The challenge is for the Singapore FA to connect with the thousands who used to fill the National Stadium and used to regularly cross the Causeway to watch away games and free ice cream won't do that.

I said earlier if I was more clinical, I would have long dropped Singapore from my football coverage. I haven't, and I have no plans to do so in the near future. Others have taken on the baton and done a bloody good job in spreading the word, be they bloggers, Tweeps, or fans on the terraces. In my 12 years watching Singapore football, I have met some top, top people with their own passion for the game in their backyard. For me, its ability to regularly shoot itself in the foot, given that most of the country remains cynical and aloof, are reasons enough to stick by it.

I have great respect for those who go against the grain at the best of times, and fans who follow Singapore football certainly do swim against the tide. Fair play to them for that. And having seen the effect Aleksander Duric had on those young fans, from hearing Chris Harvey's passion, and from listening to the lost football fan, the taxi driver from the 1990s, there are obviously people out there who care about the game. Chris, for example and the cabbie who doesn't quite get modern football yet still loves the game. And got so wrapped up in the conversation, he forgot to turn the meter on!

It's funny, but looking back on the evening, never once did we discuss where Wayne Rooney should play or how good Ross Barkley is, according to the media following the England team. Which is another funny thing. Just think about all the websites out there, all the newspapers. And they all tend to lead with pretty much the same story or stories. The football media offers up the same tales of Coach X wants to win, Player Y wants the fans to get behind the team, and Agent Z is using the papers to increase his commission. It bugs the crap out of me. I can be sitting in a bar on a Wednesday in Jakarta reading a story that appeared in an English newspaper on the Tuesday that first broke on the internet on Monday and wasn't interesting even then!

There are a heap of stories in this region that are newsworthy, but we never hear about them because editors prefer to use one or two day old wire copy from the other side of the world! Or if we hear about them there is little in the way of follow up because the next day everyone is publishing a story about how some international has the sulks because he never got a birthday cake!

Football matters everywhere. Singapore football matters but to an ever dwindling audience. Is it doomed or is there light at the end of the seemingly infinite tunnel?

2.
WHERE HAVE ALL THE HEROES GONE?

I probably visit Singapore at least half a dozen times a year and love the place, but it is fair to say the local tourist promotion board won't be calling me to act as any kind of visitor ambassador any time soon. I fly in on a budget airline, travel by bus into Joo Chiat and stay in a backpacker's type place. I move around the island on the bus or, for longer journeys, the train, known as MRT, and eat in food courts or coffee shops.

I also avoid Orchard Road, that sacred home to consumerist suckers who have sold their souls, and credit status, to emporiums flogging overpriced crap made by underpaid workers. Nope, not exactly a poster child for Singapore tourism!

My trips down to Orchard are fortunately infrequent, and usually involve catching up with someone to jaw jaw about football. They also involve me getting lost inside some frightful mall where signs and information, along with clocks, are at a premium. They have no interest in consumers, what an awful word, knowing where the nearest exit is or what the time is. Just stay and hand over your cash you mugs is their motto.

After going up and down escalators for an age, I plucked up the courage to go and ask one of those people standing behind a desk saying Concierge. 'Outside, turn left,' said the unsmiling automaton. She probably sensed no one was going to get rich quick off me.

I finally found the loathsome coffee shop where I had arranged to meet Mustafic Fahruddin, the Tampines Rovers central defender. I sat down opposite the 33-year-old Singaporean international and I swear within one minute, Steve MacMahon, sitting at another table, got up and left. One minute! Oh, the delicious irony for me, an Arsenal fan! It was worth coming into Orchard just for that!

I'd first met Farra in 2009, when he had moved to Persija Jakarta in Indonesia. It was the start of a fairly successful spell in the country. Although he was released at the end of the season, par for the course there, he was snapped up by Persela Lamongan in East Java, a small but homely club that may lack the glamour of provincial rivals Persebaya Surabaya and Arema Malang but at least the players get looked after.

The previous night, Tampines had defeated DPMM Brunei 2-1 at Clementi Stadium after coming from behind, and understandably Farra was on a non-caffeine high, describing the win as one of their best performances of the season. It was certainly an important win; had DPMM taken the three points, they would have moved nine points clear of the Stags. Fortunately for Tampines, Noh Alam Shah's winner on 68 minutes narrowed the gap to three points and the relief around the stadium was palpable.

It was only their second win in a gruelling schedule of 10 games that had seen them lose touch with DPMM at the top. But Farra was keen to point out the arrival of three new foreign signings (former Geylang United, and Negeri Sembilan's Jozef Kaplan, A-League's Central Coast Mariners' goalkeeper Justin Pasfield, as well as New Zealand's Waitakere United former captain Jake Butler) had boosted the morale in the squad and they were confident that despite DPMM's place at the top of the table, with the AFC Cup out of the way, Tampines would be able to concentrate on the SLeague and he identified Home United as their only serious rivals.

I wanted to know about Noh Alam Shah. Like Farra, a Tampines boy through and through, both speak highly of the club owner Teo Hock Seng. Indeed, when both made the move to Indonesia, they sought the blessing of Teo and were assured of a place should they decide to return to Singapore.

'Alam Shah is great, one of the best players I have ever played with. He can't play the whole game now, he is carrying a back injury, but he just gives us so much on and off the field.'

Noh Alam Shah had first made people sit up and take notice when he hit seven goals for Singapore in the ASEAN Football Federation Cup back in 2007. Two years later, he was playing in Indonesia for Arema and certainly, it was the ideal club for him; wild, passionate support. NAS, as he is known, revelled in a spotlight he had never really received in his own country.

'Did you see him after he scored? The way he was geeing up the fans?' Farra went on. 'It doesn't matter if it is 30,000 in Malang or Bandung or six people in Clementi, he is always the same. His energy, his passion, are great assets to have in the dressing room and on the pitch. He always gives 100%.'

Farra first arrived in Singapore back in 2002 with Tampines. After a season on loan with Sengkang Marine, now known as Hougang United after a series of tortuous name changes that belongs more in a soap opera that a football story, he returned to Tampines and stayed for a further five years.

2009 saw a number of Singaporean internationals make the move to Indonesia as they somehow became the flavour of the month. As well as Farra and NAS, M Ridhuan (Arema) and Baihakki Khaizan (Persija) travelled south to further their careers. One player, who nearly but didn't make the journey, was Farra's former international and current Tampines team mate, Aleksander Duric. He had been set to join Sriwijaya but the deal fell through at the last minute.

After a trophy laden spell with SAFFC, Duric made the move to the Stags and the trophies kept a coming for the veteran striker, who was the first player to hit more than 300 goals in the SLeague.

Farra is full of admiration for his pal. Well, almost. Duric is now in the last campaign of a glorious career and, with an eye on the future, has taken on the mantel of fitness coach.

'I get messages first thing in the morning from Alex saying I am going on a run, do you want to join me?' Farra grimaces at the thought.

'One time I am in Serbia and he messages me saying he is going to run a half marathon, do I want to join him? I have my feet up, enjoying a Serbian meal. What the hell do I want to go on a 21-kilometre run for?!'

As he is your mate and you go back several years, does he go easy on you in training I wanted to know.

No was the short answer. The thing is, Farra explained, he is quicker and stronger than any of us. He sets all these exercises and is always the first to finish, and he then complains the rest of us can't keep up!

The center half leans forward conspiratorially. 'I hope he is not fitness coach next season!'

He is joking, of course. The respect he has is total, as he goes off on a tirade about how nobody from the Football Association of Singapore has been in touch with Alex to find out his plans for retirement.

That doesn't surprise me. The FAS aren't great in acknowledging the efforts of players for club and country. But when you have a player who has done so much for football in the country, it is incumbent (he didn't really say incumbent, but it is what he meant!) on the people who run the game to show him some respect. Because if they don't respect a player like Duric, then who will they ever acknowledge?

Born in Yugoslavia, represented Bosnia at the 1992 Barcelona Olympics in canoeing, he hitched there from Hungary (!?), he moved to Australia in 1994 to play for South Melbourne, where he was to enjoy two spells. He also played for Port Melbourne, Gippsland Falcons, West Adelaide, Heidleberg United, West Adelaide, Marconi, and Sydney Olympics, over the next six years as well as finding time for short spells in China and Singapore with Tanjong Pagar in 1999.

He returned to Singapore the following year with Home United after the last two mentioned Australian teams, before signing with Geylang United.

And that was when people sat up and took notice. Ninety-seven goals in 126 games for the Eagles, he was snapped up by Singapore Armed Forces (better known as SAFFC before a rebrand saw them named Warriors) in 2004, when his career really took off. Remember, he would have been 34 when he signed for the Warriors, but you would never have thought it as he inspired them to four SLeague titles and two Singapore Cup successes, hitting 129 goals in 150 games during his five year spell there! Things quietened down in 2010 when he joined Tampines Rovers. Yeah, he won a further three SLeague titles, netting a further 78 goals along the way!

Singapore football needs heroes and it needs role models. In Duric and Alam Shah they had both, but it is unfortunate little was done to keep them involved in the game in high profile positions once they had hung up their boots. Football fans the world over love a Paolo Maldini, a Steven Gerrard, a Pele. Players who graced the pitch, whose exploits catapulted them beyond merely being a guy doing a job into the posters on the wall Chris referred to earlier.

Footballers don't die; instead their names and their deeds become part of the rich, ever changing fabric of a football club or nation. Bobby Moore, Franz Beckenbauer, Ferenc Puskas, these names are familiar to millions who never saw them play passed on from father to son. Not in Singapore. Last season is a closed book for many, and while the exploits of the 1994 team remain alive in the memories of the supporters, the page of local papers 20th anniversary of that Malaysia Cup triumph passed by with little in the way of official recognition. No brochure, no book, no stamps.

Unfortunately, for many in the upper echelons of the game, and I am not just talking about Singapore here, players are still seen as a necessary but unloved chattel to be traded at will, discarded at will. They see players as taking money, their money, out of the game and giving very little back in return. Odd I know but again, going back to England, things were like that there until the 1970s, 1980s. Now perhaps the pendulum has swung too far in the other direction, but at least the pendulum swung. No sign of it even moving an inch in this part of the world!

As I tap these words I am reminded of an anecdote told to me by someone involved with football in a country in this part of the world. No names, no country you understand. The club owner was moaning that the players couldn't pass the ball very well. 'When I play on my son's play station, the ball always moves smoothly,' he opined.

When you have that kind of mentality you can see there is a long way to go!

3.
A JAPANESE EXPERIENCE IN SINGAPORE

It's quite common to see one team dominate their league for years on end. Across the Causeway in Malaysia we have Johor Darul Ta'zim, which has won the Super League for five consecutive seasons. In the 2017/2018 season, Bayern Munich won the Bundesliga for the sixth consecutive season. For example, while in Scotland, Glasgow Celtic lifted the title for the seventh straight season. In Singapore itself, we have seen Singapore Armed Forces (now rebranded Warriors) claim four leagues on the spin, and more recently Tampines Rovers won it three times on the bounce with the aforementioned Aleksander Duric playing a prominent role in all seven of these successes.

As we approach the end of the second decade of the 21st century, we have a new name dominating the Singapore football landscape. Albirex Niigata aren't your typical football club. They don't represent a local community or a private company or even a government department. Rather, Albirex Niigata (S) are a satellite of Japanese side Albirex Niigata and have been competing in Singapore since 2004. There have been a number of foreign sides playing in the SLeague since it started in 1996, but Albirex Niigata are by far the longest serving and, now, the most successful.

The first few seasons were uneventful as both SAFFC and Tampines Rovers dominated the football scene but Albirex Niigata, nicknamed the White Swans, were earning a reputation for being a well-run club playing football the right way. They were only allowed to use Japanese players, and typically each new campaign would see a raft of young, new faces arrive and soon fit into the local template. A League Cup in 2011 was their only silverware in those early years, and no one really thought too much about them. The big clubs were Tampines, Home United, and Warriors. Albirex Niigata were just one of a number of foreign clubs which had provided opposition a few times a season.

All that changed in 2015 when the White Swans won the Singapore Cup and the League Cup as well as finishing third in the SLeague. With Brunei side DPMM winning the SLeague, it meant a clean sweep of domestic honours for the foreign sides. The following season saw Albirex Niigata win the SLeague for the first time as well as retaining the cups, and in 2017 they repeated the clean sweep confirming their domination of Singapore football.

The idea of a foreign team playing in a domestic league is not unique to Singapore of course. DPMM have featured in Malaysia in recent years while New Zealand's Wellington Phoenix have been part of the Australian A League for the better part of a decade. It's not a new concept either. Cardiff City, Swansea City, and Newport County are part of the English football league pyramid despite geography telling is they are in Wales, and Berwick Rangers play in Scotland despite being in England.

Despite having seen Albirex Niigata a few times I had never really made an effort to understand who they were and what were they doing in Singapore football. Just before the trophies started rolling in I decided to put that right, and so I boarded the Mass Rapid Transport, Singapore's wonderfully efficient, and air conditioned, rail network and headed west.

A short walk from Chinese Garden station is that rarest of rarities, Jurong East Stadium is a purpose built football stadium. It isn't much to behold, one main stand along one side of the pitch with an open enclosure opposite. Behind the goals there is nothing but hedges to deter prying eyes. I paid my $SG 6, foreign clubs could charge fans more than local clubs, and climbed the steps up from the turnstiles, where I was greeted by a small souvenir stall offering a small selection of Albirex Niigata scarves and replica shirts. What sporting facilities there are in Singapore are very much community orientated and Jurong East was no exception, with a gym, swimming pool, and fast food restaurants attached to the main stand. Certainly, a fan could take his family to the stadium and enjoy the facilities before, during, and after the game.

I wasn't interested in the food though. I was there to see Albirex Niigata host a struggling Woodlands Wellington, nicknamed the Rams. Woodlands were a team in decline at the time, with just two wins in their previous ten games. Coached by Aussie Darren Stewart (Sadly, as I was going through a final edit of this book Darren Stewart passed away. RIP Darren). who I used to see play for APIA Leichhardt in Australia's old National Soccer League, confidence seemed to be low and that was borne out as the game was effectively over after 17 minutes, with Albirex Niigata racing to a 3-0 lead. Admittedly, the ref wasn't up to much — but then neither were Woodlands.

There seems to be a real community feel about the club. I sat in the main stand among the WAGS with their children while one guy beat the drum. Incessantly. Poor guy, he was determined to drum up (groan) some atmosphere but the WAGS and their kids were more interested in nattering to each other and drinking cold beer! Yep, one stadium which sells beer, it's gotta be worth a visit just for that! And, for the true couch potato, pick up your phone, order a pizza and have it delivered from the fast food facility attached to the stand!

For the Woodlands game, the crowd was bigger than usual, with something like a couple hundred red clad line dancers taking up half the space allocated for the home support! Okay, so it's not quite as intimidating as Millwall, but the drummer man was in his element. Normally, he beats his drum and is basically ignored, but these line dancers obviously don't get out too much. In this ageing form, he found a captive audience; he beat his drum, they clapped their clapper/programmes and everyone posed for selfies.

At halftime, the line dancers descended en masse to the pitch to do whatever ageing line dancers do. The real drama, however, was going on in the Woodlands dressing room with Stewart, citing illness, left. His team went on to lose the game 7-1 with an abject performance, and the Australian coach was to quit soon after.

The game ended 7-1, two visiting players were sent off and the ref was dishing out yellow cards like he was a vending machine. But I wonder how many of the spectators were actually aware of the events on the field. I suppose everyone had a blast and it was a good night out for the line dancers, but this was less football and more corporate social responsibility. How many of the guests would return to a game and buy a ticket? I think we know the answer to that!

I must admit, my interest had been piqued by Albirex Niigata, and it was nothing to do with the football. They had thumped a mediocre Woodlands Wellington 7-1 but to be fair, many futsal warriors, sweating under the lights and having a fag between games, could have beaten the Rams. For a professional football club, it was a shocking performance. Let's just call it a non-performance and have done with it.

But no, controversy aside, I was intrigued by other factors. Albirex Niigata Singapore Football Club. What is it all about? There are, as I said before, other Albirex Niigatas, including the mother ship in Japan. One that plays in Cambodia, and even one based in Barcelona. But why? What is the point? For all intents and purposes, a Japanese football club playing in Singapore; just how does that benefit Singapore football?

And what about the drummer man and the line dancers! Is Albirex Niigata a professional football club or just a corporate social responsibility project? I wanted to know more. So, after the match, I headed back to my hovel in Joo Chiat and contacted the club's Vice Chairman, Koh Mui Tee, through social media and agreed to meet up the following day.

'Basically, the line dancing was a collaboration between the community Albirex Niigata is in, called Yu Han community. We (have) had a collaboration with them on two fronts. First, we donate one dollar for every spectator who comes to watch our match so that they can donate to a beneficiary.'

'For yesterday's line up performance was actually a result of this collaboration because they wanted to help us bring more spectators in and they want the community to be interested in Albirex. That's why they brought 300 line dancers with their family members to come along and cheer our match. I think it is a good initiative by them, it was purely suggested by them and so it's weird seeing line dancing at a football match, I think it's the first in the world, and I think it is good outreach by our club,' said Mui Tee, over the sound of an excited group of students seated at the table behind us.

Okay, all very nice and dandy and it looks good in company brochures, especially those pages devoted to corporate social responsibility, but I wanted to know how many of those red-clad elderly folk were likely to return to an Albirex Niigata and pay the six bucks match entrance by themselves or with their friends.

'I think I wouldn't put a figure on that, but if a few of them come back and bring their friends, we would be happy with that. The important thing is the brand awareness by us, that Albirex exists in the community and whenever (players) go around the area, I want them to be recognised and Albirex is part of the community.'

Albirex feel strongly about their role in the community and have a high profile football coaching clinic reaching out to local children aged from five- to 12-years-old, says Mui Tee, and in 2014 they were looking at 150 kids enrolled. As part of the clinic, the kids had the opportunity to walk out on to the pitch with the team before kickoff.

'Our strategy is to target the children and they can bring along their parents, so we can increase our attendance.'

Was it working, though? The SLeague have stopped publishing crowd figures on their website after much criticism. So, how were Albirex Niigata's numbers holding up?

'I cannot talk about other clubs,' said Mui Tee, 'but for our club, we average more than 1,500 every game.'

But I was still struggling to learn how a foreign team with a foreign name and all foreign players and sponsors could hope to make any real inroads with the Singaporean football fans who lived in the area, especially as the club was obviously working hard to earn a connection with the local community. Did Mui Tee foresee the day when the club did become a wholly Singaporean affair?

'Definitely, the one thing I can say is we will keep our Albirex name.' He laughed before disagreeing with my comment that the club was little more than a franchise of mother ship back in Japan. 'Franchise, franchise, no we are not franchise. We are currently owned by Albirex Japan, and we are a sister company of Albirex Japan. We are part of the group.'

Okay, so what the hell are they doing in Singapore? What is the football club's raison d'etre?

'Japan always wants to reach out to South East Asia to bring up the quality of football in this region. They always believe if their neighbours are as strong as them, Japan has been doing a lot of MOUs with a lot of South East Asian countries basically to bring up the sport. Of course, it is not so straightforward, but we are one of the tools they are using.'

It all seems very paternal!

Of course, it wasn't that long ago that a foreign team did win the SLeague. Etoile were set up to give a bunch of promising French players an opportunity in the shop window and while they were not widely embraced when they first arrived, they did go on and win the title in their first season. Like many foreign sides, they didn't last long and are now a distant memory along with Sporting Afrique, while Albirex Niigata are still going strong in their 11th year.

Four years on from our meeting and some things have changed. Albirex Niigata have been sweeping all before them, hoovering up the SLeague, Singapore Cup, League Cup, and the Community Shield in 2016 and 2017, and after an eye-watering 16 game unbeaten start to the 2018 season, it looks like their lust for trophies isn't sated yet. At the start of the 2018 season, the Football Association of Singapore announced Albirex Niigata would now be able to use Singaporean players for the first time in their history. Their first signing would be attacking midfielder Adam Swandi, who had previously spent two years with the academy of French side FC Metz, before signing for Young Lions as a 19-year-old in 2015.

As for Mui Tee, a proud Singaporean and a passionate football fan, how does he feel about the White Swans' success? 'It is up to them (Singaporean clubs) to work harder,' he says simply. The fan inside is no doubt delighted by the club's success on the field, but you get the impression he gets as much joy from Albirex Niigata's ongoing efforts in their local community as he does the conveyor belt of trophies heading their way.

Credit to Albirex Niigata for being so dominant with an ever-changing squad, but serious questions need to be addressed by those who are charged with running Singapore football. Given how poorly local sides and the national team have been performing at all levels in recent years, is it time to consider the ultimate blasphemy in Lion City and contemplate a football landscape that does not hark back to 1994?

V. Sundramoorthy and Fandi Ahmad are deservedly seen as legends domestically for their playing achievements. Both played overseas, Sundra in Switzerland with FC Basel, while Fandi had stints with Groningen in the Netherlands and OFI Crete in Greece. Both shone in Singapore and Malaysia. Both played in excess of 100 times for their country, but nostalgia doesn't guarantee trophies.

Since moving into coaching they have again followed similar career paths, working with the Young Lions, LionsXII, and the national team as well as stints overseas. But legendary players do not always become legendary managers. Look at Bobby Moore and Bobby Charlton for example, World Cup winners with England in 1966 but struggled as coaches. Conversely, neither Arsene Wenger nor Jose Mourinho pulled up any trees as players, but haven't done too badly telling other players, far more talented than they ever were, what is needed from them.

Ever since Raddy Avramovic ended his trophy laden time with the national team, Singapore have struggled to make an impression at any level in any competition. The ageing squad he left behind hasn't been adequately replaced. There is confusion over whether there is a place for naturalised players in the future, yet the default Football Association of Singapore response to these, and many other challenges, has been to fall back on the squad of 1994 in a bid to court popularity, or at least to reduce the number of angry Facebook posts. And with the national teams struggling, the domestic league falls into greater mire of apathy dominated by a team that is all but ignored.

It is easy to imagine the outcry had the FAS thinking outside the box and they tried to find a way to involve Albirex Niigata's coach from the all-conquering 2016 team Naoki Naruo, within the national team set up but results don't lie. You can't run football through the prism of a glory age a generation ago. The world has moved on and yes football has moved on. Hopefully a new FAS will have the courage to look beyond the 1990s, and foreign journeymen, when it comes to appointing the next Singapore coach. A youthful approach embracing new ideas might be just the ticket Singapore football needs, just don't hold your breath.

To give you an indication of FAS thinking, it's worth pointing out 2017 was supposed to be a special year in Singapore football. Intrigued, I went to the Football Association of Singapore's website to learn more about this and guess what? Nothing there about it. In fact, there doesn't even seem to be anything about this being the FAS's 125th anniversary, period. Almost begs the question, was anything being done by the football body to commemorate the anniversary beyond hosting Argentina in a friendly? No special logo? No special branding? No special merchandise?

A miserable looking Cristiano Ronaldo breezed through Singapore in July and no, he wasn't being linked with a move to Balesiter Khalsa. Was his visit a part of the celebrations? The International Champions Cup took place at the National Stadium, where Singaporeans were being asked to pay large sums of money to watch Inter, Bayern, and Chelsea strut their stuff.

There was also a game between ex Singapore internationals and a bunch of celebrities and their ilk at Jalan Besar Stadium. Oh, and an SLeague football fiesta was planned, involving past and present Singapore internationals washing 125 cars for charity! This soapy bonanza was scheduled to take place on the same day as, but in a different location to, Balestier Khalsa playing Hougang United, and Warriors entertaining SLeague champions Albirex Niigata, while Chelsea played Inter in the ICC!

There were 26 activities being lined up for Singapore Football Week, including non-traditional activities such as Subbuteo. For many people who come from countries with a rich football culture, it will be a surprise to learn Subbuteo is non-traditional. As you would expect most of the activities were family centered and focused on getting healthy, which was fine and dandy but as a way of promoting Singapore football they fell well short.

For starters, the activities were organised by SportsSG, a body under the Ministry of Culture, Community, and Youth, and judging by some of the scheduling there wasn't much coordinating with either the FAS or the SLeague. Why, for example, were players washing cars at the same time crucial domestic games were being played around the island? Why wasn't the opportunity taken to have an SLeague game played ahead of the ICC circus games to allow domestic players the chance to play on a big stage in front of a larger crowd? You know, increase the awareness of the local game, which is surely the whole point of Singapore Football Week rather than a handful of slapstick activities that were high on selfie moments? No doubt there would have been concerns over the pitch playing two games in a day. Bloody hell. Is it made of mud? The whole thing smacked of a box ticking exercise rather than any meaningful attempt to promote Singapore football.

4.
THE LIONS' FIRST ROAR

It's a funny thing but it wasn't until 1998 that Singapore won an international title. Yes, they had won more than 30 Malaysia Cups but given the shared history between those two nations it is hard to consider the Malaysia Cup, Asia's oldest domestic trophy, an international affair.

The Lions have never qualified for the World Cup and have only once reached the Asian Cup — and that was because they hosted it in 1984! They were drawn in a group with China, Iran, UAE, and India but despite enjoying home crowd advantage, Singapore only managed to win one game, a 2-0 triumph over India in their first game.

By the time they reached their final group stage game against Iran it seems the locals had given up on their 'heroes' and just 2,000 turned up at the Kallang National Stadium.

Ten years later, they withdrew from the Malaysia Cup, having lifted the trophy following THAT 4-0 triumph of Pahang. Twelve years later they launched their own SLeague, and 14 years later Singapore lifted the ASEAN Football Federation Championship in Hanoi, defeating the hosts 1-0 thanks to a goal by R Sasikumar.

Many deciding goals go down in a country's footballing folklore.

No Englishman will be unaware of Geoff Hurst's late thunderbolt against the West Germans in 1966 for example, nor Arsenal fans when Michael Thomas went 'charging through the middle' against Liverpool in 1989. So, it is with Singaporeans and the winning goal in 1998.

It was certainly no thing of beauty; it would not have looked out of place on a Sunday League pitch on a foggy morning, but the significance of the goal transcends its aesthetic charm or lack whereof. It broke the Lions duck on the international stage and coming just two years into the life of the SLeague, what did it portend for the future? Was it proof the city state had made the right choice by withdrawing from Malaysia and going it alone?

Since that fateful game in Hanoi, Singapore have won the ASEAN Cup a further three times (2004, 2007, 2012). But success at other competitions has continued to elude the Lions, who have not even managed to lift gold at the biennial South East Asia Games, a regional Under 23 event.

Was 1998 a false dawn? Should Singapore have gone on to bigger and better things, or is being ASEAN top dog not just the limit of their ambitions but the limit of their talent? Are fans right to look forward to the visits of the likes of Juventus and Liverpool and all but ignore the national team's chances of success elsewhere, or does tiny Singapore have the potential to match other small nations who punch above their weight on a football field?

Singapore boasts a population that is larger than Croatia, Uruguay, and marginally less than Denmark. Then again, those three countries are blessed with a footballing pedigree dating back decades and alumnus featuring the likes of Davor Suker, Luis Suarez, and Brian Laudrup. While in Singapore, kicking a leather ball around a field isn't seen as a particularly smart career move by most of the population.

I have often felt Singapore's economic success as a nation has counted against possible success on a football field. With its attachment to education and an entrepreneurial streak coursing through its veins, Singapore perhaps lacks the economic environment for people to go into football as an escape from humble surroundings that other countries have. 'Work hard, study hard, become a doctor lah (local slang used in almost any informal conversation)' seems to be the mantra among many. A mantra that means Singapore enjoys one of the highest GDPs in the world and one of the lowest levels of poverty.

Wanting to know a little bit more about what it is like growing up in

Singapore for young people with aspirations of a career in football, I decided I needed to talk to someone who had not only been there and done that but had also scored the goal that saw Singapore lift their first ever trophy. As well as scoring that goal, R Sasikumar was the first player to be transferred in the SLeague and called up for the national team before he had even made his first team debut!

That explains how I ended up in Sasikumar's office one fine day in June but doesn't explain why it took several days to get the interview transcribed. After hanging up his boots and deciding coaching was not his thing, Sasi decided to follow a fine Singapore tradition and start his own business. He now rules over a mini empire that includes event marketing and management, consultancy, advertising, broadcasting, and media.

Like many young people, Sasi just wanted to play football. So, his Dad used to take him and his brother to the park and kick around, but his first love was actually hockey and he managed to make the national Under 15 team. But for hockey at least, his growth spurt was to prove a handicap.

'I was a big guy and I couldn't afford the custom made hockey stuff and that's when I started playing football. I got picked up by the school team, combined schools team, and so on.'

With hockey's loss becoming football's gain, Sasi was able to exploit his size. 'Because of my size I was good in the air and I had some pace, believe it or not, when I was younger, so that's where I started. But to be perfectly honest I didn't have any proper football schooling; it was all accidental.'

I have occasionally wondered over the years whether there is too much coaching in the game these days. After all the likes of Stanley Matthews, Pele, and George Best never paid big sums to enroll in an academy, they learned their skills on the streets, kicking balls against a wall and doing keepie-up with a bundle of socks, but Sasi believes he could have been an even better player with a grounding in the basics.

'When I look back, if I had proper football schooling since I was six, seven, eight, at football schools and learned the right thing, maybe I could have played at a much higher level.'

Maybe that is the Singaporean attachment to education coming through but having spent some 15 years in classrooms across South East Asia, I long came to the conclusion there can be too much education and not enough experimentation, too much emphasis on good grades, and not enough on learning from mistakes.

Today of course, football academies are a growing industry with clubs like Arsenal, Manchester United, and Liverpool seeking partners throughout the region to open their own branches with varying amounts of success.

Does the fact that Michael Owen and Sol Campbell went to the English Football Association's first centre at Lilleshall point to the success of the venture or does the arrival of so many foreign players point to its failure? Was Manchester United's class of 1992, which featured the likes of David Beckham, Paul Scholes, and the Neville Brothers, a fluke that had little to do with the academy and everything to do with an extremely talented gene pool in that particular year?

A few years back, West Ham United's academy produced the likes of Joe Cole, Frank Lampard, and Rio Ferdinand, but not much in recent years. More latterly, Theo Walcott, Gareth Bale, Alex Oxlade-Chamberlain, and Adam Lallana, have rolled off the Southampton production line but that is no guarantee they will still be producing internationals in three or four years time.

Interestingly, Sasi points to one factor that helped him reach the top of the game in Singapore that probably isn't taught at any academy. 'One thing I always made up for, because I always felt I wasn't the most skillful player, was I probably had the biggest heart on the park. I got away with a lot because of sheer determination. And the will to win.'

Whenever I hear players say that I am always reminded of the story of Pat Rice, a former full back at the Arsenal. Everything you read about him says the same thing. Not the most talented of players but always ready to work hard and put a shift in. I can't help but wonder if Pat were to apply to an academy today, would he be picked up by a football club?

As a kid, Sasi didn't just play football, he watched it. Indeed, he seemed surprised that I would even ask the question. 'Of course, as a kid I would go to the National Stadium, watching the Lions play in the Malaysia Cup, that was huge.'

In the early 1990s, Sasi was living in Yishun, in the north east of the island. Back then the MRT didn't go that far so he and his friends used to take the bus to the nearest station then take the train to the stadium. He recalled 20 years on the atmosphere of walking to the stadium among thousands of other fans singing and dancing, everyone excited about the game ahead.

This was my favourite part of the interview. Sasi grew up in Singapore and has lived there all his life. Me, I grew up all over the place. His youthful experiences weren't mine: punk rock, fare dodging, finding ways to shock people, the odd scam here and there, but now we were on similar territory. Going to a football match. I loved the way it seems to have been part of his growing up and how well he remembers it. Going to the game was obviously an important part of his formative years, as it was mine, and Sasi was recalling those days with fondness much as I do.

But while at the back of my mind I would be wondering what I would do if I got caught without a ticket on the return journey, he would tell people that one day it would be him wearing the red jersey and people would be making the same journey to cheer him and the other Lions on. Everyone laughed at him of course. Youthful bravado — we have all been guilty of that at some stage or other. But for Sasi it came true!

It doesn't happen anymore though. Even though I knew the SLeague crowds were on the small side, I still expected to see one or two fans on the MRT as I ventured to my first ever game at Bedok Stadium; the East Coast Derby between Geylang United and Tampines Rovers. In my flights of fancy I half expected to see rival fans battling each other at Bedok Station as the cops struggled to keep things under control; I expected to come out of the stadium, ask some lady with her shopping where the ground was and to be told to 'just follow the crowds.' If you do that in Singapore, if you follow the crowds, you would probably end up at some shopping mall with a sale on.

There was no one on the MRT wearing club colours. No one at all. For a local derby! I made my way to the stadium, paid my money and sat behind a group of automatons who would stand on demand, chant on demand, clap on demand, and eat their chicken rice on demand at half time.

Atmosphere, there was none, and crowds there were less. I wasn't expecting much but I still came away disappointed. Where had the 60,000 odd gone who had filled the National Stadium back in the glory days of the 1990s I had heard so much about? Even the early SLeague days were filled with promise and large crowds.

It isn't just Singapore where the idea of a generation growing up with the football-going habit may be in decline or heading for one. In England, home to the Premier League, the average age of a spectator in the EPL is 40+... hardly a sustainable business model. Ticket prices have so outstripped inflation kids can barely afford it and with so many other distractions around them, all those computer games and social media sites, they can have their fun sitting on the sofa and catch the games on TV. Not the same, I know but when you know no different, what to do? But we're talking Singapore here and I wanted to know where they had gone, all those football lovers. I was hoping Sasi could tell me.

'I think a lot of people I talk to these days have fallen out of love with local football because like anything in life there needs to be continuity, you need to keep perking people's interest. Like anything in life, if you don't stay interesting, if you don't stay relevant, people are going to lose interest.'

That is an interesting point of view and certainly one I had never considered. To me, I would go to football. If I didn't go see the Arsenal I would go see someone else. To me, football was the be all and end all. Sasi is almost saying football is a product that needs to keep reinventing itself to stay in the public eye or people go elsewhere. To me, there was no alternative. It was only when I moved to this region I realised shopping was a lifestyle choice. People would do it because it was a social thing, malls always had something going on, they were a place to hang out and meet your mates. For me, shopping was a time when I bought my Frosties and milk. It was a bloody chore, in and out as quickly as possible. Different strokes, etc.

'The SLeague came along with a huge buzz and I still remember being part of the early days of the SLeague with 25-30,000 people in the stadium but what we failed to do was to keep the buzz going. We took it for granted the fans would always be there and I think that was the downfall of football here and sure enough the money started drying up... and the fans started staying away.'

'Like it or not, people like to be associated with winners, with fashion, so we failed to (keep up) and now I suppose we are paying the price.'

He has a point. Walk around town and you are going to see loads of Manchester United and Chelsea shirts, even Manchester City these days but never Derby County or Gillingham unless they are being worn by tourists. And, of course, the EPL is massively popular, ergo trendy. If the TV broadcaster announces it is going to increase the rate it charges customers for watching the games live just head straight to the letters' page of the local papers and check their reaction. Tell them how much it costs in England and they are not interested!

There is no buzz about Singapore football and there is next to no marketing. Many will not know the names of the teams and will struggle to name eleven local players!

I wanted to cheer up, so I thought I would ask Sasi about that goal. He laughed. 'Yeah, yeah, a small milestone! I think it was a combination of a lot of hard work and I think that goal sums up a lot of my career and maybe my life... from where I came and what I did. The first Singaporean to score the winning goal for his country. I suppose it is a big deal and till the day I die I will be remembered for that.'

Yet he nearly never made it to Vietnam at all as he was carrying a knock. Recalling a game in Bangkok, coach Barry Whitbread told Sasi he would be going on so Sasi rushed into the toilet and emptied a tube of deep heat on his knee. He did well in the second half and earned a call up for the AFF Championship, then called the Tiger Cup after the sponsor.

It wasn't as if Whitbread, who had been a journeyman non-league player back in England, was unfamiliar with the lanky Sasi, having worked with him in the national Olympic squad. And Sasi was playing alongside players he had played with before. So, no doubt the coach was thinking there was little risk involved. To this day, Sasi remains grateful to the coach for the faith he showed in his tall, young, 'clumsy' charge. Indeed, on one occasion, Whitbread told Sasi he felt he possessed the 'English centre back mentality.'

Going into the tournament, the Lions were confident but after a 'shaky start' against Malaysia, Sasi and his team mates grew in confidence and by the time they reached the final, in front of a partisan crowd in Hanoi against Vietnam, the plucky Sasi turned to Whitbread and said, 'coach, I think I am going to score today. I have a feeling I am going to score.' And he did.

I am sure Sasi has relived it many times, but I wanted to hear about the goal for myself. So, I asked him to talk me through it. He smiled.

'For free kicks and corners, I am always the guy going up there, making a nuisance of myself. There was an incident earlier, when there was also an opportunity for me. Kadir again put the cross in, and again I smashed the keeper and I do this every time. So, the keeper is looking over the shoulder. He went in with his knee up so we both smashed into it, fell down, got on with it.'

'Seventy-something minute, we had a similar opportunity. I stayed up, it was a corner, we still had the ball, they hadn't cleared the ball. The ball was lifted into the air, I was running on to the ball from an offside position. I am looking at the goalkeeper, he is looking at me and I am thinking he is going to take me out for sure because I did it to him once.'

Sasi braced himself for the collision. It was a cup final, he was quite prepared to go in where it hurt for his country.

'So, I jump, and I know I am going to get clattered, so I turn sideways so the impact is less. I put my hand up just to protect my head... so as I jump he is looking at me, not the ball. If I don't foul him, I am going to connect with the ball and score. All this is happening in seconds. I am trying to head the ball, but I miss because he is trying to push me out of the way and the ball hits my shoulder and then just bobbles into the net.'

'We both land and I am sure the ref is going to blow because of what happened before. No whistle, the ball is in the back of the net and everyone is looking at me! All the reserves are celebrating behind the goal where they are warming up and the ref hasn't blown up!'

For the rest of the game, Vietnam went for the jugular. The Lions had a player sent off to set up a nail-biting final few minutes, but they held on for a famous victory, and for a few moments, at least, Sasikumar was the hero of a nation. Even now, some 18 years later on, Sasi admits he gets goosebumps just thinking about it. 'You know you work hard all your life, when that happens you don't realise it happens, it is just another day.' It wasn't until he got back to the hotel room and lay down did it actually dawn on him how crucial his contribution was to the game and, of course, its outcome.

One thing that comes through when I talk with Sasi, is how often he talks about hard work. Talent is nothing without hard work. As is the case with many a player, hard work, grit, and determination, can often lead to a more successful career than a player blessed with all the skills but none of the application.

Malaysian fans putting on a show of their own before AFF Suzuki Cup Final 2014

5.
MALAYSIA'S FIRST SUPER CLUB

Heading to Malaysia from Singapore has to be one of the easiest border crossings in the world. There are numerous direct buses from Lion City to all points north, and over the years I have probably used most of them. The easiest, by far, is the 170 that goes from Queens Road to Larkin Bus Terminal on the outskirts of Johor Bahru. Frequent services take you from downtown up Singapore's spine to the border crossing at Woodlands and across the narrow causeway that links the two countries. You alight at Woodlands with your luggage, go through immigration and board the next bus that comes along, repeating the process on the Malaysian side of the border. The tourists or shoppers can walk from the immigration centre into JB itself, or you can stay on the bus to the end of the line.

Larkin is only really good for two things; catching a bus elsewhere in Malaysia or watching football. The bus terminal is a few minutes walk from the Larkin Stadium. Officially, it is the Tan Sri Dato Haji Hassan Yunos Stadium but even with copy and paste I think I will stick with Larkin and my apologies. More than once I have been staying in Singapore but jumped on the 170 just to go and see a game and returning straight after.

The first few times I did this Johor was a struggling, second-tier side bereft of money and a fan base that sometimes reached a couple of dozen, but the regal ringgit (the Malaysian currency is known as the ringgit or RM) has changed all that. Larkin Stadium has been gentrified, the club is successful and the fans are responding with an average 17,000 watching each game. Johor, traditionally, has never been a footballing stronghold. State side Johor didn't win their first trophy until 1985, when they defeated Kuala Lumpur 2-0 in the final at Merdeka Stadium in Kuala Lumpur. The Scorpions, as they were nicknamed, finished second behind Singapore in the short-lived Liga

Malaysia that season and managed to reach the Malaysia Cup final again the following season but were trounced 6-1 by Selangor.

It wasn't until 1991, the Johor faithful were able to taste success again when they won the Liga Semi Pro Division One title and the Malaysia Cup for the second time in their history, this time getting a measure of revenge over Selangor by defeating them 3-1 with a hat trick from Croatian striker Ervin Boban on a riotous night in Kuala Lumpur. Johor were on for a double and a measure of revenge against the mighty Selangor, but Australian coach Michael Urukalo had assembled a decent squad built around import players like compatriots Abbas Saad and Alistair Edwards, Boban, and local lads like the experienced Nasir Yusof.

Yusof was born into a large family in Johor Bahru, in 1961. The 10th of 15 children, he started playing the game when he was seven-years-old alongside six of his siblings at the school where his father was headmaster. He went on to sign for his local club and played a major role in those successes in the middle of the 1980s, and becoming a regular in the national team, earning the nickname, 'The Professor' from his coach Urukalo along the way.

Nineteen ninety-one was to be some year for the then 30-year-old playmaker. In July he was part of the Malaysian side, which lined up against England at Merdeka Stadium in June. England won the game 4-2 with Gary Lineker scoring all four, but it was a proud evening for Yusof and his teammates as they hosted the Three Lions for the first time in their history. And then there was the Malaysia Cup final.

Before the Semi Pro League had even finished and Johor officially celebrated their title, success rumours were swirling about a number of their big players attracting interest from other clubs for the following season. Coach Urukalo was having none of it and publicly came out slamming three clubs for their alleged interest. Selangor were reportedly keen on signing Edwards while Saad, who was to finish as top scorer with 11 goals in the Semi Pro League, was said to be interesting to Kuala Lumpur. Meanwhile, Terengganu were interested in both the Aussies!

'These people should lay off the players and leave them in peace,' he fumed. 'I am upset with such approaches, especially at this stage of the season... We have yet to complete the league season and the Malaysia Cup is yet to start.' It wasn't just the foreign players who were attracting interest. Urukalo added local players, who were also being targeted, including Roslan Hamid, who he described as 'one of the best sweepers in the league.'

The Scorpions road to KL hadn't gotten off to the best of starts, losing 2-1 in the north east away to Terengganu in a game marred by an on-field brawl that saw play held up for more than 20 minutes. This resulted in Johor's, Khalid Shadan, and, Wan Azila Daud, being sent off, but a week later they got their campaign up and running defeating Selangor 1-0 at home and a week after that beating southern neighbours Negeri Sembilan 3-0 at Larkin Stadium.

A couple of tricky away ties followed with Johor managing to hold on to a 3-3 draw away to Negeri Sembilan before losing 2-1 away to Selangor. With just five points from their five group stage games and sitting third in their group Johor faced a tough ask overcoming second placed Terengganu at Larkin Stadium in the final game while group leaders Selangor, needing a point to guarantee going through to the knock out stage, were away to bottom side Negeri Sembilan. Johor won 2-0 to secure second place while Selangor were somewhat surprisingly held 1-1 by their opponents.

Johor met Kuala Lumpur in the semi-final, winning 3-1 on their own pitch in front of an estimated 20,000 fans, but ending the game with 10 men after Abbas Saad was sent off on the hour mark for a challenge on an opponent. Edwards had given Johor the lead on 16 minutes, the first goal he had scored against Kuala Lumpur, and Boban had doubled it nine minutes after Saad had taken an early bath with a close-range finish. Playing a man short didn't seem to worry Johor and they added a crucial third on 72 minutes through substitute Annuar Abu Bakar from outside the area. With 11 minutes remaining Subadron Aziz headed a goal back for Kuala Lumpur to set up a nervy 10 minutes for the home side but they held on to the two-goal cushion to take to the nation's capital a week later.

As is so often the case, the headlines after the game revolved around Saad's dismissal. 'I was simply frustrated at all the shoving, pushing, and elbowing (Zaid Jamil) had been giving me all night,' he explained after the game. The final straw came, claimed Saad, after a challenge with Zaid left him with a bloody nose. The ref played on and a fuming Saad retaliated by shoving Zaid to the ground. Urukalo rued the dismissal, which meant Saad would be missing from the second leg and any potential final.

Johor travelled to Kuala Lumpur without Saad, knowing they faced a very dangerous opponent on their own patch. Urukalo said he expected Kuala Lumpur would go for the jugular from the start but added that his team weren't going to play safe either. 'We are not going to defend our lead at the Merdeka Stadium,' he said, 'that will be suicide. Johor will go there looking for another win.'

As expected Kuala Lumpur started the game on the front foot and went 1-0 up within the first five minutes. A second goal meant they went into the last 10 minutes with extra time beckoning. Then, with nine minutes remaining, that man Edwards scored an all-important goal giving Johor a 4-3 lead on aggregate and they managed to survive some scary moments to reach their first Malaysia Cup Final in six years. The joy at the prospect of locking horns with Selangor once more though was tempered by the confirmation they would do so without their top scorer Abbas Saad.

The Malaysia Cup Final has to be one of the biggest days in South East Asian football. The trophy itself may not have as much value as it once did. The winners of the FA Cup, for example, are the ones that get a ticket to the AFC Cup, but for the fans it is just a massive day out. Every year, around 80,000 supporters from each competing team descend on the stadium, be it Bukit Jalil or Shah Alam and fill the vast arenas with noise and colour several hours before kick-off.

To my great regret I have yet to make the game myself though I have come close on a couple occasions. The first time was in 2004. I was working in Malaysia at the time, Cyberjaya to be precise, and had a day off so ventured into Kuala Lumpur for a look around. My interest in football in the region hadn't yet been piqued. Jakarta Casual was to begin a couple years later and looking back I am sure those few hours on the streets of Malaysia's capital city must have played a role.

It was the year of the Northern Final when Perlis, playing in their first ever final, came up against Kedah, then a team on the up. There were thousands of Perlis fans in town clad in yellow, that remains my abiding memory. I had no idea where the game was (it was at Bukit Jalil) and no idea how to get a ticket (it was a sell-out) and truth be told my primary concern would have been finding a bar to watch the English Premier League games. Perlis were to win the game 1-0 and were to return the following two seasons losing one and winning one more. How distant must those memories seem for the Perlis faithful, as the 2018 season sees them playing in the third tier of Malaysian football, the FAM League.

And the second time I came close to seeing the final? Sadly, I can offer no excuse on this occasion. I had flown into Kuala Lumpur especially for the game. I had picked up a ticket for the game. I had arranged to meet a friend before the game at a fine hostelry in the Bukit Bintang area of Kuala Lumpur. My pal arrived and we enjoyed a few cold Tigers, putting Malaysian football to rights. It soon became apparent he wasn't that keen on going and the way the rain was coming down in sheets outside, I started to lose my enthusiasm. We were having a good natter after all. The beer was lovely, and did I really want to get wet? So, I chickened out and fate has yet to find me in Kuala Lumpur on match day, though I do live in the hope one day will be third time lucky.

There could be no such excuses, of course, for Alistair Edwards and the rest of the Johor team back in 1991. They had reached the final on merit, and even though they were missing Abbas Saad they still fancied their chances against Selangor.

In the dugout were two Australian coaches, with Ken Worden coming up against Urukalo. Everything else was pure Malaysia, from the crowds queuing early to snap up the 45,000 tickets to the tropical downpours that didn't stop all day. Thousands were locked out but those who did make it in to the stadium made it a day to a remember, with the Selangor faithful who had made the short journey into Kuala Lumpur along the River Klang clad in red and yellow, while the Johor masses were dressed in blue and red. On Malaysia Cup Final day, it takes more than a mere torrential rainstorm to dampen the enthusiasm of the supporters.

It was to be the Johor fans who were to celebrate first and longest, with Boban scoring a hat trick inspiring some wonderful work from the nation's copy editors in the newspapers the following day. 'Southern Comfort' was one, referencing Johor's location at the southern most tip of Malaysia. 'Boban neat with three shots and brings cheers to Johor.' A day filled with many firsts: Boban netting the first hat trick during the final in the semi pro era, Johor being the first team to win the Semi Pro League and Malaysia Cup double, and likewise Urukalo, the first foreign coach to achieve such a feat. Ten thousand fans greeted the returning heroes when they landed at Johor airport. They were then taken into the city and on to a civic reception on the back of three open topped lorries accompanied by a large informal motorcade of motorcycles and cars waving the red and blue state flag. And yes, it was still raining!

If Johor fans though were hoping this double would usher in a new era of unparallelled success, they were to be sadly mistaken. Despite holding on to coach Urukalo and the trio of imports, Boban, Edwards, and Saad, 1992 was to prove a disappointing campaign as the team finished seventh in the Semi Pro League, failing even to qualify for the Malaysia Cup they had won so triumphantly. There was little joy to be found in the FA Cup either as Johore fell to Pahang in the first round. The glory days were over. For a few years at least.

I'd first come across the name Steve Darby when I was living in Australia. I would see his name mentioned in the local football media, they call it soccer of course, and with it being a rare Anglo sounding name amid a tsunami of unfamiliar sounding Greek, Serbian, Croatian, and Italian names, it stuck in the memory. Later of course, when I was living in South East Asia he would be a frequent pundit on satellite TV, offering opinions that went well beyond the 'the defending was shocking' that is the bread and butter of so many ex pros in front of the camera.

Imagine how chuffed I was when he contacted me after he had read Jakarta Casual. Golly. This was a man whose path had, kind of followed mine from England to Australia to South East Asia, we have both spent some time in the Middle East as well. The big difference of course was he was, and remains, a proper football person and I am just someone who hands over insane amounts of cash to follow my passion.

We have met up over the years in various weird and wonderful places and I have always enjoyed our chats. He is warm, witty, and irreverent, qualities I like in a person. From Australia he has worked in Malaysia, Singapore, Vietnam, Thailand, Laos, and India, furthering his reputation as a 'player's coach.' Which is football speak for a coach who club officials don't like.

Sydney Olympic were long seen as one of the biggest clubs in the old NSL winning the title in 1990 and 2002. I used to go and see them play at Sydney Football Stadium, Parramatta Stadium, and St George Stadium as they struggled to nail down a home ground in those years, but they were always followed by a large (by the standards of that era) boisterous, predominately Greek crowd. It was one of these fans, who taught me my first, and to date, only Greek word. How I laughed when I found out it was also the name of a city in Malaysia.

'Like most Olympic coaches, if not all I was sacked, this was 1998, and then got a phone call. Did I fancy 6 weeks in Johor, Malaysia, to save the team from relegation. This happened, and we also won the FA Cup. So, I ended up 3 years in Johor.'

A lot of Australian internationals from the early 1990s were heading to Malaysia and Singapore to play in the Malaysia Cup. At the time it could be argued Malaysian football was streets ahead of its rivals in the region and clubs were investing in foreign players. Of course, the Australians came relatively cheaply but many went on to have good careers and remain fondly remembered. Names like Abbas Saad, Darren Stewart, Scott O'Donnel, Scott Ollerenshaw, were among those early pioneers and within a few years Aussies were venturing even further afield as Europe beckoned.

Darby, though, had been focusing on his career in Australia, and before packing his toothbrush and heading to Malaysia, didn't really know what he was letting himself in for beyond what he had learned from Saad and his salary would be going up! The lad from the Wirral was now 33-years-old and had come far from the cobbled streets over-looking the Mersey but Bahrain, Tasmania, and Sydney hadn't really prepared him for life in hot, steamy Malaysia. And his time in South East Asia didn't get off to the most auspicious of starts.

'I remember arriving in Singapore and the driver due to pick me up went to the wrong terminal! Welcome to Malaysia!! At least there was no media asking me to juggle a ball this time! So, I managed to get across to Johor Bahru by taxi, and the first game was that night against Perlis. I was really thrown in the deep end. Jet lag? What's that?'

Tired, though, he may have been Darby was still alert enough to recognise a talented player when he saw one. 'There was a skinny little left winger, who I thought was a great player for Perlis (I thought he was Malay) but it turned out to be Kiatasuk Senmuang, better known as Zico, from Thailand. What a player!' Indeed. Within a year he was forsaking the north of Malaysia for the north of England. What a culture shock that would have been for the 26-year-old from the North East of Thailand when he signed for Huddersfield Town before returning to South East Asia and playing in Singapore and Vietnam before going on to coach the Thai national team.

As he settled into his new home Darby recalls the help he received from a couple of players who went out of their way to help him adapt to his new surroundings. 'There were two Aussie lads in the Johor team, Darren Stewart (whom we met in the Singapore chapter), and Milan Blagojevic (later coached at Sydney Olympic), who were great Pros and I wouldn't have survived without them.'

Len Shackleton was a well-known footballer back in the 1930s in England playing for, among other teams, Newcastle United and Sunderland. He was a talented player but, like Darbs, didn't have much time for incompetent management and is perhaps best known these days not for his playing career but his memoirs, which included a chapter memorably entitled 'The Average Director's Knowledge of Football,' which ran to a single page bereft of text.

South East Asian clubs don't have directors but they do have managers, and while there are good managers out there others see themselves as more important than the football club and want to be seen as the ultimate wielder of power, quick to accept the plaudits and praise, but hiding behind the coaching staff when results don't go his way. In his early Malaysian career Darby admits he was lucky.

'I was lucky in that Malaysian Football has this ubiquitous role of the Team manager who usually was a cross between Sir Alex Ferguson and Adolf Hitler. With Hitler's football knowledge. This person usually causes 90% of coach dismissals. I was very lucky I had a highly educated CEO as my manager, who also understood football and we had 3 years together. When I was sacked (because of politics) he walked out with me.'

The Johor Steve Darby was with at the turn of the century was a very different beast to the Johor side that now dominates Malaysian football and has ambitions that spread beyond the constricting local league. Johor then were a state funded side with limited facilities. Very limited.

'Facilities then were not like Johor Darul Ta'zim' now. We trained on the Sultan's polo field, which had no dressing rooms or showers; I kept the balls, nets, and bibs in my car. The staff was me, an assistant, and a part time physio. That was it! It was frustrating as on the polo fields there was a manicured pitch with perfect goals and nets for use by the royal family. In 3 years, I never saw it used.'

The neglect extended to the Larkin Stadium, where by the sound of it David Attenborough would have been more at home than any footballing people. 'Occasionally we trained at the stadium, cleaning the dog waste off first, and then cleaning dead rats away. One day the workers were trying to clean the electronic scoreboard out as it never worked. I heard screams and saw them jumping out. A nest of snakes had set up home in there!'

Every day was an adventure and Darby would go to work not knowing what he would find. 'By accident I found an "Academy." It was a dormitory under the stand for youth players. It was a bit like the dormitory in the film, *Escape to Victory!!* Appalling unhygienic conditions, but as I was told it was better than home for some of the lads.'

On the football field, amid the faeces and the fauna, second division Johor found success with Darby helping the team avoid the drop and winning the FA Cup in his first season defeating Sabah 1-0 in the final with Blagojevic scoring the only goal just after the half hour mark. Incidentally that Sabah side featured ex Arsenal and England star David Rocastle, then at the end of his career. Darby's second season saw Johor finish top of the second division, then known as Premier Two, and earn promotion back to the top flight. Heady days for the Johor fans and an era that wouldn't be repeated until royal money and professionalism transformed football in the state.

Sadly, Darby didn't stick around much longer. Politics is never far from the football field and despite bringing success in his two seasons with the club Darby was told he had to face life in the top flight with a smaller budget. There was also some behind-the-scenes bickering between Johor and Johor FC, ostensibly a private club which had finished third behind Johor in the 1999 season, which saw the FC come out on top and Darby was gone.

In 2010, Johor and Johor FC met in the top flight after the Super League had been expanded to 14 teams. It was Johor FC who claimed the initial bragging rights, defeating their city rivals 3-0 and they completed a resounding double when they thrashed Johor 5-0 at Larkin Stadium. They finished fourth in the table, which allowed them access to the Malaysia Cup where they reached the semi-finals before losing to Negeri Sembilan 2-1 on aggregate. For the Scorpions, the season was a disaster with just five wins and 18 goals to show for their efforts in the league and they were relegated after just a single season in the top flight.

The story of Malaysian football in the last few years is the story of one football club. Johor Darul Ta'zim came into being after the Crown Prince of the state of Johor became president of the state football association at the start of 2012 and set about revamping football under his patronage. At the time there were a number of different Johor based clubs operating at different levels with Johor FC in the Super League, Johor, MBJB, and MP Muar in the second tier Premier League and none were performing particularly well, and all were struggling to attract meaningful crowds.

The new state FA set about consolidating the clubs. MBJB and MP Muar were withdrawn from the Premier League for the 2013 season, while Johor FC were rebranded Johor Darul Ta'zim and Johor would later become Johor Darul Ta'zim II implying a feeder-club status for the Super League side. Professional management became the order of the day at Malaysia's southern most club, and not just on match day with training and medical facilities improved across the board. Typically, Malaysian clubs are state football associations reliant on local government support or extensions of private or state enterprises. Either way, football clubs were vulnerable to the changing winds of political fortune or bank balances.

Malaysia is made up of 13 states (Selangor, Perlis, Perak, Kedah, Kelantan, Terengganu, Pahang, Penang, Melaka, Negeri Sembilan, Johor, Sabah, and Sarawak) and three federal territories (Kuala Lumpur, Labuan, and Putrajaya) and it is from here where most of the professional football clubs have historically been drawn. The idea of private clubs is a relatively new one. Johor FC being one of the first, and they tend not to last too long, but they sure bring some colourful names to the football landscape. Kuala Muda Naza, Public Bank, PLUS (operators of a toll road), UPB MyTeam (based on a merger between an existing club and a reality TV show), Sime Darby, T Team, and Telkom Malaysia have all appeared briefly in the top flight for example. When Johor Darul Ta'zim got up and running they changed everything. To compete it was up to the other clubs to compete or fall by the wayside. That JDT have won five Malaysian Super League titles on the bounce suggests there is a lot of catching up to do.

As I checked into the hotel, I asked the receptionist about getting tickets for the game and he said wait an hour or so, he will arrange them. I went to the stadium anyway and, six hours ahead of kick off, there were already fans queuing to buy tickets. In fact, there were more people milling around at the main entrance of the stadium than there had been at the two games I had seen previously at the ground. And everyone was wearing the red and blue club colours, bought no doubt from the small club shop. Yep, there had been big changes!

Back at the hotel and my new bestest mate, the receptionist, was as good as his word, giving me my ticket and not wanting any money for it! I got to the stadium early but already the seats in the grandstand had been taken so I stood around at the back and looked dumb. Tucked away to the right of the stand was a small band of Terengganu fans who had made the long journey south for the game and would probably get home just in time to go to work the next day. You gotta love football and the lengths people go to just to see their team in action, no matter where it is. It doesn't matter how inept the management of the game is, the dedication and passion of fans are phenomenal.

I was eventually offered a seat in the paddock by a bald gentleman, who then kept piling me with bird seed. Or nuts, not sure which. He said he was a Tottenham fan, so I got up to leave. 'No, no, it is ok, you stay here.' He had a point. There weren't many seats left and he and his friends did seem a friendly bunch.

'We are diehard fans,' he proudly told me. I told him of the last time I had caught a game at the stadium, against PPUSM in the Premier League when the crowd was only a couple dozen or so. 'No, that was rubbish. We only started coming in 2012.' Or when the Crown Prince started investing. To be fair to the guy, it was more of a footballing experience now. The stadium had the look and the feel of a football club, with its branding and colour scheme while a slick website and a regular magazine showed they were trying to find ways to connect with their fans. No programme mind!

I remarked upon the lack of a connection between the glory days of the past and the present era when I was in Singapore, how little was being done to show how football clubs are living, breathing organisms stretching back over dozens of seasons, how a club's heritage is something to be embraced as part of a club's present. Johor Darul Ta'zim have embraced this concept with legends from 1991, Boban and Edwards actively involved with the club today.

Boban, was introduced to the crowd and received a rousing reception. Everyone in the ground knew who he was and if they didn't they made sure to find out by asking the guy next to them. The crown prince arrived and received a rousing reception. Then the atmosphere dropped a notch or two for the prayer and the teams came out. The Malaysian national anthem was sung, the Johor anthem was sung, the Terengganu anthem sung and finally we were ready to play some football!

Terengganu were soon 2-0 up and, if there had been a script, I am sure that was not in it. I wasn't too worried though, mainly because I was neutral and didn't care who won but also memories of the FA Cup Final were still fresh in my mind. 2-0 against Hull City, Arsenal went on to win 3-2. There was still a long way to go and did you know it only takes a second to score a goal in football?!

There was another factor at play. JDT's coach was Bojan Hodak at the time. The previous season when he was at Kelantan, I had seen his team similarly go down 2-0 fairly quickly only to fight back and draw 2-2. Indeed, after that game when I met up with some local journalists and coaching staff from Kelantan, it became apparent Bojan's team were more than adept at late come backs. However, I couldn't tell that to the fans around me. They were going mental! The last thing they wanted was a cool head saying, 'it's ok lah, a long way to go...' It's football in the stadium and everyone hates the smart alec who absolutely refuses to get caught up in the tension and emotion.

Sure enough, JDT did claw their way back into the game, at one stage leading 4-2 before a late goal by the visitors led to some squeaky bum time for the home support. The game ended 4-3 and the fans went home happy with three points. Back at the hotel, the friendly receptionist gave me a JDT scarf and took a couple of pictures of this strange English guy who lived in Indonesia and had come to his home town to catch a football match! He didn't know the half of it!

6.
THE FAILED GROUNDHOPPER

Bukit Bintang at 5.30 in the morning was cool, quiet and dark. The area, famous for its clubs, bars, and restaurants, was settling down after a hectic Saturday night. A few massage parlours remained open, hoping to catch the last of the revellers while the odd coffee shop attracted their own audience, mostly locals, intent on watching the opening games of the 2014 World Cup.

I found a bar that was open and ordered my first beer of the night. Morning. Whatever. There were perhaps a couple dozen England fans in there, done up in shirts and flags. Well, it was a Scottish bar! Some looked like they had been on the beer quite a while! It was loud and raucous yet friendly; I guessed most of the punters were expats by their familiarity with the hard working staff which was fine by me. If they were mostly tourists, with less of a stake in harmony man, things always had the potential to get a bit lairy should England lose. And while in my early days overseas I may have fit the Brits on the Piss stereotype, age has wearied me. Nowadays, I just want to watch a game, and perhaps send a strongly worded tweet before carrying on with my life.

The teams came on to the field and all around the world, wherever two or three English folks are gathered, the words to the national anthem, God Save the Queen, blared out in unison. From Manaus to Manchester to Melbourne via Malaysia, there would have been scarves and beers held aloft as the words of the song were bellowed lustily into the evening, night, morning air. It is the beauty of football, and satellite TV, that you just know for those few moments, you are not alone.

Before the ref blows the whistle, for those final few moments while the players finish their limbering exercises, England and Italy are on level terms. Costa Rica had shocked Uruguay in an earlier game, winning 3-1, and for now those England fans all around the world were optimistic of their chances. That same blind faith that accompanies the team wherever they go, whatever competition they enter. One shrill blow on the whistle, one final 'Come on England' and we are on our way.

Things were pretty genteel in the pub. There wasn't much in the way of singing or abuse roared at the screen. In fact, I have probably seen more atmosphere at a rugby match screened in a bar than on this particular occasion. For good reason, probably. Most were too cut after drinking all bloody night!

England lost, of course. They didn't play too badly but the defeat would be picked over by the media and the pundits and the fans all around the world. This was the fourth time Italy had defeated the Three Lions at a major tournament, Euros in 2012, the World Cup in 1990, and the 1980 European Championships, but hey, optimism abounds! Anyway, for me it was supposed to be a perfect day; watching England in the early hours then heading off to catch a local game at a new ground. It was fair to say I was really looking forward to this day and there was no way I would allow the small matter of an England loss darken my mood.

The Malaysian league season is actually formatted fairly well for the fan, who likes to catch a few games a week. Typically, Monday and Thursday are Premier League days, Saturday and Tuesday belong to the top flight Super League, and Sundays are given over to the third tier FAM League. Obviously, television demands are eating into that schedule, but the rump remains constant. So, on this particular Sunday in June I planned to take in Kuala Lumpur against Harimau Muda C. Yep, C.

Harimau Muda was a development programme set up by the Malaysian FA to offer talented young players a career path to top flight football by having them play and train together for a number of years. I guess by playing together from a young age, the players can learn and grow together but it has now been stopped. There was a Harimau Muda A which covered players aged

20 and 22. At various times they have competed in Queensland, Australia, Slovakia, Singapore, as well as domestic leagues. Harimau Muda B (18-21) have played in Malaysia and Singapore competitions while Harimau Muda C (Under 19s) were purely a domestic affair.

Harimau Muda's opponents were to be Kuala Lumpur, the only football club in the nation's capital but fallen on hard times in recent years, starved of leadership, and cash. Other clubs, Sime Darby, Felda United, and PLUS spring to mind, have pre-fixxed their name with KL to emit a sense of belonging to the capital but for all intents and purposes there is just one local side. Kuala Lumpur Football Association, we'll stick with KLFA, were formed in 1979 as the Federal Territories, which makes sense from a geo political point of view but not a footballing one when you consider part of the federal territories is an island off the coast of Borneo! Rebranded as KLFA in 1987, they had a purple patch at the end of the 1980s, winning a series of trophies and featuring a number of big name players including Singaporean legend Fandi Ahmad.

If ever you want to know about Malaysian football in general, or Kuala Lumpur in particular, you could do far worse than track down Devinder Singh, a freelance writer (I feel your pain pal) and a full-time Kuala Lumpur fan since he was 10-years-old in 1988.

'Very few people realise KL missed a golden opportunity to become Asian club champions in 1987. I have no recollection of this event, but I came to read about it through my research of the KL team's history. In the semi-final group stage, KL entered their final game needing to beat Kuwait's Kazma at the Merdeka Stadium to reach the final. A 1-1 draw, however, left KL second in the group on a goal difference of one with Japan's Yomiuri, the predecessors of Tokyo Verdy, going through to a final they did not have to play to emerge champions when Saudi Arabia's Al Hilal withdrew.'

I loved the fact that Devinder was talking about doing his research about his favourite football club. When I started following Arsenal I devoured any printed material I could find about the club and soon learnt about its history, exploits, and heritage. To me, all that knowledge was an essential part of being a fan. I don't mind admitting, old fart rant warning, younger generations don't seem so interested. For too many supporters these days the club only exists in their recent memory; anything before they jumped on the bandwagon doesn't exist. I remember one time trying to give away some old Arsenal programmes from the 1980s and this lad said he wasn't interested. 'I am only interested about Arsenal after Arsene Wenger came to the club,' he told me.

'As I was too young to go to the games (my mother forbade me),' Devinder continued. 'I mostly followed Kuala Lumpur through the rare live matches, on radio, and newspapers (the predominant mode of information).'

Success eventually came to the football club when ambitious management took over. 'It was not until 1984 when the then KL mayor Elyas Omar became KLFA president did the city team's fortunes began to change. Historically state government backing has been a prerequisite for a successful football team, but as a federal territory Kuala Lumpur wasn't able to draw on local taxpayer's money in the same way other states could. A vibrant city league attracted players from all over the nation as well as from Singapore, making them eligible to play for KL. (During the amateur period until 1988, players needed to be playing in state leagues to be eligible to represent their states in the Malaysia Cup and the national league). With KL having the luxury of picking from the cream of the crop, the city team were in the ascendancy and reached four Malaysia Cup finals in five years.'

Despite the newfound success, the club found it difficult to attract fans with people still preferring to follow neighbouring Selangor with Devinder estimating crowds rarely rising above 10,000.

After finishing runners-up of the top flight of Malaysian football in 1982 and the Malaysia Cup in 1985, KL lifted the Malaysian League in 1986 and 1988 and the Malaysia Cup in three consecutive years from 1987, with 1988 being a particularly special year adding the Charity Shield to make it a clean sweep of domestic trophies. The Malaysia Cup, of course, was the big one and having finished second in the group stage in 1987, the City Boys brushed aside Kelantan and Perlis in the knock out stages scoring 13 goals along the way and setting the stage for their second final appearance.

Kuala Lumpur had the advantage of playing the game at the historic Merdeka Stadium right in the heart of KL, a short walk from Chinatown. It was here that Malaysia declared its independence from Great Britain in 1957, it was here Muhammad Ali fought Joe Bugner in 1975. The stadium is no longer used for sports apart from a one off game back in 2015 when KL hosted Sabah, though a few big name international artists have performed there in recent years. However, before the construction of more modern facilities in Bukit Jalil the Merdeka Stadium was the venue for the nation's showpiece events. And in the mid-1980s there was nothing bigger than the Malaysia Cup Final, especially when the local team were eying their first ever title. Singaporean international K Kannan's goal just before half-time was enough to send the home support into raptures as Kuala Lumpur defeated Kedah 1-0 to end their Cup drought and keep the glory years ticking over.

Twelve months later they were back in the final after finishing top of the group stage with 11 wins and just one defeat from the 16 games, four points clear of Singapore. They carried that form into the play-offs, defeating Penang 3-0 on aggregate, Subradon Aziz, and Singaporean Fandi Ahmad, scoring on the island with Aziz making sure back in the Merdeka Stadium.

In the semi-finals, Kuala Lumpur were drawn against mighty Selangor from along the Klang Valley with both legs being played at the Merdeka, which doubled as Selangor's own home ground in the years before their Shah Alam Stadium was built. It was advantage Selangor after the first leg. Zainal Abidin Hassan had given them the lead on the hour mark, but the reliable Aziz had pulled one back within a few minutes. Dollah Salleh made it 2-1 in the last minute, leaving the Red Giants, as they are known, with the narrowest of leads going into the second leg. The two rivals lined up again just three days later and Kuala Lumpur soon raced to a 4-0 lead with goals from that man Aziz, two from Fandi and S Balachandran. Selangor pulled back two late goals in the last five minutes to set up an exciting finale, but KL held on and got to meet Kedah for the second time in the final.

Kannan had moved back to Singapore at the start of the season but there was still a strong Lion City thread running through the City Boys line-up with Malek Awab giving them the lead early on. As you would expect, the prolific Aziz scored on 34 minutes after Singaporean Malek Awab had given KL the lead on five minutes. Malek played over 100 times for Singapore during his career and was a long-time teammate of Fandi, but while Fandi has remained at the forefront of the Singapore football story as player, coach, and father to a couple of promising young players (Irfan and Ichsan Fandi), Malek has kept a lower profile post-retirement, showing little interest in coaching. Maybe it is the writer in me, but I am always looking for patterns and it intrigued me that 22 years after Fandi and Malek were leading KL to glory another Singapore duo, this time Noh Alam Shah and M Ridwan, were playing a leading role in guiding another foreign team, Arema Malang in Indonesia, to success!

Devinder's time on the KL terraces will be familiar to supporters of under-achieving clubs around the world. 'Being a KL fan is not for the timid. We lack the numbers to make ourselves heard, but we have the run of the stadium when playing teams other than Selangor (away teams had significant support but not as many as Selangor used to have). With a capacity of 45,000, the Merdeka Stadium looked deserted at most KL home games, thus allowing the KL fans the freedom of running along the terraces. We usually sat on the upper tier and rained down insults on the away fans occupying the lower tier. Nothing untoward ever happened, as it was all good fun.'

Still, anyone can support a successful club. It takes a certain commitment and stubbornness to follow a team that doesn't expect to go anywhere. I may be an Arsenal fan but I cut my teeth, as it were, on the East Bank at Aldershot in the old Division Three and Four in England. Over the years I have come across die-hard fans of clubs like Oldham Athletic, Rochdale, and Wrexham. So, I can totally understand where Devinder is coming from when he says, 'a good thing about being in such a cavernous yet empty stadium (such as Merdeka Stadium) is being able to hear what is said on the pitch. Sometimes, you can even hear the coach yelling from the opposite side of the pitch. On one such occasion, the then KL coach, Chow Kwai Lam, was so angry with his players that he volleyed an out-of-bounds ball to the corner flag at the other end of the pitch, drawing a big cheer from the crowd.

In one FA Cup semi-final, Chow again drew applause from the fans when he bellowed to the KL player Adilson Roque to take a free-kick. 'Adilson, come take this!' Chow shouted for everyone in the stadium to hear. Roque scored from the kick some 35 metres from goal.

Most of the highs I enjoyed came in the early years of being a KL supporter and the lows mostly in the latter years, the worst being relegation to the third division in 2013 on the back of a match-fixing scandal. But it was also during this period that I grew to know better the KL legends through my work as a sports journalist. It was a great honour and thrill to have made the acquaintances of Razip, Tang, Mat Zan, Fandi Ahmad, Subadron Aziz, Ramlan Askolani, and S. Balachandran, among others.'

And as any supporter of a lower league or unfancied club will tell you, there is nothing like the feeling when you beat one of the top clubs. 'Johor Darul Ta'zim came to the Kuala Lumpur Football Stadium in 2018 and their fans occupied 90 per cent of the venue. Needless to say, that did not stop KL from winning 1-0.'

Why haven't KL been able to attract fans in large numbers and keep them? Part of the reason is historic. Selangor are massive and have been around for a long time. They are the most successful club in Malaysian football history, and there is that tradition of people following a family tradition by supporting the team known as the Red Giants. Granddad used to. Father took son. Now, son takes his son and the familial attachment continues. KL were the new kids on the block.

Devinder feels there is another reason why his beloved Kuala Lumpur have struggled for their moments in the spotlight; demographics. Malaysia's population is mostly Malay but there are sizeable numbers of Chinese and Indians who came to the country back in the colonial times. And like capital cities all around the world, Kuala Lumpur is a cosmopolitan potpourri with the Chinese and Indians rubbing shoulders with Malays from all over the country. People would leave their towns or villages in other states like Kelantan, Perlis, or Johor, and head to the capital city in search of a better life in the city.

Settling down in Kuala Lumpur, they would marry and have children, but they would not forget their roots. 'The newcomers retained their allegiance to their state of origin,' says Devinder. 'This is nowhere clearer when teams like Kelantan, Terengganu, Kedah, and Johor visit KL and the home team fans are far outnumbered by the away supporters, many of whom lived in the city. Given that they do not get many opportunities to watch their own team play, they turn out in droves when their teams visit KL. As the immigrants laid roots in KL, their offspring too support the state teams of their parents.'

Then there is the delicate issue of race. Outside of Kuala Lumpur the local Malays are in the majority, but in KL the numbers are more equal with the Chinese and Devinder says much of the KL fanbase was drawn from the Chinese community. 'But these dwindled when Malaysian football turned professional in 1994, with many Chinese players choosing not to pursue a career in football. The lack of Chinese players had a knock on effect on fan support. Many Chinese fans turning to European football, which by this time was ubiquitous on television, thanks to ever-expanding satellite broadcasts. A bribery scandal of 1994-95 also had a major effect in driving fans away.'

'With the Chinese fans gone, those that continued to support KL were overwhelmingly Malay, but their numbers were too few. Even with a present-day population of 1.7 million, KL would be lucky to get 1,000 fans coming to games, excluding the away support.'

For the remaining KL faithful, those days, all that silverware must seem like a distant dream and one which has no commemorative DVD to ease the pain. Starved of cash, the club have been in freefall with the nadir coming in February 2014, when the complete playing squad was found guilty of match fixing and banned from the game for varying amounts of time. Five players and three club officials were banned for life, while a further 17 players received fines. It was revealed during the hearing that some of the players had been threatened and beaten up if they didn't go along with the fixers' demands or showed any kind of dissent.

It is all well and good to pontificate about match fixing, but it is very unlikely many of the pontificators have been put in a position where a complete squad is bent and physical violence was just a hesitation away. What would an English player have done in the circumstances? Could someone even get away with bribing a whole team without the media picking up some clues on their highly-tuned antennae. What would any of us have done? Would we have gone public, for the good of the game, and taken a baseball bat breaking a few limbs as the price to pay? Or would we have considered our family and our less than bulging bank account before deciding the idea of throwing a football match for a few quid was worth the risk?

In England, for many of us, the class system, at least, on some level is gone. When we say, 'we don't give a shit,' we sometimes even mean it. We are no longer so easily cowered by some powerful, rich, landed dude and his goons. But in a part of the world where society is still based on hierarchies, both visible and invisible, what to say, what to do? Connections remain important as a means of self-defence as much as anything, and players may be loathe to put their careers at risk by offending some local big-wig just for some match fixing, which they may see as a victimless crime anyway.

I have witnessed games where you just knew something had been fixed by someone somewhere. Be it players, coaches, match officials, whoever, it stunk. The odour hung around the stadium, the result, and the subsequent match report. The problem with knowing the match, or a part of a match, has been fixed is of course it can be pretty hard to prove it. It is very hard to find anyone involved to stand and say, 'you know what, I actually took some money to throw that game because I needed to buy a new car or put some food on the table because my club hadn't paid me for a few months.'

There are supposedly experts out there who can identify, somehow, when a game is at risk but then not everything I imagine goes through online betting websites. What about on the ground, at the game itself when, for example, not only every 50/50 goes in favour of the home team but every 40/60 and 33/66? How will that show up on any spreadsheet somewhere? And what about mysteriously long periods of extra time or sudden goal fests that would have the Famous Five and Timmy salivating at the prospect of another mystery for their hols.

I have talked to a number of people in the game, who have told me they just try not to think about it. You work all week trying to get things right for the match and at the back of the mind lurks the knowledge that you may not only lose to a ref's bad decision or an error from your own team or a piece of magic by one of the players on the pitch; they are all hazards of the job. You could also be undone by someone or some people who really don't give a shit about football and fancy making a few bob on the side.

It's unfortunate. Every European club with their eye on their revenue streams, is eyeing the South East Asian market, and its cash, yet the local scene lacks credibility in the eyes of many for its lack of legitimacy and transparency.

As the coach says, if we thought about it too much then we would all pack up and go home. In the same way that in England, football finally reclaimed the game from the hooligans (perhaps it can next be reclaimed from the corporates!), and Australia's managed to put together a league that is challenging the more established football codes. I am confident that one day, football lovers in this region will reclaim the game from the smoky backrooms and the nefarious influences that currently rule the roost.

Anyway, back to the game we love. The FAM website had the Kuala Lumpur down as being played at the mini stadium in Persada PLUS. Nope, I had never heard of it and nor had the taxi driver who proceeded to take me to a totally different arena, MBPJ Stadium, rather than admit he didn't know where I meant!

I showed the guy the address according to the website and he still wasn't sure, but off we set again. More by luck than design, we found a mini stadium right by the toll road, PLUS is the name of the road that goes right along the length of the Malay peninsula, but there was little life there beyond a helicopter. The driver went off to ask the security guys while I sat in the back seat and played the dumb tourist role to perfection while wishing my hangover away. Needless to say, the security guards knew nothing either and I could see the little group kept glancing in my direction with smiles on their faces suggesting my quest to find a football match had brightened up their Sunday. The driver returned to the car. 'Better we go to the FAM (Football Association of Malaysia) building and ask them,' he says, and away we go. Fair play, I have been known to whine a bit about taxi drivers, but this guy was more willing to go the extra mile. Mind you, the meter was ticking over nicely!

Of course, what with it being a Sunday and all, there was no one at the FAM and of course the security there knew nothing about any games being played anywhere. They did, though, make a phone call and we finally learned from Devinder the KL game had been moved to Bangi, which was bloody miles away. There was still something like an hour to go till kick-off, but I was sure the drive out to the rearranged venue would be long, tortuous, and expensive. The enthusiasm I had felt at the start of the day was slowly being sapped and I was losing the will to do much beyond return to the humming air conditioning in my hotel room and get some sleep. But I was like a dog with a bone. If I couldn't see Kuala Lumpur, then goddammit I would see another game.

'We'll go Subang Jaya. There is a game being played there,' I said. So, the driver agrees, turns around and we are on the road again. All this for a bloody football match in the third tier of a league that the FA can't even be arsed to provide accurate info about! The stadium at Subang Jaya was really just a running track, a field, and a stand. That was it. I paid off the cab and went inside, noticing a couple of European-looking folks arriving just as I was.

I've seen some great teams and games over the near 40 years of watching football. Bayern Munchen, Arsenal, AC Milan, Ajax, St George, in the old National Soccer League in Australia. I've also seen a few odd ones. You know, like 1FC Garmisch Partenkirchen in the German Alps or the Westfield Sutherland Shire Soccer Sharks in the New South Wales State League. Now, at least according to the FAM website, I was about to see MISC-MIFA host PBDKT, a mid-table clash in a league that gets next to no publicity even from the organisers at a stadium that is miles from anywhere! God, I love football.

I walked around. Things were a bit quiet. Hot, humid but quiet. Odd, with about 15 minutes to kick off, you would think the teams would be out warming up, wouldn't you? There was no indication of a game, the dressing rooms were locked, and the staff didn't have any idea what was going on. The latter didn't worry me, no one ever seems to know anything! But a locked dressing room, now that was a cause for concern.

One of the foreigners approached me, wondering if I knew anything. Of course, I bloody didn't! He and his mate were a couple of Austrian ground hoppers, in town for the game. Before, they had been to see Negeri Sembilan and Sriwijaya in Indonesia. After a few games in and around KL they were heading down to Singapore for an SLeague fix but for now they were milling around Subang Jaya in the hope of a game. So, picture the scene. Suburban KL, two Austrians and me placing our faith in the FA website, each of us making long, painful journeys to catch a game between a bunch of random letters that fell off a scrabble board.

Halfway through what would have been the first half, even I had to admit defeat in my quest. There wasn't going to be a game and the people, who were now venturing to the venue, were more interested in stretching their limbs on the running track as a slight breeze made some inroads into the heat. I finally got another taxi, after a bloody long wait, to the nearest railway station and took the train home. It was Father's Day. Back in Jakarta my son had thrown a can at his grandma while his old man had spent way too much time and way too much money in the pathetic pursuit of a football match only for the day, much like England's World Cup quest, to end in glorious failure.

7.
THE STORY OF SUPER MOKH

The forty-yard pass split the Arsenal defence and the diminutive striker in the number 10 shirt raced through the gears driving home from just outside the penalty area. A Malaysian Select side had just gone 1-0 up against the Arsenal in front of 30,000 fans at the Merdeka Stadium and some Europeans were being made aware for the first time of a very special talent. Sadly, in 1975, there was no internet and there was no blanket coverage of football. All that remains is a grainy black and white video showing a somewhat bemused looking Arsenal being beaten 2-0 in Kuala Lumpur, with both goals scored by Mokhtar Dahari.

Malaysians, of course, knew all about Mokhtar, and had known since he had made his debut for his home state Selangor, as an 18-year-old in 1972. Mokhtar was born in Setapak, some four and a half miles north of the Merdeka Stadium, where he was to grace for so many glorious years. When he was 11-years-old he moved with his family to Kampung, Pandan, and started going to the prestigious Victoria Institution. A school that had opened its doors in 1894 and could boast a number of prominent politicians and business people among its alumni. I have always been fascinated by history and while Kuala Lumpur may not have the historical reach of a Bangkok or a Jakarta, as it was only settled in 1857 by a gang of tin miners, plenty of research exists on its formative years, with the prodigious J M Gullick, prolific contributor. In 1911, the Victoria Institution was at the heart of a scandal that rocked colonial Malaya to its core.

It was located on High Street, approximately where Kinabalu roundabout is today. Its fields backed on to a bend in the river where masters used to go shooting crocodiles, while the area nearby was a notorious red light district. Despite this, or maybe because of, the school proved an instant success with student numbers rapidly increasing and headmaster Bennett Shaw took to returning to the UK to recruit suitable teachers, one year returning with a William Proudlock.

By all accounts Proudlock was an all-round good egg. Good at sports, involved in the fire brigade, active in the choir, and popular with students. So, the whole KL community, no doubt, was chuffed when, in 1907, he married Ethel Charter, described as an attractive blond Eurasian. Such was the good Proudlock's status that when Shaw took leave in 1911, he left the school in the safe hands of the all-round good egg. Proudlock, wife Ethel, and 3 year-old-daughter Dorothy moved into the headmaster's bungalow set back from the main road and backing on to the Klang.

On the evening of 23 April, William was dining with a colleague in Brickfields, the same area as the glitzy, glossy new railway station. Ethel was at home alone when she had a visitor. Mining consultant William Steward turned up on a rickshaw, bidding the rickshaw wallah wait outside. Next thing the rickshaw puller hears is gunshots and sees Steward stagger from the bungalow and fall to the ground. Ethel following, standing over the hapless Steward still shooting.

Proudlock returned to find his wife hysterical and Steward dead. It was to become the OJ Simpson trial of colonial KL. The Malay Mail, at the time, described it as, 'in the history of the Federated Malay States the case is without parallel,' with allegations of impropriety, illicit affairs, and the race card thrown into the mix. If they had had CNN back then, Larry King would have been reporting daily from the courthouse along with a gaggle of high profile lawyers adding their sixpence worth. Enough dirty washing came out at the four week trial to keep Persil executives rubbing their hands in glee.

The case rocked the colonial community. One did not entertain men when one was married, one certainly did not kill one of one's own class, one did not bring shame on one's community, one was English with all the moral baggage that came with it. The days of Swettenham and Douglas, doughty pioneers in their way who had overlooked any amorous discretions with locals, had gone, replaced by a world of assumptions and mirrors. Ethel standing over William on that April eve pumping bullets into the inert body had shattered the mirror.

First, of course, and what guaranteed the case made the headlines was Steward. What was he doing calling on a married woman, home alone, especially at night time. It came out in the trial that he kept a Chinese mistress at home. The curtain twitchers raised their collective noses at that because, of course, one did one's best but one most assuredly did not fraternise like that with the locals. So, was Ethel having an affair with an older man who had a mistress? But there's more.

Like who exactly was Ethel? Her birth certificate said nothing about her mother. Therefore, she was born out of wedlock, therefore she was universally damned by the oh so prim and proper matrons of the time who took solace from the fact that, 'she isn't one of us after all, she's Eurasian.' After all, went the reasoning, why hide the mother's name unless she was local?

Her defence rather predictably was that Steward had forced himself on her, she had backed off, found the gun by some chance and shot him, that she had acted under great stress and was extremely scared, made worse by an embarrassing gynaecological problem. She could not explain why she had followed him out of the house and continued firing into his body as it lay on the ground. The press lapped it up; no doubt Bennett Shaw on leave in England followed the case in the papers, wondering just what the bloody hell was going on in his school.

The solicitors who worked on the case were in no doubt Ethel was guilty and sure enough she was soon found guilty in a trial that lasted just 10 days and sentenced to hang with a recommendation that mercy be granted. But the damage done to British self-esteem was incalculable. So, was the murder done in a moment of jealous xenophobic rage? A spurned lover raging at being rejected for an Asian? However, even on death row she managed to upset western sensibilities by appealing to the Malay Raja for clemency, which she duly received. One can imagine how she was mightily relieved to leave that cloistered world.

A later headmaster in an altogether different Malaysia on the eve of independence met a VI old boy who had been a student at the time and the old boy offered an intriguing twist to the tale. On the night of the murder a fully clothed European was seen swimming across the river behind the headmaster's bungalow. In those days it would have been a real river, in April flooded, and home to crocodiles. One does not just swim across such a river, the theory being Ethel was protecting a third party. Another lover perhaps or maybe even Proudlock? Another theory, put out by Ethel's employer at another school was that Proudlock knew more about what had happened than he let on and that Ethel was protecting him.

The truth, like the headmaster's bungalow, has gone forever. Proudlock followed his wife back to the UK, where they moved on to Canada and America. He finally settled in a school not dissimilar to VI in Argentina. Students there recall a poem he used to recite about his days in Malaya.

When I was in Malay

I killed tigers twice a day

Now I'm not in Malay

I kill children twice a day

Mokhtar went to the school a couple generations later, when Malaya had become independent Malaysia and while the history buff in me would like to think he was aware of this story, the realist appreciates there were more pressing matters for the student than the antics of colonials half a century earlier. Mokhtar had friends to make and, of course, football to play and the latter he did pretty well. In 1971 he started to make an impression, not just locally but on the country.

Years later, in an interview he did with the school magazine, Seladang

Mokhtar, recalled his time at the school. 'I entered VI in Form One. It was 1966 then. I stayed there for about four years until 1970.'

Mokhtar's humility stands out through the snippets of interview that have been passed down to us. 'Well, the truth is I was just an average player,' he recalled. 'My position was left wing striker. Even now I feel that the training methods of my days were very raw. There weren't any qualified coaches at all. But Cigku Othman Mohd Ali, our school coach, was really something. We were very disciplined and individual fitness was maintained. Sometimes, we even had centralised training when we had to stay in the school!'

It's interesting what we choose to remember from our school days. I hated mine and have tried to erase them from my mind though a few moments, not always pleasant, cling on. Mokhtar's memories of school beyond the football field don't seem to be very positive either! The prefects! 'They were a strict bunch,' he told the magazine, no doubt with the journalists nodding and smiling in knowing appreciation. 'They were strict bunch. They even warned me for having my bicycle modified! I was sent to detention class once or twice, where I had to polish hinges! My worse experience was when I failed two subjects and the report card given out on the same day I was supposed to play against PMC in the finals. A couple of whacks from the headmaster was enough to put some fire into my playing and we won the match as expected.'

Back in 1961, the Malaysian national team coach of the time, Choo Seng Quee, was sent to England to study some coaching techniques on a six month secondment, spending time with a Burnley team, which at the time was the reigning league champions. On his return to Malaysia the Singaporean born coach was presented with a trophy by Burnley to be presented at a Malaysian game played between a couple of Under 19 sides. So, it was that Mokhtar, representing Selangor in the Burnley Cup in 1971 first made people sit up and take note of his blistering pace and ability. Soon after, he was representing Selangor in the league and the Malaysia Cup and a year later he made his debut for Malaysia against Ceylon (later to be renamed Sri Lanka). The Super

Mokh legend was born.

He was the heartbeat of an impressive Selangor side that won the Malaysia Cup an impressive 10 times in 15 years and was at the core of what many Malaysians consider to be their finest ever national side. Beyond defeating the Arsenal in that friendly the Malaysians triumphed in the South East Asian Games twice (1979 and 1981) as well as finishing third in the 1974 Asian Games.

Despite his status as the star of both club and country there was little opportunity for Mokhtar to play the big time Charlie. There was no Bentley or Range Rover to cruise around town in. Like other players of his generation, football wasn't a career move. Mokhtar's day job came in a bank and he used a humble motorcycle to get him from home to office to training field. His motorcycle was the thread that joined the different parts of his life together and with no motorcycle his life would come crumbling down. Which is what happened early in his career when it was stolen. Super Mokh was distraught and decided he would quit football. The bank was his livelihood, he needed that income. He would sacrifice football, a game he truly loved, and which was growing to love him. Fortunately for football, people rallied round in his time of need and in an early example of player sponsorship a motorcycle manufacturer stepped forward and gave him a new two-wheeler. Super Mokh was back and revitalised, he went on to score the goals that helped Selangor go on to win the Malaysia Cup.

As Mokhtar's fame grew there were offers to move to different clubs but the number 10 would never entertain them. For him it wasn't ever about the money. It was about playing for Selangor and Malaysia and being close to his family.

There was something about number 10, about Mokhtar. He was squat, had thick thighs, and could run. His electrifying pace was coupled with immense body strength much like Diego Maradona, and it was quite appropriate the two players would one day meet on the pitch at Merdeka Stadium when

Selangor hosted Boca Juniors in a friendly in January 1982. The 19-year-old Argentine was just beginning to make a name for himself while Mokhtar was undoubtedly at his peak, but still little known beyond Malaysia. And yes, it may have only been a friendly but for those few moments when Mokhtar and Maradona shook hands in the centre circle Malaysian football fans truly believed their Super Mokh was with an equal.

Everyone can recall the goal Maradona scored for Argentina against England at the World Cup in 1986. No, not the one he scored with his hand, the other one where he set off on a mesmerising run leaving a number of England defenders in his wake to score the 'goal of the century.'

I wonder if Mokhtar, and indeed the watching England manager, allowed himself a wry smile as he watched the game on television, recalling a similar incident against a similar opponent eight years earlier. In May 1978, an England B team set off for a tour of the Far East and New Zealand with Bobby Robson as manager. The B team was a squad usually made up of players who were under consideration for the full squad and this particular travelling party included the likes of goalkeeper Joe Corrigan, defender Viv Anderson, and striker Paul Mariner. The game ended 1-1 but for those who were there it will be Mokhtar's goal which will live long in the memory. Receiving the ball in his own half Mokhtar put his head down and started running, leaving the England defenders like Anderson struggling to catch up. From 18 yards his shot flew past the despairing lunge of Corrigan, and had there been social media, the Malaysian striker would have gone viral. Big players perform on the big occasion, and while the Arsenal and England B teams may have had their minds elsewhere on their post-season tours. Make no mistake, in the days before the English Premier League set about colonising the hearts and minds of South East Asia, here was one of their own showing what he could do against some of the best in the world.

Mokhtar finally hung up his boots in 1986, and though he dabbled in coaching he soon complained of illness. His wife took him to London for a check-up and it was revealed he had motor-neuron disease, which affects people's bodily movements. He died tragically early in 1991, aged 37, but lives on in the collective soul of Malaysian football as a true great of the domestic game. As Singaporeans like to recall 1994, Malaysia has Mokhtar. He represents a golden age when Malaysia and his club Selangor were at the peak of their powers and their fulcrum was the small, speed dynamo they called Super Mokh.

While his exploits live on in the memories of those lucky enough to see him play or the occasional black and white clip on YouTube, his name continues to be associated with football with an academy that bears his name. The Mokhtar Dahari National Football Academy is based in Kuantan and was founded in 2014. While it is too early to see the fruits of this project bloom, the Under 14s did make some waves early in 2018, when they won the Whitsun Under 14 Championships in Dortmund, Germany defeating FC Midtjylland 4-0 in the final. Days later, the Under 15s triumphed in Maastricht, Netherlands. The Under 14s proved Dortmund was no fluke as they won the Vogido Championship defeating KRC Genk 1-0 in the final. They were unable to keep the good form going as they struggled in their next competition, but they returned to Malaysia in June not just with the medals and trophies earnt, but experiences Mokhtar could never have imagined about while he was learning the game on the playing fields of the VI.

8.
FOOTBALL'S UNIFORM FETISH

For some reason I have never been to any of Malaysia's really big games. I haven't seen a Selangor game in front of a packed house at Shah Alam Stadium, neither have I seen a Pahang or a Kedah let alone Penang or Melaka United. I have, though, seen the likes of ATM, PDRM, and Felda United, and no one can take that away from me!

On one of my spins through Malaysia I managed a uniform double catching PDRM and ATM on consecutive nights. Both games were important in the scheme of things regarding their respective leagues, but both were worth catching on their own merits. And let's face it, who wouldn't want to catch a game between the police force and a government department that dealt with relocating people around the country!

PDRM v Felda United was a top of the table clash in the second tier Premier League, and Felda had been Flashing the cash, snapping up two of the best foreign players in Indonesia, Liberians Zah Rahan, a midfielder, and striker Edward Wilson Junior. The two imports have been at the heart of much that has been good from the team, guiding them to their first ever FA Cup Final, narrowly losing to Pahang in 2014. Going into this game, PDRM had already made sure of finishing in the top two and earning, both, promotion back to the Super League and their place in the prestigious Malaysia Cup, the longest running football competition in Asia. They were also scoring goals for fun, averaging three a game and conceding one. Sorted, a 3-1 win for the home team then!

Like their opponents, Felda, PDRM, Polis di Raja Malaysia or Royal Malaysian Police to give them their full title (they are nicknamed the Cops), had invested heavily pre-season, including bringing in highly rated coach Dollah Salleh from Pahang.

The Melaka-born coach has been one of the most successful coaches in the country over the last 15 years or so, having brought success to MPPJ (Malaysia Cup, Premier League, Charity Shield), Selangor (Premier League, FA Cup, Malaysia Cup in one season) and Pahang (Malaysia Cup). I guess that little haul can go some way to disproving the old notion that the best players don't always make the best caches.

As a player, Salleh played for, and won trophies with, Johor, Selangor, and Pahang, as well as playing for home town club Melaka, and Negeri Sembilan, netting 143 goals in 257 games. He also did the business on the international stage, scoring 48 goals in 97 games for Malaysia.

So, the stage was set for a match-up between the top two teams in the Premier League. The crowd was around the 1,500-2,000 mark perhaps with home team PDRM fans vastly outnumbering the Felda support, which is odd because Felda have been using the same stadium this season for their home games. And they recently received an allocation of 30,000 for the FA Cup Final. At this game there were perhaps 0.5% of that number!

There were cops everywhere and not because they expected crowd trouble. I counted 10 lorry loads, you know those military style trucks, while a few more coaches had also been booked. And of course, the fans were cops!

There were cops in r and r clobber and there were cops in neatly pressed white shirts and ties. There was a cop band featuring saxophones, French horns, and bagpipes, honest guv. There were cops on-duty doing crowd control and there were cops who escorted the match officials to and from their changing room at half-time. (This last is a normal occurrence in Malaysia and is probably a reaction to the rampant match fixing that has plagued the game here.)

It was all a bit much. At one point, I tried to return to my seat after a visit to the toilet, but my way was blocked by two burly cops who told me that as I was a Felda United supporter I had to sit on the other side of the grandstand!

A Felda fan?! What the hell was all that about? So, I sat with the Felda fans, who at least made some noise, had some scarves and shirts and stuff, and tried to generate some atmosphere of their own and not under instruction from some guy with pips on his collar.

PDRM fans were dressed up in official clobber but there appeared to be no place outside selling merchandising for the rare enthusiast, though one or two fans had broken from the mould and were wearing replica shirts.

The Cops, the ones on the field, had plenty of possession but Felda defended well and it was no real surprise when Liberian international Zah Rahan, who used to play for Sriwijaya Palembang and Persipura Jayapura in Indonesia, scored with a sweetly taken volley in the first half. The silky midfielder was a lively threat all game, and it was Felda who held out for the 1-0 win to end PDRM's unbeaten run. After the game, the cops supporting the Cops dutifully boarded their lorries and buses and headed home, politely saying hello to the fat white guy waiting for a taxi. One fan said good morning, which was just about the funniest thing since Monty Python's parrot sketch according to his mates, who repeated the punch line about 60 squillion times as they wiped the tears from their eyes.

Coming from England, it is difficult to get excited about a police football team. I was one of those teenagers who used to walk the suburban streets after the sun had gone down and the commuters were in the armchairs watching their favourite soap or out having affairs. We were too young and too skint to go to the local pub too often or the local off licence, and uninterested in doing our homework — gosh what rebels — so we walked the streets. People didn't walk round my way, they had cars. So, when the middleclass twitchers, behind their lace curtains, heard the sound of people talking out on the street they were on the blower to PC Plod. This, of course, was back in the day when there was a cop on duty in the evenings!

I wouldn't say I was naughty and I wouldn't say I was targeted but with my Doc Marten boots, leather jacket, and messy hair (I never used combs), the local residents sized me and my mates up, added it to the stories they read in the Daily Mail or had seen on Nationwide and came up with 99bloody9. So, no, my early memories of the old bill aren't that good though not bad enough to go and get ACAB (All Coppers Are Bastards) tattooed inside my lower lip! But no way could I follow a football team with their roots in nicking people! There is a Metropolitan Police team playing in one of England's lower leagues, but they are only of interest to ground hoppers and those in search of a game, like me one December evening back in 1988!

In this part of the world, they are more common. Singapore has Home United, formerly known as Police but rebranded to become a hub (!) for the fire and ambulance services as well, while Thailand has Police United who signed former Queens Park Rangers and Sunderland defender Anton Ferdinand once upon a time. In fact, the owner of Police United later took over Championship side Reading!

Home have been one of the most successful teams in Singapore since the SLeague began, lifting the trophy on a couple occasions as well as being the holders of the Singapore Cup but their attendances, as in the rest of the league, remain small. They do, however, seem to play an active role in the community and I have often seen them bus in old folks from retirement homes to catch a game, reinforcing a point I made earlier about Albirex Niigata being as much a CSR exercise at times than a full blown football club — and I don't mean that in a cynical way.

The problem with clubs like PDRM, Home, and Police United is their natural fan base, serving cops, their families, and retirees, is going to be narrow. Usually football members of the security forces are rarely seen in a good light (witness Indonesia where a police side Bhayangkara and military side PS Tira have failed to attract any meaningful support). So, a fan growing up and seeing guys in uniform take liberties are not going to look favourably on a football team bearing their moniker. It will be interesting to see how the future treats these football clubs.

Clubs like Johor Darul Tazim, Kelantan, and Pahang, have shown the potential of football in Malaysia. It remains to be seen whether or not those that are for all intents and purposes an extension of a government department, and that includes Felda United, can match their vision and appeal to a wider base.

ATM are the armed forces team. If you want to search for them on the internet, make sure you are looking for ATM Malaysia adding the word football, or you will be taken to pages of cash dispensers. As of 2018, they are in the third tier FAM League, but it wasn't that long ago they were rubbing shoulders with Malaysia's very best in front of fairly decent crowds.

In 2014, they narrowly escaped relegation from the Super League, and in the run to the season gave title chasing Johor Darul Ta'zim, a shock beating them 2-1 at home in a rip-roaring affair. It was end to end game in front of 6,500 (ATM's largest crowd of the season), with JDT opting for a four man attack, including Norshahrul Idlan and Yahya Amri down the flanks and Argentine imports Luciano Figuero and Diaz down the middle. Seriously, if this was at the World Cup, the press and twitter would be reaching for superlatives.

Coaches, however, watch a different game to the rest of us and judging by Bojan Hodak's body language in the second half, he was less than impressed with the match officials' performances, feeling a couple of penalty appeals were given short shrift. As JDT trooped down to the dressing room, coach Hodak cast a disconsolate figure. Victory, he believed, would have set the team up nicely for the title run in. But ATM had done Selangor last week, perhaps there was no surprise they were too much for JDT.

While it was hard enough to turn your eyes away from the game, the action on the terraces was just as thrilling. JDT had brought perhaps 3-4,000 thousand supporters with them and comfortably outnumbered the home support at the Selayang Stadium, north of KL, but both sets of supporters kept the atmosphere at boiling point all through the game.

Being an armed forces team, it was perhaps no surprise that most of the home support was drawn from the military. Indeed, among the hard core there was evidence of a uniform with the ATM home shirt being worn along with camouflage trousers. And unlike the PDRM fans yesterday, these guys kept the racket going all game, accompanied by a military style band that featured drums, trombones, cymbals, and god knows what. They even had a small posse of head-scarf-wearing girls joining in the fun. And it was fun.

JDT's support was a more traditional football following, including doing the Poznan when the teams came on the pitch ahead of the kick off. At the end of the game, despite the loss, the players stood to attention, facing the travelling fans as they belted out their anthem while the home fans, buzzing after a famous victory, watched politely. It's these little touches that make football, the global game, so local.

Considering the large away contingent, there was never any indication of crowd trouble and the security presence was minimal. Certainly, had this been Indonesia, there would have been hundreds of robo cops on duty. I guess no one wants to mess with a battalion of highly trained soldiers at a match!

Despite the Poznan, replica shirts, and scarves, this was most definitely a football experience crafted in Malaysia. Outside, the ground ahead of kick off there were some JDT fans praying outside the petrol station opposite, while fans of both sides mingled with no sign of trouble and JDT's two club coaches were untroubled and unharmed. All a far cry from the security and remoteness all too common in the English Premier League.

There was one ticket tout trying to flog tickets next to the queue at the ticket box! I guess he had overlooked the location, location, location class at business school. Mind you, he was doing a bit better than one guy I encountered at a game in Indonesia who was selling his wares at less than face value!

Touting is hardly the big business it can be in the west but when it does happen many locals feel it is the result of a collusion between club officials and their 'mates.' I recall going to an AFC Champions League tie once and when I approached the ticket office they told me with as much disinterest as they could muster, all tickets were gone. I had to buy one from one of several touts milling round the forecourt. I wonder what the AFC would have made of that?

There was also the time when Indonesia reached the final of an Under 19 competition, which was being held in Sidoarjo, East Java. With a large crowd expected, fans were advised to get to the stadium early, which they did. Of course, when they arrived they found the ticket outlets had the 'Sold Out' signs up while plenty of scalpers had plenty in their grubby little mitts. Being a cynical bunch, the supporters assumed the match organisers were trying to make themselves a tidy little profit. So, they went on the rampage, burning some outlets and attacking the touts. In England we would just roll our eyes, say, 'what can you do,' before heading to the nearest pubs, pausing long enough to send a couple of irate tweets.

Meanwhile back in Malaysia, there were a few women who had set up a souvenir stall within the petrol station itself and seemed to be doing a pretty healthy trade.

I headed back to my hotel in a taxi, necking a deliciously cool isotonic drink I had bought at the petrol station. It gets hot and humid in those stadiums, and as ever the driver struck up a conversation.

'Who won?' was the opening salvo.

'ATM,' I replied, watching the mirror for any sign of a reaction. Often cabbies just like a natter to break the tedium of a long, dull old day but the smile on this guy's face told a different story.

'Who do you support?' I asked him.

'Kelantan!'

I understood. Ex Kelantan coach Bojan had lost and his team had been knocked out of their stride on their way to the title and that was enough to bring some cheer to my taxi driver. This was pure schadenfreude, and it was a feeling most football fans are familiar with.

Many is the time I have headed home from a game not particularly enjoying the bitter taste of defeat even if it was washed down with a cool lager, but the taste would magically improve if I heard Tottenham had lost or one of our other rivals. On the other hand, when my team loses one thing that makes the defeat even harder is knowing our rivals have won and their supporters will be just impossible to deal with for a few days.

Malaysian football is in a state of flux at the moment. On the one hand, you have Johor Darul Ta'zim who have won the Super League every year since 2014, and even became the first South East Asian team to win a continental trophy when they lifted the AFC Cup in 2015. Then you have, well, nothing much. No club seems to be able to match JDT and their deep pockets on or off the pitch. Perhaps more importantly, no other club seems to be able to match the southern team's professional set up off the field which is setting the stage for a successful club in the future. Other clubs' fortunes ebb and flow at the whim of the local political situation, meaning each new season pretty well sees a new club for all intents and purpose. Forward planning is a luxury most clubs can only dream about.

The promise shown by the national team also hasn't been built upon. The golden years when Malaysia triumphed in the SEA Games twice and won the AFF Suzuki Cup for the first time in 2010 are but a distant memory as Malaysia, like the rest of the region, wait for any scraps left over by the Thais. A humiliating 10-0 loss away to United Arab Emirates in a 2018 World Cup Qualifier. In 2015, was a new nadir for the national team in a year when they also lost 6-0 at home and away to Palestine and a pitch invasion by disgruntled fans in a qualifier against Saudi Arabia saw them forfeit that particular game.

The answer, as ever, lies in youth development and the successes over the summer of 2018 by the teenagers of the Mokhtar Dahari Academy showing the talent is there. Sadly, it looks like there is no clear career progression as they get older, as so many clubs are run on such a short-term basis. There are efforts in place to try and improve the game's creaking infrastructure but there is no quick fix. For a proud football country, the jewel in the crown is JDT but the lingering question must be what is the rest of the crown made of?

To close the Malaysia chapter, I will return to my interview with Steve Darby and his experiences after he left Johor for they are instructive.

He chose to return to Malaysia when Perak, from what was now known as the Malaysian Super League, came calling in 2005. After three years with Johor and Home United, Darby, was to stay with Perak for another three years and he feels it was no coincidence he stayed so long at those three clubs.

'I learnt that the key to success for, both, the team and as a coach is the quality of management. If you can't manage upwards in Asia, you don't last long. Also, you have to win early. There are no projects or philosophies in Asia except win... and win again next week. Where I had quality management I lasted three years, a long time in Asia. When megalomaniacs came in, results and myself suffered and it was time to go.'

With Kedah and Selangor so dominant in Malaysian football at the time, Darby struggled to replicate the success he had enjoyed with Johor but the club stuck with him because they could see his efforts bearing fruit in other areas. It also helped that his time at the club got off to a flying start.

'The first game v Selangor was in Bukit Jalil in the Super Cup final, where everything went right, and we won easily 4-1 in front of 100,000 fans. That gave us a winning platform. We had great characters such as Ahmad Sharul, Khalid Jamlus, and foreigners such as Keita Manjou, Vedran Kucok, and Troare. All quality players on and off the pitch.

'Also, the Malaysian Cup final in 2007 was great, with again 100,000 at

Bukit Jalil v Kedah. We were deservedly beaten by an excellent Kedah team coached by a top local Coach Azrai Kor. Khyril Muhymeen Zambri opened the scoring for Kedah and the prolific Marlon Alex James added two more. Sadly, we lost out captain after 17 minutes to his first tackle and a red card.

'A few other strange decisions and it makes you wonder should referees have a big game as their last game? There is no comeback. Over the years we heard many rumours about the officiating in this game, but we were well beaten so I don't blame it for the result. We also lost out to Kedah by two points for the premiership. Again, there were some unusual scores in the run in! I have to say that I don't believe Azrai or the players were involved. As they say in Malaysia, unseen hands may have been at work.'

Among those 'unusual results' Darby refers to was Perak winning 9-0 away to a Melaka side, which was eventually relegated having conceded 72 goals in their 24 games! Kedah enjoyed their own goal fests in those last few weeks of the season, beating Pahang 4-1 and Negeri Sembilan 7-0 to overhaul Perak, who had been held by Negeri Sembilan 1-1 in their last home game of the season to clinch the title.

Darby describes the first three Perak club presidents as 'brilliant.' Like most state sides in Malaysia, Perak relied on local government funding channeled through the state football association. With political appointees often placed in charge of the football association, coaches are reliant on good will from the man with the purse strings to do their jobs properly. When the manager is willing to give a coach the freedom to act as he sees fit then the club takes on the sheen of professionalism but is rarely able to take a long-term view. The problem with democracy is all those damned elections giving people the opportunity to elect their representatives, and when a new party takes over in the corridors of power they set about cementing their power base by appointing their favourites to key positions. Sadly, this includes football.

Following elections in 2008, a more conservative party took over the political reigns in the state from the United Malays National Organisation in Perak and they set about imposing their authority. Steve Darby takes up the story.

'(They) decided to stop paying wages! The new football association president was the state prime minister. So, I went to see him and said you have to pay the players — and me! He replied we should be playing for honour. I asked him if he was prime minister for honour!! So, I knew there would be no contract for next year! I ended up having to pay some of the young lads their wages out of my own pocket as they literally had no money.'

Although Darby wasn't able to win any trophies during his time with Perak, he did lead them to the quarter finals of the AFC Cup in 2008, despite getting thrashed 6-1 at home by Singapore Armed Forces (now known as Warriors) with veterans Aleksandar Duric and Therdask Chaiman netting five between them. Perak finished second in the group, level on points with SAFFC and earned a spot in the quarter finals where they were drawn with Lebanese side Safa. The first leg was played in Ipoh, the state capital of Perak, and the visitors won 2-0 giving them a strong advantage going into the second leg to be played in Beirut a week later.

'I had to arrange the cheapest flights. I took 15 players, three substitutes, and a keeper sub, and three staff including myself. We arrived at the airport and six committee men turned up flying business class and spent three days shopping in Beirut and Damascus! So much for piety and equality that was widely promoted in their manifesto!'

With such a public show of support from their club officials it is little wonder the team were beaten 5-0 and so ended their AFC Cup ambitions and Darby's time with Perak.

Anthony Burgess once wrote a book called, *The Malayan Trilogy*, looking at the end of British rule in what was once known as Malaya and the changeover to independence. It follows the adventures of Victor Crabbe, a history teacher during those tumultuous times. Steve Darby could well pen his own Malaysian

Trilogy as following his success with Johor and his relative success with Perak, he returned to Malaysia in 2014 for a brief coda with Kelantan. In a way, Darby's time in Malaysia parallels Victor Crabbe. Unfortunately for Darby, he doesn't look back fondly on his north eastern interregnum. For starters, the warm relations he had enjoyed with club management in Johor and most of his Perak spell wasn't replicated in Kota Bahru, where the football association president at the time, Tuan Sri Annuar Musa, was very hands-on.

Still, the 'noughties' proved to be the most successful in Kelantan's history as B Sathinathan, M Karathu, Peter Butler, and Bojan Hodak guided the Red warriors to unimagined success. They were crowned Super League champions twice, FA Cup winners twice, Malaysia Cup winners twice, and lifted the Super Cup for good measure. However, their last trophy came in 2013 when they defeated Johor Darul Ta'zim 1-0 to win the FA Cup, but they were being left behind as JDT had come along and were blitzing the rest of Malaysia football out of the water with their ideas they were adopting from the western super clubs. Professionalism, nutrition, science, data. JDT had taken football into the wifi age while Kelantan were still on dial up; their decision to allow a skin whitener company to become the major sponsor and change their club colours and name showed how far they had fallen in such a short period of time.

It seemed a match doomed to failure. Their colourful chairman at the time, Annuar Musa, liked to make his feelings known, as did Darby.

Darby loathed interference from up high when it came to doing his job. Annuar Musa felt that was his job. Darby was outspoken in his criticism of interfering club officials, Annuar felt he was the main man at the football club. Darby lasted less than six months!

'After three great years in Thailand and others in India and China I was offered a contract by Kelantan. It had changed a lot from when I was there with Johor. The dressing rooms now were not cockroach infested, but we still trained on a school field with no showers and, of course, there was still no cinema in Kota Bahru as that was banned by the religious clerics, which ruled the state! But I was fascinated by the number of cars that used to travel from this state across the border to Thailand. It must have been for the quality of the rice!'

'The players are usually no problems, but this time I had a complete team signed before I got there and there had been no homework done on the players. Whilst the foreigners were quality players, the off field behaviour??? was different, though I have to say Mohammad Shawky the Egyptian International was one of the best pros I have worked with. By coincidence he left soon after me! This time I was saddled with a team manager who was constantly interfering and mixing socially with some of the foreigners. I speak reasonable Bahasa and I could understand many things he was saying behind my back.'

It was a recipe for disaster and it wasn't long before the pot boiled over. 'Many political stories from within the club and this alone could fill a book!' teases the coach as we end our interview.

Bangkok Glass fans making a noise away to BEC Tero

PART 3: THAILAND

9.
JUST A FOOTBALL FAN HANGING OUT ON PATTAYA BEACH

Every time I approach Bangkok airport I have a Cold Chisel song playing in my mind, you know the one about this town and me sharing a bit of history. Oh yes, me and Bangkok go back a long way. I first visited Thailand in 1987, on my way to Australia and moved there to work in 1994. Back then I wasn't really interested in the local football, which at the time consisted of teams like SET, BBC, and TFB. I watched the odd game on TV and promised I would catch a game live one day but never did.

In those days TFB, or Thai Farmers' Bank, was one of the biggest clubs in the region. They even boasted a small shop in Siam Square and despite visiting it in a number of occasions, I never opened my wallet to buy anything. To be fair, if I had opened my wallet there would have been nothing in it!

In the 1990's, Thai Farmers Bank strode majestically across not just the Thai scene but also Asia. They won the Thai League four times in six years (1990, 1992. 1993, 1995) and the Queen's Cup four times (1994, 1995, 1996, 1997). They also won the Asian Champions League twice in 1994 and 1995, the only South East Asian to have triumphed. Indeed, no team has won the trophy more than TFB, though, several have also won it twice. Selangor from Malaysia were beaten finalists in the inaugural tournament losing to Hapoel Tel Aviv of Israel!

But there's more! The winners of the Asian Champions Cup used to play off against the winners of the African Champions Cup for the Afro Asian Championship and Thai Farmers Bank were victors in 1994, beating Egypt's Zamelak on away goals. A year later they were beaten 4-1 on aggregate by Tunisian side Esparance, the first leg being held bizarrely in provincial Suphanburi. Or maybe not so odd. Thailand's Prime Minister at the time was the dimunitive Banharn Silpa Archa and his constituency was... Suphanburi!

Judging by their record, Thai Farmers Bank gave up sponsoring its football club probably about 1997 or 1998, when the Asian economic crisis struck. The shop closed down and I never got to see probably Asia's most successful club side in action!

It wasn't till 1997 that I saw my first game, at the Supachalasai Stadium next door to MBK shopping mall in the centre of Bangkok. Thailand were playing South Korea in an Olympic Games qualifier and they lost 3-1. That was also the second year of the Premier League and the teams that took part then make interesting reading and suggest why they struggled for fans back then.

RTAF (Royal Thai Air Force)

Sinthana

Bangkok Bank

PAT (Port Authority of Thailand)

Tero Sasana

TFB (Thai Farmers Bank)

BMA (Bangkok Metropolitan Authority)

TOT (Telephone Organisation of Thailand)

RTA (Royal Thai Army)

UCOM Rajpracha

PCA (Police Cadet Academy)

RTN (Royal Thai Navy)

More familiar names like TTM (Thai Tobacco Monopoly), KTB (Krung Thai Bank), and BBC (Bangkok Bank of Commerce), were in the second tier at the time. And yet those teams managed to come together to produce players like Kiatisak and Tawan and Piyapong, who would go on to become icons of the local game as players and coaches.

I have probably been through Don Muang more than any other airport but now, with a new facility catering to international and domestic flights, it is used only for budget airlines and strangely quiet. Okay, maybe the recent coup and curfew as well as the ongoing political stalemate kept visitors away!

Finding a taxi, I gave my instructions in my rusty Thai. 'Take me first to Leo Stadium, then we go to Pattaya.'

'Ah, Leo Stadium,' the driver repeated with authority, 'Muang Thong?' It's not, of course. Leo Stadium, home of Bangkok Glass, is to the north of the airport and Muang Thong is to the south. It didn't matter anyway because the driver decided to head straight to Pattaya anyway and off we went. I was tired, it had been a long day, and I was frustrated because I was going to miss a football match. I was also scared. Thai taxi drivers love to put their foot down whenever they spy a bit of open road and this chap was no exception.

He was no Lewis Hamilton either nor Jeremy Clarkson. For this driver, wing mirrors were just another irritant along with seat belts and speed limits. Having a large white guy in the back seat who knew a few Thai words, now that was interesting. So, there we are hacking it down the toll road at 120 kilometres an hour with this driver turning round to ask me what Thai food I liked or if I thought Thai ladies were pretty, while keeping one hand on the steering wheel and talking to his mates on the phone. '*Farang phud Thai*,' he would tell them excitedly while I cowered in the backseat looking nervously in the central reservations for the debris of previous lunatic drivers. With great relief we arrived at the hotel in Pattaya in one piece and as I slid off the seat my driver asked me if I wanted to go on a tour or should he wait for a while. I smiled. 'No thanks.' Trying to sound as friendly as I could.

Pattaya is the kind of place where you get out of a taxi and a tout asks you if you want a taxi. Where you are wearing sunglasses, and someone asks you if you want to buy some sunglasses! My first visit there was in 1989, and I was there a week before I knew the place had a beach! Pattaya is not many people's idea of a fun place, certainly not mine. In all the time I lived in

Bangkok, you could probably count my number of visits on two hands. If you are not there for the jet skis, propping up beer bars, or seducing ladies from the villages of the north east there isn't much to keep you entertained. Me? I was there for the football of course!

It has made efforts to transform itself into a family destination but at its heart it is still what it is and unashamedly so. Pushing a toddler in a pram along its potholed pavements is not my idea of fun but for the ageing folks who call it home or visit regularly and enjoy wandering the *soi* (narrow lanes that lead off larger roads), hopping from bar to bar with their best Hawaiian shirt exposing a bit of bling and a bit of hair, it is everything they look for in a destination. And let's face it. Leaving a cold, depressing European winter for sun, sand, and sea is not a bad way of life, is it? I needed a beer.

Growing up in England in the late 70s, early 80s, if you were a punk, a skin, or a football fan, you were perceived as the lowest of the low. All three were associated in the minds of Daily Mail readers as gutter trash and thugs. Well, I grew up with punk, had a skinhead when my floppy mohican fell off and travelled the country following my team. Unfortunately for the stereotypers, I was tall, skinny, ungainly, and wore NHS specs. Hardly hardcore material.

I would be at concerts or football, get home and hear all about the riots. I never saw them but hey, middle England needed someone to fear so it was punks, skins, and football fans. So, your clothes and your lifestyle marked you down as a 'threat' and you were treated accordingly by the authorities... read the police. Fast forward 30-35 years and not a whole lot has changed, has it?

There was a lot of hooliganism around in those days and let's face it, the football was so grim at times, many supporters would hope for a brawl to break out just to give them something to talk about.

Some of the better known hooligans, top boys, became the thing of urban legend and the rest of us would go silent as they walked past. People feared them yet at the same time there was a tinge of envy. These guys would go to all the games, some even had superb programme collections, and would be the first to get stuck in when it kicked off. I guess, if you want to get all romantic about it, there was a camaraderie about them many of us envied. Don't get me wrong, I'm not condoning rearranging someone's face with a beer bottle but there have been times in some of football's outposts I and no doubt many others were glad they were around!

Chelsea had one of the most active firms as well as some of the most creative wannabes, especially during the 1983-84 season when they were in the old style Division 2 and took bloody thousands to every away game (it must be true, my Chelsea supporting mates told me at the time!).

In response to the ire of a football loathing prime minister, Margaret Thatcher, the cops started clamping down on the hooligans. They got organised on match day and started going undercover. Previously, the attitude had been more of a 'boys will be boys' thing and lads involved would get away with a slap on the wrist and that was about it.

As the police started coming under increasing pressure, they turned to grasses and to fabricating evidence, a common enough occurrence in the UK legal system as those campaigning for justice for the victims of Hillsborough and the Guildford 4 trials can attest. The wheels of justice move slowly indeed when the wrong people are convicted.

Two Chelsea fans were found wrongly convicted, were released and given a pay-off. They retired and moved to Pattaya where they opened a bar, '*The Dog's Bollocks*,' and set about enjoying the warmer climes of their new home. Great story!

Headlines followed them though; and in 2002, ahead of the World Cup, an undercover reporter spent a couple of days in the bar talking to the regulars and the owners before writing a story about vicious English football hooligans looking to cause trouble in Japan. Faced with banning orders back home preventing them from flying direct to Japan, the fans planned to holiday in Thailand and get organised there. The Chelsea fans, so the story goes, would organise onward flights to Japan and match tickets with the game against Argentina a target. Oh, and they were going to sell fake football shirts as well. The story of course took off, playing as it did into the fear middle England had of marauding football thugs causing mayhem on foreign shores and journos raced to provide the most sensational headlines.

The anticipated trouble never happened but there was one unexpected windfall as, *The Dog's Bollocks*, grew in popularity with more and more holidaying hooligans lining up to have their picture taken at the now infamous bar. In a town notorious for alleged mafia types and villains it is a football-themed bar that attracts notoriety! Still shaking after my taxi driver from hell I walked into the narrow bar much like any other narrow bar down the soi, pulled up a stool and ordered a cold beer. The waitress took one from the fridge and asked me if I wanted a condom! Of course, I wanted a condom and she wrapped my beer in a stubby holder to keep it cool.

I talked football with some regulars and took in the newspaper reports that were still on the wall as are the photos and the flags devoted to Chelsea, Rangers and England; it is almost a museum to a certain era in English football. The bar has changed ownership over the years and it may still attract a hooligan element, it may not, but so what? Now it is just one of several English themed bars in the area catering to regulars and visitors alike and it is not a bad place to watch the football in the evening.

Indeed, given the bar's reputation it seemed a tad incongruous when the staff started handing out neatly cut triangle shaped sandwiches to its customers!

Pattaya is on the province of Chonburi and the story of Chonburi is the story of one man. Chonburi is one of Thailand's richest provinces and certainly one of its more interesting ones. For the tourist, for example, it offers a number of beach resorts including Pattaya, Sri Racha, and Bang Saen. For the football fan it has a number of professional teams like Chonburi, Pattaya United, and Sri Racha.

It also has a fascinating political history revolving around one family that grew from humble beginnings to become a major influence on national politics. It is the kind of rags to riches tale the Americans like to think they have a monopoly on with their 'American Dream.' But Thailand, with its economic growth dating back to the 1970s, also has its fair share of local guys made good. And rich. And very powerful.

The story begins back in the 1960s when Chonburi province was still a quiet backwater and the American military had yet to get involved in the quagmire that became Vietnam. After dropping out of school young and spending time as a soldier and a monk, Somchai Khunpluem got involved with a French national who was involved in fishing the resource rich waters off the coast before branching out into other business and by 1968 had become a village head, an important position in Thai regional politics.

With the U Tapao air base, Sattahip naval base and its close proximity to Vietnam and Cambodia, the province was ideally placed to benefit from the escalating war in the conflicts blighting Indo China, and Somchai seized the opportunity with both hands, illegally smuggling goods into the stricken lands.

In the 1980s, the Thai economy was booming and so was Chonburi. Tourists were flocking to Pattaya, and foreign companies were racing to set up shop along the highway from Bangkok. Again, there was Somchai, known by his nickname Kamnan Pho, to facilitate the development with his contacts at the local level and his increasing influence in the corridor or power.

It was certainly an unconventional way to the top and one no business school would advise it, but Kamnan Pho became very rich off the back of war, smuggling, and an economic boom just by being in the right place at the right time. For all that it may be unconventional, it was not unique as other strategically located provinces like Buriram and Suphanburi fell under the spell of a rich family with contacts and contracts seemingly on tap. Thailand was developing at a fast pace and these families were at the forefront of that development.

If you read some of the quotes attributed to Kamnan Pho you end up with a picture of an almost romantic figure, near Robin Hood, who fought his way up from being a bus conductor through some pretty violent times to a pillar of the community happy to spread largesse among the villagers and sending his children off to the US for higher education.

Following the murder of a business rival, Pho was quoted as saying, 'in Chonburi, bad guys must die.' On another occasion he said he was, 'semi businessman, semi gangster.'

He was also dismissive of government and what he saw as its limitations. Civil servants, he said, didn't earn very much. On the other hand, he had a lot of money and he made sure people knew he was well off.

He would help build new shelters at the side of the road, new temples, and help improve the infrastructure in his area; all jobs that should have been under the remit of the government. He filled a void and people in turn recognised him as a good man, a man of influence who could get things done. And it kept politics very local. Despite a democracy going back several decades, for Pho, 'we go for friends and not for the party.' And what Pho said went for most of the residents who looked up to this country bumpkin made good.

Sitting on key corridors to neighbouring countries with whom Thailand didn't always have harmonious relations, Pho and others like him were king makers in more ways than one. While the kingdom has boasted universal suffrage since the 1930s, when it came to elections, people in the villages voted for their local person of influence and power, a *phu yai*. So, when the *phu yai* decided to throw their weight behind a certain political party, that carried not just the rich family's votes but also the vast majority of the province's residents.

While neither Kamnan Poh nor his offspring have ever made it to the top position in the land, they have helped others get there including Banharn Silpa'archa, patriarch of Suphanburi province, who became prime minister in 1995. In this respect, they are similar to the Chidchobs, another powerful family, this time from Buriram, which has historically carried a large number of followers among politicians making them a valuable asset when it came to forming a coalition government.

Coincidentally, or not, the Chidchobs (Buriram United), Silpa'archas (Suphanburi), and the Khunpluems are the driving forces behind their local football clubs; the Khunpluems in fact have two, Chonburi and Pattaya United each being run by sons of Kamnan Poh.

Buriram United have enjoyed enviable success since they were formed from the merger of Buriram PEA and Buriram FC, while Suphanburi have been enjoying large crowds as they experience top flight football. Chonburi have a reputation for being a well-run club while not splashing the cash like Buriram United and Suphanburi. Patttaya United have spent the last few seasons yo-yoing between the top two divisions.

There used to be a football club called Coke Bang Phra. They came from a small town in Chonburi province called Bang Phra and were for all intents and purposes a works team for the local Coca Cola plant. Nothing unusual in that, of course, in the annals of football. Consider Bayer Leverkusen in the Bundesliga for example. Or, for those with longer memories, Ferranti Thistle were a work team formed in Edinburgh, Scotland, in 1943. When they joined the Scottish League in 1974, they were forced to change their name to Meadowbank Thistle. They are now known as Livingstone.

Here in Asia there are a number of teams who take their name, or share their name, with a company sponsor or owner; Semen Padang, of course, springs to mind in Indonesia. While in Malaysia, there was a team called KL PLUS; they were owned by the company that built a toll road!

Mind you there is one club that returned itself to the fans. KFC Uerdingen

05 are not a fast food franchise, but a football club based in Krefeld (and now plays in the Bundesliga fourth division). Not too long ago they were known as Bayer Uerdingen.

Or there are a number of teams in England that started out as a bit of fun for firm employees before moving on to bigger and greater things. Arsenal, for example, started life in an armaments factory. Manchester United can trace their origins back to employees of a railway company.

Coke Bang Phra were a nothing team going nowhere particularly fast until the Khunpluem family, the province's ruling dynasty, decided their number one international beach resort, Pattaya, needed its own football team. So, they rebranded and relocated Coke Bang Phra, giving them a name that would ensure global recognition — Pattaya United. Coke Bang Phra had finished second in the second tier Division One, earning them promotion to the Premier League (TPL) and the prospect of local derbies against Chonburi.

After one season in the TPL, when they finished 11th, the Khunpluems got involved and introduced the new name, badge, colours, and stadium, at the same time keeping the old club's red and black jersey as second choice kit. Pattaya United finished 4th in 2011, their best ever finish, before slipping down the table and getting relegated in 2013.

I arranged to meet a Pattaya United fan of long standing — five years in Thai football counts as long standing — in one of those depressing open air beer bars in downtown Pattaya. Willy has been living in the resort town for the better part of a decade and is a football nut. A fan of VfB Stuttgart in his native Germany, Willy had no problem being encouraged to follow the Dolphins, especially as their tidy Nong Prue Stadium is not too far from his home.

What Willy doesn't know about Pattaya isn't worth knowing and he puts his knowledge of Thai football to good use, contributing to the excellent bilingual www.thai-fussball.com Thai Fussball website. And Willy was not a happy chappy when it comes to the goings on at his club though he assured me he still goes to the games.

He arrived on his motorcycle, resplendent in a Kaset Sart replica shirt and we settled down for a good old fashioned natter while the girls literally girls, or women? behind the bar tried to entice more customers with their gravel voices and the lure of cheap beer and endless games off Connect 4.

'Many people have stopped going to the games. They don't think it is the real Pattaya United,' he started. 'It's all politics here, you know.'

Immediately, my ears pricked up. Not at the politics bit, jeez. I been living and working in Asia for more than 20 years and I am familiar with the Khunplume brand thanks to my prodigious reading of books by Chris Baker and Pasuk Phongpaichit. Both are excellent resources for background on recent Thai politics and a fascinating insight to the names behind some of the biggest football clubs in the country. Read their books and nothing will surprise. Nope, it wasn't the politics Willy mentioned that intrigued me. It was the comment about Pattaya not being the real Pattaya United.

'Pattaya United is now just a Sri Racha team,' he went on. They are based there and train there, only to coming to Pattaya for their home games. They used to be in Pattaya but no more,' he explained.

Mind you, if I was a coach of Pattaya United, would I want the team based in the resort many foreign visitors like to call Sin City? Could I trust healthy young men with plenty of free time to keep themselves fit and healthy with all the attractions on offer?! Anyway, there is a delicious irony in fans of a club that were taken bibs, balls, and cones from Bang Phra to Pattaya getting upset because they have shifted base one more time! And there is a further argument here. Are fans staying away because they protest the move to Sri Racha or are they staying away because the team got relegated and are playing shite?

When they are doing well, Pattaya could tap into the large number of foreigners who call the town home. I have seen them play a couple times in Bangkok, and each time there was a healthy number of expats in their travelling support who had crossed the Bang Pakong River for a day in the capital.

The first game came in 2009, when Pattaya played Chula United at the Chulalongkorn Stadium in the heart of Bangkok. The visitors certainly outnumbered the home fans. Chula are one of the smallest clubs in the country and were later renamed BBCU and did their best to drink the stadium dry. In common with many at Thai football, the foreigners were clad in replica shirts with one gentleman wearing a dolphin on his head. Fortunately for him, the club aren't nicknamed Pigeons. Football, eh?

The last time I saw Pattaya was at PAT Stadium in Klong Toei, a far more intimidating venue if you believe some reports. But the Pattaya faithful still turned up in numbers, drank their beer, sang their songs, and generally had a good time in the stand with one guy wearing a stuffed dolphin as a hat while on the field their team played dreadfully and lost.

The idea of several foreigners going to a football match and getting well lubricated in a public place seems fairly well entrenched in Thailand and especially Pattaya. But would it work in other countries in the region? You rarely see many foreigners at games in Indonesia, for example, and you couldn't imagine a group of well-oiled expats giving it large at places like Banda Aceh or Jayapura, throwing beer down their necks outside and inside the stadium!

Back to Pattaya. While other clubs owned by dynastic provincial regimes have benefitted from local largesse, money at Pattaya United has been tight. No big name players have pulled on the less than famous sky blue and white hoops — former Queens Park Rangers defender Richard Langley, former Home United striker Kengne Ludovick, and former Gombak United striker OJ Obatola apart. And despite earlier, optimistic talk of a new stadium, the Nong Prue arena will probably be more than enough for the next few seasons. A small, tidy little ground, it sits among a temple and a local school on the other side of the highway from Pattaya. It boasts one main stand and an open temporary looking affair opposite and that is about it. Nothing behind the goals. An anonymous, unambitious ground, it seems a perfect fit for its current tenants.

Willy seemed depressed just thinking about the plight of his team. 'We could even be relegated, that is how bad we are.' Shuddering at the thought of his beloved team playing in the nether regions of the Regional League.

We headed off to a German-themed open air beer bar and as the beers went down, the despondent Pattaya fan livened up.

As a brand, Pattaya has to be one of the highest profiles in South East Asia but is it enough to host a top flight, successful football club? Yes, it may attract a few homesick expats and beered up youths on holiday but any club needs to have, at its core, its local community and Pattaya is made up of large numbers of people who have come to the beach resort from other areas of the country in search of money. It's a transient place, which was little more than a fishing village half a century ago with plenty of neon along the main strip but that's about it.

Imagine, though, if it could add world class sporting facilities to its other attractions? Training pitches, a top class international stadium; would the Pattaya brand be able to attract touring sides from Australia or Japan or South Korea or even further afield? It's unlikely the city fathers have any such long-term vision for the place. In the thirty years I've been visiting, more and more bars and restaurants are the only changes to the city scape.

The 2018 season ended with suggestions Pattaya United were to be taken over by another club and relocated along the coast to Samut Prakan.

10.
CHONBURI & THE RISE OF REPRESENTATIVE FOOTBALL CLUBS

When I am in Thailand, I try to catch up with a Chonburi game, preferably in Bangkok. The first Chonburi game I ever saw was when they played away to Thai Port in 2009, the year Thai football was invented??? and daft bastard that I was/that I am, I took a bus from Bangkok to Sri Racha to get picked up by a guy I had never met before. Football, eh? I had been speaking on line with Dale Farrington for a couple years and recognised a kindred spirit, even in cyber space. He had been following Chonburi since 1997, when they had started, and stuck with them ever since, following them over land and even to Singapore at one stage.

I was spending a few days in Bangkok, so I got in touch and hey presto, we met up in his home town of Sri Racha. Had a natter and a beer then took a supporter's bus back to Bangkok to the PAT Stadium, literally a couple bus stops from the hotel I had checked into earlier that morning!

The connection we had made on line continued in real life on that bus journey as we found out how many times our paths had crossed or nearly crossed in years gone by. He had been a punk, I had been a punk, he had seen a number of the bands I had seen, we had been to see Thailand play South Korea back in 1997, for both of us our first game in Thailand. And as a mad Oldham Athletic fan, he was present at the few occasions I had seen the Latics, including a Friday night at Brighton and Hove Albion and a league cup tie at Highbury against the Arsenal that was to be my last game at that venerable home ever. Wipes away tear and moves on.

Two thousand and nine was the year football in Thailand came of age. The Football Association of Thailand (FAT) decided clubs needed to be more representative of their communities and not be seen as government departments. Chonburi had been the first club to take this path a decade or so earlier and now the floodgates opened as private companies saw their chance to develop the domestic game. Dale, as befitting someone who saw all the punk bands in their early days when they were at their prime, had been going for several years and had seen Chonburi go from playing in front of one man and his dog, to crowds of several thousands and a few titles along the way. There was hardly a stadium he hadn't been to when the league was still a thing for Bangkok and its environs, and there was hardly a game he missed. As the league grew in popularity, he became the go-to man for the foreign market now able to combine their Thai holiday with a bit of footie!

As the only foreign football fan in the league, he had become quite a well-known sight, this strange, beer swilling northerner with his Oldham Athletic flag. He was soon approached by the makers of the Chonburi match day programme to add a few columns. Yep, Thai clubs have programmes, you know, little magazines that provide light reading on match day and allow fans to identify which player is wearing which number shirt, 'cos guess what, you public address announcers in Singapore, Malaysia, and Indonesia, after you run through the line-ups ahead of kick off, we, the paying public find it bloody difficult to keep up. Serious we do.

Later, as I could get press accreditation, I was able to get team sheets, but these are only really available to the media; clubs, and leagues no doubt convinced we, the fan, have little or no interest in who is playing. And sometimes, people can get pretty anal about team sheets. At the SEA Games in Indonesia in 2011, I asked one of the organisers for one during the game. He had a massive wad of them and there was sod all media at the game, but he just looked at me like I had been crawling round in poo all day and sniffed, before saying, 'only for the media' before walking away!

Back to Dale. The first time we met, I asked if he had any plans for a blog as quite a few foreign fans in Thailand had gotten in on the act, but he was adamant. Not as in Adam and the Ants, but adamant his computer skills, even for Blogspot, were useless. I remember thinking at the time someone who grew up with the whole do-it-yourself ethos of punk, fanzines, and three chords was not as neanderthal as he was making out and sure enough, a few months later he was making his first foray into cyberspace!

I interviewed Dale for Jakarta Casual TV early 2010, against the backdrop of noisy fans ahead of a game between Chonburi and Thai Port. He was positive about the direction Thai football was taking, while being a little peeved it was his Chonburi that was being usurped by the freshly-minted Muang Thong United.

So, what about this Damascene conversion that saw him go online?

'What happened was the lad who done the programmes asked me to contribute a few pieces but as space was always an issue, things were not always used and at the same time I was getting messages through the Thai Football message board asking for information about Chonburi... I thought I already had made a start, I might as well get the info out there,' he said, while supping his beer in the car park of Chonburi's stadium.

Around us, fans of both teams were mixing together and enjoying the variety of food and, of course, drinks on sale while just over Dale's shoulder, the club shop was doing a roaring trade. Everyone once in a while, a half-hearted chant broke out and at one point some firecrackers took centre stage. It was all very polite, very twee. There is no doubt the Thai football experience can make for a very pleasant family day out with plenty of food stalls and beer on sale outside the grounds.

As the website goes from strength to strength, Dale refuses to acknowledge any improvement in his keyboard skills while reluctantly admitting his finger typing speed has improved.

'Computers still remain as much a mystery to me as they did (the previous year when he had first met), absolutely hopeless.'

Four and a half years later, the website is still going strong and we meet up in the car park of another stadium, this time the relatively new TOT Stadium in Lak Si, just off the Vipawadee Rangsit road out to the old airport at Don Muang.

There was another fine drizzle and behind the away end, roofed but open to the elements, the grass had turned to mud. If you could overlook the 28 plus degrees temperature, the rain and the mud would have you thinking you were back in England at some grim northern footballing outpost on the edge of, oh I don't know, some desolate moor perhaps!

As ever, Dale had driven up from the eastern seaboard with some mates and they were enjoying a few beers before going into the ground. In the car park by the main entrance there was a neat row of Minis, while a group of motorcyclists made sure we all knew they had arrived by revving their engines loudly.

There was a small club shop, but it was probably the least busy I had seen in my travels to Thai games but then TOT weren't no super club. One of the older clubs in the Thai Premier League, they have stubbornly resisted the move to rebranded and remain what they have always been, the football club of Telephone Organisation of Thailand. In recent years they have flirted with playing in the town of Kanchanaburi, towards the Myanmar border, and even ground shared with Muang Thong United but they have struggled to build up any kind of fan base.

At one stage, they were even called TOT-CAT. Do you really want me to spell that out? Okay, deep breath. Telephone Organisation of Thailand Communications Authority of Thailand. Happy? Good, all together now, give me a T. They soon reverted to plain and simple TOT, playing in a tidy little stadium on the land of TOT and not too far from Lak Si station, if you were that way inclined!

For the Chonburi game, the crowd was around the 1,200 mark, and when you consider the visitors brought perhaps 300. You can see TOT are one of those clubs being left behind in this brave new world of Thai football. Who wants to support the telephone company? Thai Port can survive because they are from Klong Toey and they are easily recognisable as from the docks in that working class area. But TOT and their ilk?

By Thai standards, though, they do have a bit of history. After they won the FA Cup in 1993, back in the days before there was even a proper national league, TOT were rewarded with a place in the Asian Cup Winners' Cup. Today, there is a burgeoning buzz about the AFC Champions League and increased TV broadcasting of the AFC Cup is increasing awareness of the lesser competition but 20 odd years ago there wasn't so much interest in continental club competition.

Several clubs were given byes in the first round but TOT were drawn against Indian side East Bengal and summarily thumped them 4-1. There was no second leg! Why? Sorry, no idea. There just wasn't. In the second round TOT were drawn against Quang Nam Danang from Vietnam and had no problem overcoming them, winning 5-2 at home and 3-0 away.

Three wins and TOT were buzzing! Maybe. They were in the next round and drawn against Kuala Lumpur, who back then were a top side in their own league as was have seen. You think the phone men worried about that? Nope, not an iota as they cruised to a 5-3 aggregate win setting them up for a trip to the Middle East and the semi-finals.

After playing home and away games to get this far, TOT were now faced with a one off semi-final against Yokohama Flugels. The Thais lost 4-2 and finished the competition in fourth place after they lost the 3/4 place play-off two days later against Al Ittihad on penalties.

For an unfancied arm of the central government, it had been a glorious cup run on the international stage, but I guess their exploits have been long forgotten. Certainly, in a country famous for its marketing skills, the club shop has nothing to record those heady days, which is a shame though given their turn out on this particular evening. No real surprise.

Dale had been feeling a little despondent before the game and while the 1-1 draw did go some way to cheering him up, he was still a bit negative about the direction the game was taking in Thailand. All the money, the multiple replica shirts, the fact you now had allocated seats at some clubs and you couldn't just sit with your mates like before and the ever increasing prices.

In a way, his arguments are the same many put forward about the English Premier League, but no one is listening. Having been there from its early days, Dale has seen the game go from nothing to a popularity no one could ever have envisaged and, as an ageing punk who saw the Clash early in their career, it's always the early days that are the best. Come on… what do people want to listen to; London's Burning or This is England? That's a major problem with getting old. We used to moan about it when we were growing up, old farts going on about how much better things were back then. Experience is great, but nostalgia can be a bit one-eyed.

The arguments he puts forward about the game in Thailand mirror mine about the EPL. And Chonburi in a way mirror Arsenal. They aren't competing with the deep-pocketed clubs and instead try to bring through their own players. When it doesn't work, then the league sucks!

Back to the game. Chonburi have this Brazilian lad called Jaime Braganca, a 31-year-old midfielder. When he signed for the club, Dale had been in touch asking if I knew anything about him because he had a spell with Persija Jakarta, the Indonesia Premier League version, but I couldn't recall him.

Certainly, Braganca's career has taken him round the world. Nothing remarkable in that, there are for more journeymen pros than there are Jamie Carraghers out there. Braganca started in Portugal, as you might expect, before moving to clubs in Bahrain, Germany, Kuwait, Bulgaria, Indonesia, Romania, and then of course Thailand. If no one in Indonesia remembers him, it's because he played in a league no one really gave a hoot about for a team no one ever went to see in a town far from anywhere, but Chonburi fans have quickly turned him into a cult figure, very probably the first in the country. Against TOT, fans were chanting his name long before he came on as a second half substitute.

'Watch this,' advised Dale, and sure enough it wasn't long before the powerfully built Portuguese was showing off his talents. Well, the odd step over and feint coupled with flicks. Rarely the easy ball. 'You should see his YouTube channel,' said Dale and laughed. I did. He, the footballer not the blogger, likes Barbie shows!

Chonburi in a way, were the trailblazers. They were one of the first teams from the provinces to enter what was pretty much a Bangkok league despite the name Thailand that featured prominently in the name of the league. They were pretty well funded and tapped into the local market by allowing fans, for pretty much the first time, to identify with their local team in ways clubs like Thai Farmers Bank and BEC Tero would never be able to despite their success on the international stage.

This is how the first Thailand wide league ended in 1997, the year both Dale and I attended our first ever game.

#	TEAM	P	W	D	L	F-A	PT
1	Thai Farmers Bank	34	18	10	6	56-25	64
2	Telephone Organization of Thailand	34	17	11	6	61-35	62
3	Bangkok Bank	34	17	11	6	54-34	62
4	Stock Exchange of Thailand	34	17	9	8	59-31	60
5	UCOM Rajpracha	34	16	12	6	62-36	60
6	Sinthana	34	17	6	11	45-45	57
7	Royal Thai Air Force	34	14	12	8	60-50	54

8	Royal Thai Army	34	14	12	8	60-50	54
9	Royal Thai Navy	34	13	12	8	44-29	51
10	Police	34	13	11	10	53-39	50
11	Port Authority of Thailand	34	9	14	11	44-39	41
12	Singha Tero Sasana	34	9	14	11	37-44	41
13	Thailand Tobacco Monopoly	34	7	14	13	37-44	35
14	Osotspa	34	8	10	16	41-73	34
15	Bangkok Bank of Commerce	34	7	11	16	34-47	32
16	Rajvithi Agfatech	34	8	8	18	43-71	32
17	Krung Thai Bank	34	5	9	20	32-54	24
18	Sinhga Thamrongthai	34	1	6	27	26-111	9

TOT called it a day after being relegated from the top flight in 2015. Sinthana has morphed into BBCU via Chula Sinthana and Chula United before withdrawing, RTAF are now Air Force Central, RTA are Army United, and Navy are called Navy after spells as Raj Navy and Siam Navy.

Police became Police United before merging with BEC. Tero to become Police Tero, PAT are Port and Singha. Tero Sasana became BEC Tero. TTM and KTB (Bangkok Glass) have already been touched upon while Osotspa became Osotspa Saraburi, before relocating to Mahasarakham in the north east and renaming themselves Jumpasari United. It doesn't take a genius to work out a league with teams like that would never really catch on! The team from Chonburi broke the mould and helped football clubs connect with their communities for the first time.

Chonburi made their bow as it were in Division One and were known as Chonburi Sanibat Samut Prakan, and in 2002 they split from the Sanibat Samut Prakan and joined a rival league where they were known as Chonburi

Code Red.

In 2005, they won the Provisional League and were promoted to the Premier League for the first time and since then have been one of the more consistent teams, not allowing the likes of Muang Thong and Buriram, winning the TPL in 2007 and never finishing outside the top half of the table. Indeed, for an eight year spell they never finished lower than third though they had just the one title to show for their efforts in 2007.

'In the early days our big rivals were BEC Tero because they were what we aspired to,' recalls Dale. 'Later on, it became Muang Thong because they became what we felt we should have become.' Adding games against MTU can get a bit lairy, with even the odd bit of crowd trouble. And, of course, there is the hatred for Pattaya United. Dale objecting at the way they bought their way into the top flight while his own team did it the hard way. So, perhaps a certain amount of *schadenfreude* at Pattaya's troubles this season down in Division One!

For me, a sign of a well-run club in South East Asia, where clubs notoriously operate on a season to season basis is how long it can keep its best players. Typically, players only sign 12 month contracts and are moved on at the end of the season as a new coach comes in and does his own thing. Chonburi, by that measurement alone must be a well-run club. Striker Pipob On Mon joined the club in 2005, for example, and in 2018, he was coaching the B team. Goalkeeper Sinthaweechai Hathairattanakul joined in 2007, from Persib Bandung, and apart from a further loan spell in Indonesia in 2009, stayed with Chonburi until 2015.

Central defender Nattaphong Samana was with Chonburi from 2007 until 2014, while silky midfielder Adul Kahso joined the club in 2004, and apart from a short spell in Japan remained until the end of 2016. Meanwhile, Suttinan Phukhom has been with the club since 2008, though injuries have curtailed his appearances in recent years.

You get the point? And that does not include Therdsak Chaiman, who arrived in 2010, when he was 37-years-young after several years in Singapore and Vietnam. At the time, Dale told me if Chonburi could get one more season out of the silky skilled Therdsak, they would be doing well. He finally hung up his boots at the end of the 2017 season and is now, of course, on the coaching staff of the club!

The other side to that longevity, of course, is they are players who have grown up and aged together... and not won anything! Time to break up the spine or keep it and build around them? There is a saying in football that a team can only last three years. I have no idea where I read it mind! But Chonburi, despite the new mega rich, have done well to keep some of the best players in the country and to keep challenging for honours. But is there any desire to push them on to the next level?

11.
BANGKOK'S FOOTBALL MILE

Ramkhamheang is an area in eastern Bangkok famous perhaps for a long road, several sois, lanes running off the main road, and a university. There is also a fairly large Muslim population, long settled in the area. In fact, I lived down by the canal for a while and the apartment block was owned by a family who told me because of the Buddhist strictures against taking life, many Muslims worked the local abattoirs!

I first visited the area in 1994, when I went to meet someone at an office just off nearby Sri Nakarin. I was still a Bangkok newbie, wet behind the ears, and permanently short of cash to fund the local friendly bar owner's lifestyle. Taxi rides were beyond my budget, so I took an all-chugging all-polluting river taxi to Klong Tan. My contact said get off there, walk along the road and turn left, you can't miss the company's offices. So, I did what she said. And I walked. And walked. And walked.

Back then, the area was still fairly undeveloped, meaning there were massage parlours, but little in the way of high-rise. The way she gave directions, it didn't seem far at all and to be fair, it wasn't a long way if you were being shuttled around town in an airconditioned Mercedes like she was. But when you are walking? Sod that for a game of tic tac toe. It took well over an hour and I was sweating like a proverbial when I finally arrived at the office, only to shiver from the onslaught of the air conditioning.

To me, back then, Sri Nakarin was the eastern most limit of Bangkok and Ramkhamheang was the last area of substance before you entered the boonies. But I guess the Asian Games of 1998 changed all that with money piling into infrastructure, elevated roads, and sports facilities, and beyond. I cheated and took a taxi back, drinking in my first sight of the Rajamangala Stadium, little realising, of course, how I would be returning to that arena on more than one occasion in the future. Life, eh?

The Thais love their flyovers. I often think if Jakarta had half the flyovers Bangkok has, the congestion would be cut quite substantially but they don't seem to like driving in the sky in the Indonesian capital too much. Something else Jakarta doesn't seem to like too much is sports stadiums. Jakarta has half a dozen or so across the whole city. Bangkok has three in about a mile along Ramkhamheang Road! The road also boasts a fairly decent sports outlet, called FBT, on the opposite side of the road. An emporium offering the best in local and international sports gear of varying quality and pricing, and in recent years been the official kit supplier to national teams like Thailand and Bhutan while also providing clubs sides from Thailand to England via the Maldives and Bangladesh.

The ground floor, for example, has a whole area devoted to replica Thai football shirts and on this visit, a whole heap of BEC Tero shirts. There were red shirts, black shirts, blue shirts, white shirts, and orange shirts. At least, I think there were... I lost count and soon went colour blind. Suffice to say there were probably more BEC Tero shirts in those few square feet than there are fans of the club in the whole country — not many people have taken to supporting a football club part named after a TV station I guess.

There were other shirts including Rayong, Suphanburi, Bangkok United, and Bangkok in varying quantities but remember, this was only the ground floor. Up the escalator and there was a small stand-alone outlet flogging Muang Thong United gear, shirts, scarves, key rings, as well as Thai language football magazines and DVDs. And up on another floor was an area selling the big name brands, mostly the international ones which included Bangkok Glass shirts.

I don't know but I think the Bangkok Glass shirts over the years have been some of the coolest around and though I am not really a fan of shirts even I succumbed and paid 800 baht (about 16 quid!) for a green and white striped number a few years back. I even paid 350 baht for a bunny, the club's nickname is the Glass Bunny, wearing the same shirt for my son! If Thai football were a punk band, Bangkok Glass would be The Clash bassist Paul Simonon!

Most Thai clubs have their own retail outlets flogging the usual array of stuff, especially replica shirts. These have become a cash cow and over the years I have seen the prices rise as clubs change shirts each and every year, some clubs producing three, four, or even five a season. I remember buying a Thai Port shirt back in 2009, and I paid 450 baht. Today, some clubs are charging, and getting, over 1,000 baht!

When it comes to marketing and selling, the Thais are streets ahead of their rivals. Even smaller clubs like TOT and Air Force have a small selection of stuff on sale at games. Finding club gear in Singapore is a chore, while you get a people flogging stuff at games in Malaysia and, of course, Johor Darul Tazim have a small shop in their main stand at Larkin Stadium.

And Indonesia? Nope. Clubs seem reluctant to sully their hands with something as crass as trade. Everyone going to games in Indonesia wears club colours, but they buy stuff from other fans and to the observer it all seems slap dash and chaotic. But you would think in a country where so many clubs have difficulties paying salaries, you think they would recognise the benefits of alternate cash flows even if they have to sub-contract the work out to the fans. But oh no, better to just carry on regardless and whine it is so hard to find money!

Directly opposite the FBT store, over the conveniently located footbridge, lies the first of the three stadiums. By Bangkok standards it doesn't amount to much at all, just one stand, but by Jakarta standards it is bloody amazing. Even the playing surface looks billiard smooth. It may be none of the above, of course, but if you are coming from Jakarta you too would be excited! Next door, kind of, is the massive Rajamangala Stadium.

One of those newish stadiums with a wavy design — not sure why so many people went for waves, it is mostly open and holds about 50,000. It seems to have usurped the Supachalasai Stadium as the venue of choice for big games, and small teams like the ill-feted BBCU have also used it for home league games. I first visited Rajamangala for a friendly against Arsenal in 1999 but, unless you live in the east of Bangkok, it's a long way from anywhere and getting transport after a big game can be a chore if you are not familiar with the local buses. I used the non-airconditioned 115 which passed outside the stadium for more years than I care to remember on the way to and from teaching gigs in the eastern suburbs. So, I was well-acquainted with the area when I started watching football there.

Then we have the Ramkhamheang University Stadium which can be found at the back of the uni of the same name and knocks spots off any venue in Jakarta, with the possible exceptions of the Bung Karno and Lebak Bulus. I once saw Air Force United play a game there against Raj Pracha in Division One and despite two of the country's more traditional clubs taking the field, the crowd was on the (very) low side and in fact as I tried to find the stadium with my pidgin Thai, no one seemed aware of any game at all!

What of Thai football?

I meet many people on my travels and they all tell me the same thing. Thai football is where it's at. I am not so sure. Yes, players get paid on time and those at the big clubs get the big salaries but, outside of Muang Thong and Buriram, clubs are scrambling for the leftovers.

And oh boy they do seem to have some of the most technically gifted players in the region, with a work ethic and discipline to harness that talent. Without doubt, the Thai league has some of the best players in the region. I am talking players like Datsakorn Thonglao, Therdsak Chaiman, Theerathon Bunmathan, Kawin Thamsatchanan. While the 2018 season has goalkeeper Kawin playing in Belguim and Theeraton, Chanathip Songkrasin, and Teerasil Dangda playing in Japan.

In the same way, Johor Darul Ta'zim have outgrown Malaysian football. So, the Thai national team has outgrown South East Asia. They go into the 2018 AFF Suzuki Cup as hot favourites, having won the last two editions and the conveyor belt of talent shows no sign of abating with the Under 23s triumphant in 13 of the last 15 SEA Games. The Thais have qualified for the AFC Asian Cup 2019, for the first time since 2004 (they qualified as co-hosts in 2007), where they have been drawn with hosts United Arab Emirates, India, and Bahrain. The World Cup, though, continues to evade them. They reached the third qualifying round for the World Cup in Russia only to finish winless and bottom of their group behind Japan, Saudi Arabia, Australia, UAE, and Iraq. Likewise, six-time league champions Buriram United have struggled to make an impact in the AFC Champions League, reaching the quarter finals on just one occasion back in 2013.

You can't help but feel the Thai league is a millstone dragging the top clubs and the best players back. How can Buriram United really go toe to toe with the best from South Korea, Japan, and China when they are playing against the likes of Air Force Central, Navy, and Police Tero week to week? Beyond Muang Thong United, there is no club in a position to duke it out with Buriram United consistently. Yes, some clubs have their moments in the sun enthused with cash from their backers, but they never offer a sustained challenge and as we have seen even Chonburi have been slipping behind in recent seasons.

While it's great to see players like Chanathip and Teerasil ply their trade overseas they can't be expected to take Thai football to the next level, to reach a World Cup, or to challenge for the group stages in the AFC Asian Cup, in the way Kiatisuk and Tawan helped launch the Thais onto South East Asian dominance back in the 1990s. Undoubtedly, they will improve as players in Japan but were they to return to Thailand, which clubs could sign them? In all likelihood just Buriram United and Muang Thong United, and so the cycle continues.

It's not just me from afar who has this downer on Thai football. Average attendances have been falling since a peak of 6,295 in 2015, and while the Buriram v Muang Thong clash regularly tops 30,000. Most attendances are in just four figures, and only Buriram consistently average over 10,000. Would success in the 2019 AFC Asian Cup provide a springboard for renewed interest in the domestic game? It would be nice to think so, but I am always drawn back to the same argument. Thai domestic football is just too new to have taken root. And since 2009, so many clubs have come and gone, ebbed and flowed. It is difficult enough for the hardcore fans to keep up. What about the football crazy lads in the provinces where local sides last as long as their backers feel up to it? Take for example Songkhla United in the south of Thailand. They were originally from Buriram but were sold in 2012 to the southern city and renamed Wuachon United. The local folk were obviously delighted to have such a big club land in their laps, and more than 30,000 saw them play Muang Thong United in a league game.

The following year Wuachon United merged with local side Songhkla to become Songkhla United but the initial buzz soon faded and at the end of 2014 the new team were relegated to the second tier Division 1. At the end of 2017 they were relegated again, this time to the rebranded League 3 and the 30,000 that had witnessed a game in 2012, had been whittled down to a hardcore average of 1,000. However, there was more indignation to come when they failed to pass the league's licensing and they received a two-year suspension from football. They can return in 2020 in League 4 (South). An extreme example perhaps but an indication of the uncertainty that surrounds much of Thai football. Against that kind of backdrop, how can football clubs develop the shared heritage and memories that play such a key role in developing and sustaining a fan base? Is it any wonder supporters are reluctant to get behind their local team?

PART 4: INDONESIA

Persija fans in Solo for a game

12.
A LESSON IN GEOGRAPHY

Indonesia and football. Where to begin? If someone were to approach Hollywood and say, 'hey listen, I have an idea for a movie about football in Indonesia. You see, there are two leagues. We have two national teams, including one playing Sunday school teams in Australia. There is no money. One team wants to sign Dennis Bergkamp, even though he doesn't like flying. They are putting in a World Cup bid for 2022. Fans travel to games on top of buses and trains. A coach got fired because no one could find his contract...' Let's face it. They would wonder how the hell I got past the secretary.

But it's all true I swear, and so much more. In fact, it is hard to know just where to begin. As I was brainstorming this book I thought I would have to devote one entry to explaining the difference between Persiba Bantul and Persiba Balikpapan but believe me, the different Persi's are nothing compared to the reality of the beautiful game. Then again, it took me the better part of a year to get my head around them. So, for the newbie to Indonesian football, I will take thee on a journey across 17,000 islands, three time zones, and god knows what else. Before we begin, might I suggest a map of some kind to help with the bearings?

Okay. Going from west to east I will divide this up into a number of zones relating to absolutely nothing more than an ease to approach such a massive task. Sumatra, long, thin, and pencil shaped, it appears in the news frequently for things like earthquakes, haze, and tsunamis. We will begin at the northern tip of this island that runs almost parallel to the Malaysian peninsula just the other side of the Straits of Melaka. In fact, you may even wonder how this island can have any connection with those further east when it is so close to Malaysia. Blame the British! Nope, for once it is true. Back in the early 19th century, the British and the Dutch were busy conquering the local fiefdoms and potentates and absorbing them in their own empires to be ruled from a far.

To cut a long story short, the capture of Singapore rather stirred up a hornet's nest. Which island belonged to which white country? Important questions of state back then I guess. The competing European powers hit upon a simple but ingenious solution. Looking at a map of the area, they decided everything on the left of the Melaka Strait, as you sailed south, would be British, everything on the right would be Dutch. So there. The white folks had spoken and to hell with the consequences, especially for the people who lived on the islands to the south of Singapore and now found themselves under Dutch rule despite the fact they considered themselves subject of the state of Johor which came under British rule.

Anyway, back to the northern tip of Sumatra and the province of Aceh boasts a number of football clubs; Persiraja Banda Aceh, Aceh United, PSAP Sligi, PSSB Bireuen, and PSLS Lhokseuwame. North Sumatra has PSMS Medan, PS Kwarta, and PSDS Deli Serdang. The observant will soon notice the letter P prominent. PS is an abbreviation of Pesatuan Sepakbola, which translates literally as Association Football. So, PSMS is in effect the Medan Football Association; an equivalent would see Surrey FA, London FA, and Nottinghamshire FA competing in the English Premier League. Each FA is at the apex of a regional association, which features a number of clubs under their umbrella and many FAs will hold their own internal competitions, which pass with little publicity.

Moving south along the island of Sumatra, PSPS Pekanbaru come from Riau province while Semen Padang come from West Sumatra, and Sriwijaya Palembang come from South Sumatra.

At the tip of Sumatra is the port city of Bandar Lampung and their team. PSBL, while there, is also a Lampung Barat (West Lampung) out there somewhere as well, and Persilat.

Now, we cross the Sunda Strait, bypassing the infamous Krakatau volcano and land on Java, one of the most crowded pieces of real estate in the world and my home for a wonderful 15 years. Heading east on the highway from the ferry terminal, we pass through Cilegon United and Serang, home to Perserang. Tangerang, an industrial city close to Jakarta, is a two team city with Persita and Persikota. For half a season of the Indonesia Premier League they had three teams, with Tangerang Wolves competing in that short-lived affair.

Next up is the capital city, Jakarta, which also has two teams, Persija and Persitara; the latter come from North Jakarta. There is also a South Jakarta team, PSJS. There used to be an east Jakarta team as well, Persijatim but they are now Sriwijaya after a short hiatus in Solo.

West Java surrounds much of Jakarta and is home to a number of large towns and cities, with their own football clubs. Persib Bandung sits atop the province as we shall discover in these pages, the Apex Football Club. Then we have Persika Karawang, Persipasi Bekasi, Persikasi Bekasi, PSB Bogor, Persikabo Bogor, Persikab Bandung, PSGC Ciamis, and Persipur Purwakarta.

Next up is Central Java, and for convenience I will include the teams of Yogyakarta in this group. Deep breath. Persis Solo, PSIS Semarang, Persip Pekalongan, PPSM Magelang, Persiba Bantul, PSIM Yogyakarta, PSS Sleman, Persiku Kudus, Persik Kendal, Persibat Batang, PSIR Rembang, Persipur Purwodadi, PSCS Cilicap. And there are more! Basically, if you arrive in Yogyakarta during the football season for a holiday, and it is a popular tourist destination in its own right, then you stand a good chance of finding a game locally.

Persebaya Surabaya, Arema Malang, Persema Malang, Persekam Metro Malang, Persik Kediri, Persikoba Batu, Deltras Sidoarjo, Persida Sidoarjo, Gresik United, Persela Lamongan, Persid Jember, Persewangi Banyuwangi, Persekabpas Pasuruan, Madiun Putra, Persebo Bondowoso, Persepam, Madura United, PSMP Mojokerto, Persinga Nganjuk, Perseta Tulungagung,

Persibo Bojonegoro, Persipro Probolinggo... can we just say there are a lot of football clubs in East Java!

The island of Kalimantan, maybe better known to many as Borneo and famous for its abundant natural resources, disappearing rain forest, and orangutans. And football teams? The province of East Kalimantan is, by some standards, the richest in the country and boasts a number of teams including Persiba Balikpapan, Mitra Kukar Kutai Kartanegara, and the very difficult to get to Bontang FC. More recently, there is a Pusamania Borneo FC, formed after Perseba Super Bangkalan (East Java) sold their licence to Pusam fans, who were disappointed with the way their club was being run!

Bali had nothing to write home about until recently. Deltras started life there and recently Persigi were in the second tier, but that is about it while Bali DeWata appeared in the short lived IPL for half a season. There are teams based around Denpaser and Badung but it is all very low key, amateur stuff. Once, Bali did host a World Cup qualifier between Timor Leste and Hong Kong though, but no, I did not go! Now, we have a Bali United who appear to be settling down for the long haul, investing in their stadium as well as a number of academies.

Sulawesi is that funny shaped island in the east of the country and while PSM Makassar is one of the oldest clubs in the country, the island does have a number of other teams that, for some reason, remain inactive in the top two divisions, for now at least. When I kicked off Jakarta Casual, there were teams like Persma Manado, Persimin Minhasa, and Persibom, all from the north of Sulawesi. There was a Persigo Gorontalo in the second tier, but they recently relocated to East Java and are now known as Semeru!

And finally, we have the vast expanse of water with a few islands sprinkled around in the far east of the country. The Malukus and Papua remain little understood even by Indonesians. They are just so remote and difficult to get to. A direct flight to Jayapura, for example, can take seven hours or more from Jakarta; it is quicker and often cheaper to fly to Hong Kong or Beijing! And

Jayapura is relatively easy.

Even now, after eight years, I do not always know where some of these clubs are actually from!

Persiter is quite easy. The island of Ternate is a mere pin prick compared to Java and Sumatra but was one of the original spice islands that attracted the Dutch here all those centuries ago. Persemalra is a team for North Maluku but ask not where they are based for I know not.

Papua, of course, is home to one of the most successful clubs in the country in recent years, Persipura Jayapura. Then we have Perseman Manokwari, for whom ex Arsenal striker Christopher Wreh had a short spell, Persiwa Wamena, Perseru Seru, Persiram Raja Ampat, and Persidafon Dafonsoro.

With all those resources to draw upon, you would think Indonesia would be a world powerhouse in the game, wouldn't you? Well, think again. For a number of reasons, logistical, administrative, financial, the country has struggled to make an impact domestically, let alone internationally. While tiny Singapore, the little red dot, has won the ASEAN Football Federation Championships on a number of occasions, Indonesia has yet to lift the trophy even once. This inability to impose itself regionally even extends to the South East Asian Games for the Under 21s. They did reach the final in 2011, played in Jakarta, but froze when it came to the penalty shoot outs, allowing Malaysia, their dreaded foe, to lift the title.

In 2007, Persik Kediri represented Indonesia in the Asian Champions League and to be fair acquitted themselves pretty bloody well. Coached by Daniel Roekito, the little heralded team from East Java played a flamboyant, swashbuckling type of football where the goalkeeper, Kurnia Sandy, was pretty much left to his own devices while Uruguayan born striker Cristian Gonzales, Brazilian born Danilo Fernando, and Argentine Ronald Fagundez, spun their Latin magic, ably supported by the flair of Indonesian born Budi Sudarsono.

Persik were drawn in a group that featured regional heavyweights Sydney, Urawa Red Diamonds, and Shanghai Shehua. They finished third with two wins and a draw from their home games but lost all their away games. Still, it was a pretty good effort from the unfancied Persik, who had been forced to play all their home games at Solo because the AFC deemed their own Brawijiaya Stadium did not meet their criteria.

In the same year, in the sort of political compromise that football just loves, Indonesia, along with Malaysia, Thailand, and Vietnam, co-hosted the AFC Asian Cup. Based in Jakarta of course, Indonesia were grouped with Bahrain, South Korea, and Saudi Arabia, and were not given much chance by anyone really.

They started well, defeating Bahrain 2-1 in their opening group game but then came undone against the Saudis and the Koreans despite putting up heroic resistance. Certainly, against South Korea, Indonesia worked their socks off closing down their fitter opponents, but it was never going to be enough. It was impossible for them to keep up that work rate for the full 90 minutes and they went down 1-0.

Attitude is important in football and you do get the impression this is one area where Indonesia does fall short. Soon after the Asian Cup, Lebak Bulus Stadium in South Jakarta played host to the AFF Under 16 Championships and being at a loose end I decided to catch some games. Ultimately, it wasn't events on the pitch that caught my attention but what happened off it.

There were two games each match day. So, you would often see players from the teams not playing catching snippets of the other game. The Indonesian lads would sit in the stand, talk with their mates, mock goalkeepers who were marshalling their defence, and play with their handphones. The Malaysians would have bits of paper and clipboards and were engaged in taking notes and asking their coaching staff questions.

Malaysia won the SEA Games in 2009, the AFF Cup in 2010, and the SEA

Games again in 2011.

For a few glorious days in December 2010, Indonesia seemed to be on the cusp of something beautiful. Alfred Riedl was coaching them at the AFF Cup and they breezed the group stage, in Jakarta, crushing Laos 6-0, Malaysia 5-0, and drawing 0-0 with Thailand. Irfan Bachdim had come in from the Netherlands and was thrilling the fans, and celebrities, with his pace and good looks while Oktavianus Maniani was another who had the fans on the edge of their seats with his blistering pace and his penchant for the spectacular in the most inconvenient places.

And up top was Cristian Gonzales, the ex Persik striker who had taken Indonesian citizenship and was now playing for his adopted country.

Indonesians love a winner as much as anyone else and people who didn't know their Hamkah Hamza from their Ponaryo Astaman, were suddenly rushing to catch this rarest of sights... an Indonesian football team winning. Celebrities, with their fake eyelashes, had their minions rush out to buy replica shirts and tracksuit tops so they could look the part, while their agents called in the TV stations and said, 'oi, she will be at Bung Karno tonight, send a crew and some photographers sharpish.'

The semi-final was against the Philippines, with both games played in Jakarta; Manila lacked a stadium that reached the minimum standard, and two large crowds of more than 90,000 came along expecting to see Indonesia become world beaters. Or at least Philippine beaters. It didn't happen, two dour games were settled by a single goal by Gonzales and Indonesia were through to the final against the same Malaysia they had beaten so convincingly in the group stage.

Expectations were high but ahead of the first leg in Kuala Lumpur there were concerns raised over the use by Malaysian fans of laser beams to distract players. In fact, so distracted did the Indonesian players seem by this threat it seemed to consume them, and they were soon 1-0 down at the Bukit Jalil

Stadium in front of more than 85,000 fans. At one stage, they threatened to walk off their field in protest at the distractions.

Indonesia fell apart. They lost 3-0 and while some 17,000 of their countrymen did their best on the terraces, the players offered little and the final was effectively over. Since that initial rush of 11 goals in their first two games, they had managed just one in 360 minutes of football. Only the most optimistic fan believed they could net four times without reply at the Bung Karno.

Unlike in KL, where Indonesian fans were here, there, and every bloody where, caused in no small measure by the large number of migrant workers, in Jakarta any visiting fan kept a low profile. Every once in a while, relations between the countries would become strained as politicians would seek to score a few points by explaining Malaysia stole land, food, and culture, from Indonesia and they were in fact just bullies. So there. Extremists would go to the Malaysian embassy, burn their flag, and chant a few ditties, all the while budget airlines would flit between the two countries carrying an ever-increasing number of tourists and business people. Ah the fetid aroma of nationalist politics.

In front of perhaps more than 90,000 at the Bung Karno Stadium, Indonesia did restore some pride, winning 2-1 but the damage had been done in the days ahead of KL when the focus had been allowed to move from football to laser beams. But in the months that followed, rather than build on the success of the AFF Cup run, football imploded. Some new people took over the football association, known as PSSI, and sacked Riedl, claiming they couldn't find his contract, and at one stage Indonesia were humiliated 10-0 in an Asian Cup qualifier by tiny Bahrain.

Incidentally, the two semi-finals against the Philippines, and both legs of the final against Malaysia, attracted somewhere in the region of 360,000 fans!

For about six months, Irfan Bachdim was the poster child of Indonesian football. Girls and sponsors loved his cherubic good looks and his model girlfriend, he later married but as with the national team, it never lasted. Just 18 months later, I saw Bachdim come on as a sub for his team Persema, and the crowd was not worth counting. The so-called celebrities had moved on to a new craze and Bachdim was left to try and rebuild his career, first in Thailand and more latterly In Japan before settling down with Bali United far from the glare and hype of 2010.

Okta Maniani's career flickered during those seminal nights at Bung Karno and he has struggled to reach those heights again. At one stage he took up a job as a civil servant as he moved from club to club before ending 2018 as top scorer with Perserang in Liga 2

And that in a rather large nutshell, is Indonesian football. Success, or the promise of success is fleeting. Andy Warhol said everyone has 15 minutes of fame. I guess he had never been to Indonesia, where people were lucky to get 15 seconds. Short-term political thinking will always trump long-term football planning. Football remains a hostage to the fortunes or brickbats of others. It is never entirely its own master, and while everyone involved in the game shrugs their shoulders and says, 'this is Indonesia.' Nothing will change.

13.
DOUBLE TROUBLE

It was deep into injury time of the Asian Cup qualifier between Indonesia and Oman at Bung Karno Stadium in downtown Jakarta back in March 2009. The home team were losing 2-1 and resigned to yet another disappointing campaign. They had drawn their first two games, away to Oman and home to Australia yet that promising start had foundered with a 2-1 loss away to footballing powerhouse Kuwait, despite Bambang Pamungkas giving the merah putih (red and whites) the lead on 33 minutes.

Victory against Oman could well have reignited their campaign, but it never happened and come injury time there was a look and feel of resignation around the cavernous arena filled with 45,000 souls.

But wait a minute, what is this? Charging through the middle, a solitary red shirt. He is forced wide and while his ball control wasn't the best, his attacking purpose exceeded much of what the home team had shown all evening. He cut inside, leaving the Oman defence in his wake but took too many touches and his finely effort on goal, and yes, it was on goal, was easily saved by the Wigan Athletic goalkeeper Al Al-Habsi.

The problem for Indonesia was Hendri Mulyadi was not a name on their team sheet for the game. Indeed, he wasn't even on the bench. Hendri was just one of the 45,000 fans at the stadium that night pissed off with his team's performance in particular and the state of the game in his country overall. But rather than boo, hiss, and throw plastic bags filled with piss, Hendri opted for a more direct course of action. An action that pretty well summed up the state of the beautiful game in Indonesia.

Despite all the fences and the security present at the stadium, Hendri was able to get on the field at the opposite end of the stadium and run through Indonesia's defence. There was a half-hearted challenge in the middle of the park but Hendri just switched outside. The players gave up and watched this unexpected intrusion while one security officer did run on the pitch, but he was even slower than the invader.

After fluffing his shot, Hendri was finally apprehended by the gallant officer, one handed because he didn't want to drop his communication device. Then, all of a sudden, crowds of security from the area behind the goal who had previously done nothing, suddenly piled in and rugby tackled Hendri to the floor before, mob handed, escorting him off the field.

Indonesian football was sick, and it had taken a bespectacled young man to show how sick to the world. Suddenly, football was front page news and even politicians started taking an interest.

Earlier in the year, January to be exact, Indonesia's football association (known locally as PSSI) had surprised many people in the football world, as well as Indonesians, by entering the fray to bid for the 2022 World Cup. With their bid proposal, they promised the world's first 'green' World Cup!

Candidates were required to have around 12 stadiums that could hold 40,000 or more spectators to host a world cup. At the time of the bid, Indonesia had just two, Bung Karno in Jakarta and Palaran Stadium in Samarinda (East Kalimantan). But that wasn't seen as an obstacle to the bid organisers at the time.

'Ten years are enough for us to build, renovate, or expand our stadiums, to meet the requirement,' the PSSI secretary general at the time Nugraha Besoes said.

Among those stadiums planned for upgrades were Jakabaring Stadium in Palembang (South Sumatra), home of Sriwijaya, Si Jalak Harupat Stadium in Soreang (West Java), and used by Persib Bandung and Persikab Bandung Distric,t and Maguwoharjo Stadium (Yogyakarta Special Region), home to PSS Sleman and Persiram Raja Ampat in the current Indonesia Super League. Mitra Kukar's Aji Imbut Stadium (also in East Kalimantan) was also slated for an increased capacity under the plans.

Bung Tomo Stadium in Surabaya (East Java), Pekanbaru's Rumbai Stadium (Riau), and Lautan Api Stadium in Bandung, were also included in the list of proposed stadiums but were not completed at the time of the bid while new stadiums were planned for Jakarta, Tangerang (Banten), Medan (North Sumatra), Bali, and Balikpapan (East Kalimantan).

Not just stadiums. There would need to be a whole heap of work carried out on infrastructure as access to many of the stadiums was, shall we say, not the easiest. The new stadiums are marked by poor access and infrastructure; the Palaran Stadium is in the middle of nowhere and is positively scary after a night game due to the lack of lights in the car park and the stadium approaches; Si Jalak Harupat is reached by a narrow, potholed road that soon fills up when Persib are at home, so the team buses require a police escort to clear a path.

The bid was dead in the water within 12 months, with the government saying they preferred to develop the country and the people rather than splurge all that money for a World Cup.

Football remained on the front pages of the local media, however, as the government kept the pressure on the PSSI to sort itself out after years of perceived failure in running the game.

In March 2010, just days after the government formally advised FIFA it would not be backing the World Cup bid, a conference on the state of football in Indonesia was convened in the East Java city of Malang amid much fanfare. The media converged on the city as the president at the time, Susilo Bambang Yudhoyono, flew in to town and watched the game between local side Arema, then on their way to their first ever ISL title, and Persitara Jakarta North.

The National Football Congress, which the PSSI refused to recognise, came up with seven recommendations to improve football in the country:

- Reform the PSSI.
- Improve the sports infrastructure, especially football, in the country.
- PSSI needs to improve communications with all stake holders in the game.
- Develop youth football through academies and a national football centre.
- Sports development needed to be a part of the national curriculum.
- Use national and provincial budgets to improve targets.
- To develop a programme that would see Indonesia SEA Games winners in 2011.

A group of individuals got together and formed Indonesian National Football Reformation Movement (which fortunately can be abbreviated to GRSNI), to put together more detailed proposals aimed at improving football in the country.

In July 2010, the GRSNI put together a white paper, which they presented to the government that built upon the Malang Congress and formulated a road map to carry the game forward. Chief among their recommendations was the formation of a new league.

While all this was going on, PSSI remained at a respectful distance, pointing out once in a while that they, and they alone, were responsible for the game in Indonesia, as per FIFA regulations that only recognised one governing body in each country, and that while they would listen to proposals from other bodies, they would not guarantee to accept or implement any of them. So there.

For many, however, the PSSI were the problem and they were the ones that needed to be replaced before any meaningful change could happen.

At the time they were being led by a gentleman named Nurdin Halid, a businessman politician from South Sulawesi who had been jailed a couple times for his involvement in bribery cases elsewhere. Despite FIFA statutes clearly stating member associations could not feature folks with criminal records, for some reason they seemed to tolerate Nurdin staying in his job.

For example, back in 2007, they issued a statement stating Nurdin could not stand for re-election.

FIFA sent a letter to the Football Association of Indonesia (PSSI) in June 2007, indicating that the association must re-organise elections, as the electoral process that took place on 20 April 2007 — the day after the ratification of the updated statutes — was not conducted in line with the timelines stipulated in the PSSI statutes. The committee ratified this decision and also decided that in accordance with the statutes, a person who has been convicted of a crime, and is currently in prison, would not be eligible to stand for election.

No one, though, was listening. The PSSI saw no problem with having Nurdin in jail and they had no plans to replace him. Indeed, they cited the example of another gentleman who was chairman of the Amateur Athletics Association and had the misfortune to go to jail!

The clincher came when the secretary general of the PSSI at the time, Nugraha Besoes, was asked whether they were worried Nurdin being locked up would damage the image of the body. 'There is no need to worry about it. The image of the state is already bad, after all.'

Four years later and he was still at his post, writing a letter, to a government ministry saying there were a number of foreign players in the new LPI rebel league who had been granted legal status by the PSSI and had broken the terms and conditions of their permits. He added the presence of the LPI was a threat to Indonesia for 'opposing the rules and regulations issued by the AFC and FIFA.'

So confident did he feel, he was even reported to be pushing himself forward as president of the ASEAN Football Federation, and it wasn't until

April 2011 that FIFA finally took action and dissolved the PSSI leadership, saying it was no longer in control of the game and it had lost credibility!

In their white paper, the GRSNI highlighted a number of issues where they directly or indirectly accused PSSI officials of culpability.

After a number of match fixing and bribery allegations during the 2009/10 season, the PSSI set up an Anti Bribery and Referee Mafia Task Force to look into allegations involving a number of clubs. The white paper claims that by the end of that campaign, the task force had not reported its findings.

Another gripe mentioned by the GRSNI was the tendency for senior officials within the PSSI to overturn decisions made by other members of the organisation, for example the disciplinary committee. The white paper gives an example of when Christian Gonzales, then of Persik Kediri, was banned for 12 months from the game by the disciplinary committee, a suspension upheld by the appeals committee. All that was overruled by the head of the PSSI, who overturned the sentence and Gonzales carried on playing.

'No legal certainty has ever been established in the cases of indiscipline occurring in national football.' So, begins a chapter in the white paper about the culture of violence in Indonesian football, going on to suggest a lack of any enforcement, 'is one of the main factors in the burgeoning of the culture of violence existing in Indonesian football.'

While that section refers mainly to incidences of violence between supporters, there was enough examples of violence on the pitch for the authors of the paper to have a special paragraph devoted to 'police intervention at football matches.'

One example given was when police detained a referee and his linesmen after a game between PSIS Semarang and Mitra Kukar. The chief of Central Java police felt the match officials had shown bias in their decisions, so decided to haul them in for questioning while confiscating all the 'equipment used during the match to the Semarang Police Headquarters.' Eventually the officials were released after nothing was proved.

Around this time, I attended a game at Manahan Stadium in Solo, which came under the jurisdiction of the Central Java police. Before the game, I had spoken with a friend of mine who was quite active within the Persija support and I asked if he could get the travelling fans, there were several thousand who had made the journey for the game against Persik, to sing their version of, You'll Never Walk Alone, as I thought it would make a good video. Sure enough, the fans started doing their bit, but they were drowned out by the chief of police who was passing on his instructions to the fans on how they were expected to behave!

But the fact that the police felt they could even intervene in such a manner suggested the football authorities were not fully in control of events going on in and around the games they were supposed to be responsible for.

Then there is the issue of players, contracts, and salaries, and this could be a book on its own. Brendan Schwab is familiar with the shenanigans that are par for the course in the Indonesian football. Among his many jobs, he is the Chairman of FIFPro Asia, the players' union that seeks to safeguard players' welfare in the region. He is also a member of the FIFA Dispute Resolution Chamber and was instrumental in the setting up of the Indonesian Players' Union, APPI, under the leadership of Arya Abhiseka and Veneard Hutabarat. 'This work exposed me to the financial problems of the current league, and the vast potential of Indonesian football,' he told me in 2011

It didn't take long for the affable Australian to realize the structural problems underlining the game in Indonesia. In fact, he had seen nothing like it, saying that 'the circumstances of contract breaches in Indonesia are the most serious I have seen in football anywhere in the world.' Citing one example of a player who signed a contract for 275 million rupiah (about $300,000) but only received 175 million.

Schwab was actively involved in the setting up of the LPI as an adviser. Working alongside Arya Abhiseka, who had been appointed General Manager of the new league, Brendan provided Australia's experience where a moribund league body had voted itself out of existence and a new federation was set up to develop football in a country where different Rugby League, Union, and Australian Rules were predominant.

What the LPI was attempting could conceivably cause a lot of headaches. With the PSSI withholding recognition of the league, players, coaches, and officials, faced the very real threat of sanction from the authorized governing body. With the PSSI leadership currently in turmoil ahead of leadership elections due this year, they have proffered very little beyond expressing their distaste at the new league and restating the official FIFA view that only member Associations can run professional football leagues. They see the LPI as a distraction, and an illegal one at that.

Schwab was disappointed with PSSI's stance. 'In my view, PSSI should be open to endorsing the LPI and working together to promote football in Indonesia. The LPI aims to run football on a commercial basis to ensure the clubs and the game can operate in a financially viable and independent manner. Commercial viability is essential if football is to grow and achieve international success in any country, including Indonesia.'

Given the animosity between the two camps and their backers, any cooperation seems most unlikely. The FIFPro Chairman believes that the LPI can continue without any official recognition but, 'clearly everyone wants all football to be played within the official football family.'

Since then, little, and much, has changed. Footballers still struggle to get clubs to fulfill their side of the bargain, sometimes with tragic circumstances, while at one stage the PSSI recognised an Indonesian players' union, called APSI. (Now there is just APPI.)

I touched upon tragic circumstances in the last paragraph. I first came across the name Diego Mendieta when he was playing for PSSB in 2007. It was a name I clung on to because it was easy to remember at a time when I was still new to the game and struggling multi-syllable names of local players. After a short spell with Johor FC, before the Crown Prince got involved and changed their name to Johor Darul Ta'zim, he returned to Indonesia and in 2010 was looking for a new club. He trialled with Persikota before eventually signing for Persitara and then moving on to Persis Solo. The 32-year-old Paraguayan died in a hospital in Solo and his final days are a tragic end and a sorry indictment of how footballers are treated.

As Indonesia were preparing to play Laos in the ASEAN Cup in Kuala Lumpur, the Persis fan site, *Pasoepati,* reported their former player had been hospitalised with Typhoid and they were concerned enough to raise funds for the player who had, apparently, gone four months without receiving any salary... an all too familiar occurrence here.

During his final days Mendieta moved hospital three times; he had no money to pay the bills. The *Pasoepati* raised about 300 USD for their ex player but no sign of his outstanding salary; thought to be about 12,000 USD.

As the end approached, Mendieta was quoted by a local paper as saying, 'I have no money. I want a ticket home. I don't want to die here. I want to be with my mother.'

Persis fans were quoted on Twitter as saying he had lost 17 kilograms in weight and a final picture shows a cadaverous young man wearing a Real Madrid shirt.

It's impossible to try and imagine his last few hours. Lying in a government hospital, far from family, dying a slow death, with a few Persis fans for company doing their best to let the world know of his tragic plight. A tragic way for anyone to go; especially a footballer in good condition.

Not much to add really. Except perhaps to compare Mendieta's situation with that of Fabrice Muamba. When the Bolton midfielder collapsed at White Hart Lane the world went into mourning. #prayforMuamba was tweeted around the world by people who had never heard of Bolton Wanderers, let alone the former Arsenal player. With the oxygen of publicity that comes with the English Premier League, Muamba made headlines round the world with thousands of Indonesians passing on their best wishes. Mendieta had none of that. No one knew really beyond Solo and their amazing fans. No RT's, no hashtags, no Facebook pages. Just the ignominy of moving from one hospital to another to escape the mounting bills.

Let's talk potential. Average attendances in Indonesia's Super League are the highest within South East Asia while trailing more powerful neighbours like Australia, South Korea, and Japan. Yet the 11,000 plus who go to games in Indonesia, do so in spite of poor dissemination of information, poor facilities, and often a poor showing on the field.

In the first half of the 2018 season, Persebaya were averaging 31,000 at each home game; Persib were getting 21,000. The largest crowd of the season thus far was the 62,000 that saw Persija play Arema. In Thailand, only Buriram United can average over 10,000 for home games, while Muang Thong United and Nakhorn Ratchasima have the potential to pull five figures on a regular basis.

Malaysia has a number of clubs that can pull big crowds, Johor Darul Tazim, Pahang, Selangor, and Kelantan, spring to mind while others have too narrow a supporter base to expand much more. And Singapore? They no longer release attendances following criticism as to the way they were calculated.

Indonesia's appeal has been belatedly recognised by the great and the good of Europe with clubs like Arsenal, Chelsea, Liverpool, and Ajax hitting the shores for high profile friendlies. Arsenal, in particular, have embraced Indonesia, boasting an Indonesian language Twitter account with Manchester City following suit.

But it is the domestic game that has the biggest potential. Games shown live on TV regularly draw more viewers than even the top European games (free to air broadcasts). Yet back when a broadcasting contract was drawn up, it worked out at a meager $2-3,000 a game! According to GRSNI's white book, the two clubs playing in a game broadcast live on TV received nothing! Little wonder then at the most basic level, clubs have no cash to pay salaries or even invest in new facilities like dressing rooms or a decent training ground.

When I was talking to Johor Darul Tazim coach Bojan Hodak, who was showing me pictures of the facilities his players now enjoy.

'How do those facilities compare with clubs back in Croatia?' I asked him.

'Many Croatian clubs don't have anything like what we have here,' he replied proudly.

Of course, not every football club can boast the deep pockets of a crown prince but then clubs in Thailand and Malaysia have been able to attract serious money. Indonesia, not yet, even though businessman Erick Tohir has taken over Italy's Inter Milan. But for some reason, the serious local cash is staying away. Persib's coach Mario Gomez spent the first few months of the 2018 season bemoaning the lack of infrastructure at his club; he is well placed to comment on South East Asian football having coached Johor Darul Ta'zim to success domestically and internationally. But then JDT have royal backing. Even Persib with their reach, don't have access to regal rupiah and they are one of the better run clubs in the country. They do have some wealthy, influential backing but most clubs don't; they are still beholden to local politicians whose focus may be more on the election cycle than the transfer market.

By the second half of 2010, criticism of the PSSI was mounting from all quarters but they stood their ground. Then came talk of a new league. A rebel league set up and funded by a businessman to rival the PSSI. In short, Indonesia was entering a period of uncertainty with two rival leagues yet only one would be recognised by FIFA and that was the one operated under the auspices of the PSSI. FIFA made it clear they opposed the new league, called Liga Primer Indonesia despite the moral ground it claimed. FIFA, for all intents and purposes, was saying it didn't care what PSSI had done in the past, they would remain behind them.

Meanwhile, this new thing called social media was all aflutter. We were introduced to hashtags and *#changethegame* became the siren call from the LPI people. Football descended into good and bad and for the twitterverse, good was most definitely the LPI.

Three teams, PSM, Persema, and Persibo left the PSSI set up and joined the LPI, which was promising all sorts of wonderful things like paying players on time, no match fixing, and clean administration. Eventually, 16 new teams joined the three renegades for the season, which began early 2011, with a game between Solo Ksatria and Persema in front of a full house and a live TV audience at the Manahan Stadium. A new era was dawning, and heaven forbid any cynic should see the rain that fell that day as an omen!

The other teams that joined the league were Atjeh United, Medan Chiefs, Medan Bintang, Minangkabau, Tangerang Wolves (I have no idea whether wolves were ever found in and around Tangerang but hey, it sounded fun), Jakarta 1928, Batavia Union, Bogor Raya, Bandung, Semarang United, Real Mataram, Solo Ksatria, Persebaya 1927, Bali Dewata, Manado United, and Candrawasih Papua.

They were heady days. Money seemed to come from nowhere and, of course, where there is money there are people who will happily spend it. Nary a day went by without some outlandish names being linked with this new upstart league including, and I kid you not, Minangkabau expressing an interest in the non-flying Dutchman Dennis Bergkamp!

I had just joined Twitter and I was having a blast, though my cynicism was rarely appreciated by the *#changethegame* converts who berated me for my lack of optimism. But amid the hype, there was an elephant in the room that was constantly being ignored. In a country where nothing ever got done about the poor state of the roads and floods were an annual menace, suddenly football would clean up its act? Just like that? In that kind of environment? Football and only football? It didn't seem likely to me, but others were swept up in the moment. Anyway, people were assuming it was all about football. It wasn't. Indeed, there are some people who would suggest the whole circus was never about football but was just one more battlefield in the political sparring that was going on at the time.

When the IPL kicked off, I gave it three months. I was wrong. It lasted about five months. Even though FIFA belatedly gave it its blessing in April 2011, come the halfway point of the season, it ended and all those *#changethegame* kind of disappeared from whence they came.

#	TEAM	P	W	D	L	F-A	PT
1	Persebaya 1927	18	12	4	2	42-12	40
2	Persema	18	12	4	2	35-17	40
3	PSM	18	10	4	4	36-18	34
4	Jakarta 1928	18	9	5	4	33-20	32
5	Medan Chiefs	18	9	5	4	26-20	32
6	Batavia Union	18	8	7	3	32-23	31
7	Bali Devata	18	8	5	5	22-17	29
8	Persibo	18	8	5	5	25-22	29
9	Semarang United	18	9	1	8	18-21	28
10	Minangkabau	18	7	6	5	21-20	27
11	Ajjeh United	18	8	2	8	23-24	26
12	Bintang Medan	18	6	4	8	29-30	22
13	Bogor Raya	18	6	3	9	22-24	21

#	TEAM	P	W	D	L	F-A	PT
14	Solo Ksatria	18	4	4	10	19-29	16
15	Bandung	18	4	4	10	22-23	16
16	Real Mataram	18	4	4	10	27-41	16
17	Manado 9 United	18	3	6	9	19-36	15
18	Tangerang Wolves	18	2	5	11	19-36	11
19	Cendrawasih Papua	18	1	4	13	18-44	7

With the sheen of an officially recognised league, the 2011/2012 campaign kicked off with 12 teams in the top flight and 28 joining a newly formed second tier split among three regions. The new clubs set up for the LPI disappeared with the exception of Bogor Raya and Bandung who 'merged' with Persijap and Persiba Bantul respectively. The new season was full of familiar faces for fans.

#	TEAM	P	W	D	L	F-A	PT
1	Semen Padang	22	13	7	2	46-21	46
2	Persebaya 1927	22	12	2	8	31-23	38
3	Arema Indonesia	22	11	4	7	42-26	37
4	Persibo	22	11	3	8	31-24	36
5	Persiba	22	10	5	7	27-23	35
6	PSM	22	9	7	6	29-26	34
7	Persema	22	10	4	8	32-32	34
8	Persiraja	22	9	5	8	27-30	32
9	Persija	22	7	7	8	38-34	28
10	Persijap	22	4	5	13	18-38	17
11	Bontang	22	4	4	14	21-43	16
12	PSMS	22	2	7	13	17-39	13

What a season this was! What I call the time of plenty! There were two Persebayas, two PSMSs, two Persijas, and two Aremas, but at least the season did finish this time, with Semen Padang by far the best team.

The wheels finally came off in 2013, not that they were ever fully on the rails despite the claims of legitimacy. Persija were forced to play games outside of Jakarta and were told to change their name; they didn't. Persibo embarrassed the nation with a series of inept performances in the AFC Cup, in contrast to Semen Padang who reached the quarter finals, while some clubs just seemed to give up as the final table shows.

#	TEAM	P	W	D	L	F-A	PT
1	Semen Padang	17	14	2	1	48-7	44
2	Pro Duta	21	13	4	4	40-11	43
3	Perseman	20	12	3	5	39-15	39
4	Persiba	19	11	2	6	41-21	35
5	Persebaya 1927*	20	10	5	3	38-23	35
6	PSM	21	11	2	8	32-17	35
7	Persepar	22	10	5	7	29-25	35
8	PSIR	21	10	4	7	34-42	34
9	Persijap	20	9	3	8	32-19	30
10	Persiraja	21	8	5	8	28-30	29
11	PSLS	21	7	5	9	31-29	26
12	Arema Indonesia*	19	5	2	12	19-43	17
13	Bontang	19	4	2	13	21-54	14
14	Persema*	15	3	0	12	16-41	9
15	Persibo*	15	2	1	12	6-37	7
16	Jakarta 1928*	15	1	1	13	11-41	4

*means the team were disqualified; usually for failing to fulfill their fixtures.

Persema, Persibo, and Jakarta 1928 were all disqualified after the halfway stage as the league descended into farce. The promise of 2011 had long faded; clubs were left with bills they couldn't pay, and, in effect, nothing had changed. Football had been used as a political tool by elites and the game was left in a worse position than ever.

Once it was decided the two leagues would merge in 2014 the LPI was finished. Its irrelevancy had been officially recognised and despite plans to finish the season there was no appetite and it expired with nary a whimper. Oh, so different from the hullaballoo that surrounded its launch just two and a half years earlier.

If people had really wanted to #changethegame, there were a number of things they could have done with all that money. Unfortunately, they didn't. The money disappeared into players, agents, and officials pockets and pretty much everyone was taken for a sucker. By 2013, the money had dried up and you got the impression everyone wanted out. It was all kind of like punk rock in 1978! The LPI was a corpse that needed putting out of its misery.

The politicians, who had been so supportive and so keen to be associated with the game back in 2010 and 2011, had moved on. The teenyboppers, who had followed the league's first glamour club Persema (with their youthful coach Timo Scheneuman and young players with good looks like Irfan Bachdim and Kim Jeffery Kurniawan), had found new heroes for their bedroom walls with K-Pop. Even a prime early mover behind the league, a former players' union official, had gone under murky circumstances.

The new league had become worse than the old league and no one cared. The last IPL game I went to was between Persema and PSM at Malang's Gajayana Stadium in 2012 and it was a tame affair indeed. Bachdim, the poster boy of 10/11, came on as a second half substitute but apart from me and a crowd of perhaps two dozen, nobody else noticed.

In a bar after the game, I picked over the bones of the IPL with a couple of friends and it was all pretty morbid. Many had been taken in by the promises and many had been let down.

The white book, so lovingly prepared, reads like a fairy tale; of a game that was to be rescued by a gallant knight on his white charger taking us on to a new Valhalla with its talk of development and youth. It was all very gallant, very Arthurian. And all very unlikely.

14.
FOOTBALL ON THE BIG SCREEN

For all intents and purposes, I left England in 1987. Football was fun. There was none of this membership scheme nonsense, just Luton Town, and all ticket games were rare. You could usually just turn up on the day, have a few beers, pay at the gate and stand with your mates. Little wonder then that, I, like so many from that generation, look back on them as golden days.

It wasn't perfect of course. You risked getting your head kicked in, at the least, if you told someone the time in the wrong accent and there was still plenty of crowd trouble to keep the police occupied and Daily Mail readers hiding behind their lace curtains on match day.

There were changes afoot though. Big clubs, plus Tottenham, were pushing for a more exclusive super league that would see them take more money from TV and the fans, while prime minister Margaret Thatcher was determined to introduce identity cards for football fans, and football fans alone, and to hell with civil liberties. The Heysel crowd trouble where 39 fans died in Belgium ahead of the European Cup final in 1985 and the Bradford City fire disaster that took 56 lives were fresh in people's minds and everyone knew something needed to be done to make football a safer environment.

Against this backdrop, fanzines started appearing. Magazines about football, obviously, put together as a labour of love by dedicated fans. They provided a voice that was not being heard in the corridors of power. The first one I found was at Wimbledon; I later discovered Sports Pages in London and soon that was part of my match day experience, catching up in the latest *When Saturday Comes* et all.

Fanzine editors, writers, compilers, whatever, were my demographic. They had grown up in the punk years and seen that if you wanna do something then bloody well do it yourself and if it offends the suits and the bores then even better.

Fanzines raised issues we discussed in pubs, trains, and stadiums across the country but whereas before it could be written off as beer talking, now it was down in print. It's a funny thing but Twitter does something similar today but back then you would never get major news outlets saying, '27% of Arsenal fans want xxx out.' Today, don't they just love to come out with drivel like, 'blah blah has posted on his Twitter account,' and use it as a 'trustworthy' piece of news!

The magazines were well put together, some looked pretty professional, and talked about high ticket prices, unsympathetic policing, inconvenient kick offs, and clubs adopting a high-handed approach to their fans. Much the same things people whine about today. So, I guess they have no power or influence at all!

Read a fanzine, the team are crap, the stadium is crap, the police are out of control, the ticket prices are too high, see you next game! God, I miss all that!

Back then, there was no inkling of the cultural change that was about to embrace the game in England for better or worse. When I started following the game, football literature was pretty well limited to *The Football Man* by Arthur Hopcraft (1968) and Brian Glanville's *Puffin Book of Football*, plus, of course, the *Shoot* annuals!

I was away when it started to change but even those back in England have difficulty pinpointing the moment football started to become more gentrified (a polite word meaning expensive). Certainly, Nick Hornby's *Fever Pitch*, later to become a movie, was a pivotal moment but then so too were England's reaching the World Cup semi-final in 1990 and hosting the European Championships in 1996. And we cannot forget the moment when English football was invented by Sky in 1992 and beamed to the world.

I read *Fever Pitch* with dismay; bang went my idea for literary greatness thanks to a bald-headed guy who lived a few miles away from me

The Tarquins and the *Johnny Come Latelys* had discovered the beautiful game, they painted their faces, wore jackets with leather elbow patches, and told everyone how much they loved 'footy.'

I do know when I left England, there was sod all about football on the shelves of WH Smith, and when I returned in 2002 they were creaking under the strain as every Tom, Dick, and Harry was adding their two penny worth. And not just the players. Coaches, fans, celebrity fans, and even former hooligans were having their say. Thug lit, one time top boys with their tales of hooligan chivalry, never done, never run, fare dodging, cheap shags, and a line or two of marching powder to keep the momentum going.

All that was missing from the burgeoning football lit scene was the inside story of a lottery ticket seller for Hartlepool United telling us what it was really like standing outside the main stand trying to flog dreams of easy cash as a biting wind came in from the North Sea that was so cold and so harsh, even the sea gulls stayed home. Or the inside story of the little old lady who sold Wagon Weels and piping hot Bovril from a shack behind the terraces.

From the books, it was not a big step to movies and following on from *Fever Pitch*, we have seen the likes of *Football Factory* and *Damned United* lead the charge to the big screen. Well, I haven't. We don't get them movies in Indonesia, although I have heard people tell they can be bought on pirated DVDs for about 35p, but I will have nothing to do with that, oh no siree.

Then we have Indonesia. Here, they have missed out the fanzines and the legions of books and gone straight to movie making, thanks to the efforts of a man named Yusuf Andibachtiar. Indonesia has yet to have its own Fever Pitch moment. The game remains widely loathed by the chattering classes until it comes to politics and remains decidedly un-mainstream. Much like the game in the 1980s in England!

The liberal luvvies in their armchairs sipping coffee in swanky malls who dictate much of the arts scene see no great value in football, preferring syrupy soap operas featuring lots of piano, eyes moving slowly, and rich people with white skin.

Yusuf swims against the tide and for that he has my respect. At the moment, he is on a 19 hour boat journey to a remote island to carry on filming his latest tome, about the national Under 19 team, a journey no self-respecting limelight seeking luvvie would countenance. Nor me, if truth be told!

The bespectacled Yusuf is no Danny Dyer or Nick Love. He is a passionate football fan who has followed his own team near and far. So, there are perhaps a couple of parallels with Cass Pennant but only a couple! I am not aware of the former West Ham United lad getting a slap at one of his screenings!

Movies should be a voyage of discovery, a learning experience for the viewer of something new, not a spunkfest for spotty, sweaty animation geeks, and special effects freaks who are not sated unless something, somewhere is getting blown up. Yusuf looks at people and tells the tale of people with football as a backdrop. Much like writers did in the past, someone like, you know, Charles Dickens for example. He told of dramas, poverty, greed, and the like, and didn't feel the need to imbue every tale with a proper exciting horse chase.

The Jak marked Yusuf's cinematic debut; a documentary about Persija fans. It was certainly no *Fever Pitch*. He talks about Jakarta as a melting pot with people seeking an identity and features a guy, who is one of the most violent fans yet is also an activist for a political party and would campaign for them come election time. He doesn't have the kind of income to allow him to mix with the mall folk and even if he had, I am not sure he would want to. Instead, the money he makes from selling tofu goes on supporting his football team around the country and he talks about why he feels the need to fight to 'preserve' his space in one of the most crowded cities in the world. It talks about an underclass of society shut out from economic development and given little opportunity to express themselves.

The Conductors was something very different. Where The Jak is raw and in your face, much like Jakarta is raw and in your face, *The Conductors* takes us on another journey with a couple of leading characters. One a conductor of a large orchestra of people dressed in suits playing to people in suits at prices only people in suits can afford. The other character delivers water in a kampung and is devoted to Arema football club in Malang.

The toff conducts orchestras of up to 100 musicians and can earn $10,000 a month, the waterboy, on the terraces of Kanjuruhan Stadium, conducts several thousand fans clad in Arema blue before and during the game and takes home perhaps $100 a month.

Then we have *Romeo and Juliet*. There is no way this movie could have been filmed in Singapore or Thailand! There is more to come from the rivalry between Persija and Persib in this here diary and let's just say the movie did not go down well in Bandung! Indeed, at an attempted showing there, Yusuf was jostled and slapped by angry Persib fans who felt the film should not have been made at all and as far as I am aware, no efforts were made to show it again. The movie was banned across much of the provinces of West Java and Banten, where there are large numbers of Persib fans.

A forbidden love story between a boy who supports Persija and a girl who supports Persib, it follows the William Shakespeare original with the names obviously changed to reflect the Jakarta/Bandung characters and of course, the Old Bard never had much of an issue with rampaging football fans when he was penning his stuff on the banks of the Avon! Persib fans see the movie as Jakarta elitist propaganda, showing the capital city to be some smooth, sophisticated place while looking down on Persib as a city full of country bumpkins speaking a funny language.

This idea of Jakarta cultural superiority is one I have come across a few times. Recently, I was down in Yogyakarta, a city famous for its Javanese soul and the most visited city on Java by foreign visitors. A friendly young local was telling me how Jakarta made TV shows often depicted people from Yogyakarta as traditional, dressed in traditional costumes, and following old traditions with the air of a country bumpkin!

The movie starts with a bunch of Persija fans attacking a bus load of Persib fans. As they battle away, bringing traffic to a standstill on the highway, smashing windows, and kicking the living crap out of each other, a Persija thug sees a Persib lass and, amid the mayhem their eyes meet, cupid fires off an arrow and they are in love. He can't believe it, she can't believe it. The eyes don't lie. And for the next few minutes they bore their friends shitless with their amour carved in the trenches of Indonesian football's bitterest rivalry.

Does the Persib fan swoon out of an open window, beseeching, 'Romeo, Romeo where for art thou you Persija bastard?' Not as far as I can make out but when they do finally meet up, their first words to each other are, of course, to slag off their respective football teams! And on such lovey dovey foundations does a long lasting relationship develop? For that, you will need to watch the movie!

15.
JAKARTA, THE FOOTBALL CRAZY CITY OF MALLS

It doesn't matter how many worn out cliches you can think of regarding Indonesia's passion for football, when it comes to sporting facilities, Jakarta and its surrounding areas are a veritable wasteland. New stadiums have cropped up across the country in recent years, most notably in places like Banda Aceh (Aceh province), Bandung and Bekasi (West Java), Pekanbaru (Riau), Samarinda and Balikpapan (East Kalimantan). But Jakarta? Nope.

In fact, the capital city is probably deemed to have too many stadiums because it wasn't that long ago, one was torn down (Menteng Stadium) in an old money area of the city, to be replaced by a park catering to the local residents. The park by the way, hit the headlines when it featured for a while a statue of Barack Obama who went to school in the area and was deemed worthy of recognition. Football, obviously, was not deemed worthy of recognition.

When the old stadium, it had been constructed in 1921, was demolished to make way for a park, it was not just a football stadium that was lost. It was a living, breathing entity that made up a football club as these quotes make clear.

'The designated relocation site, Roxy Stadium (formerly known as VIJ Stadium and used by Persija until 1950 when they too were known as VIJ), is too small for the subdivision competition, while Lebak Bulus Stadium is reserved for the main division,' said Ridwan Ramli, an official with Persija at the time.

'Hopefully we can find a new field of stadium in Central Jakarta as it is the most strategic area for most of our players to reach. If we relocated to South

Jakarta, for example, many of our players would have to commute from far away and it would become exclusively the southern players' territory,' he added.

As a football association, the Persija league boasted about 70 teams at the time including some 40 junior clubs with several hundred players each! No compensation was paid apparently.

'I am afraid that the junior and child players will fall into drug abuse, drink alcohol, and commit crimes while waiting for the competition to resume,' Ridwan said.

One of Persija's junior teams was Putra Dewata, established in the 1950s, who were forced to move to a district military-owned soccer field on Jl. Jenderal Urip Sumoharjo in Jatinegara, East Jakarta.

'We can only practice at this Jatinegara field. However, we can't use this field for competition as there is no seating for supporters,' said Dino Asmuni, 52, who trains goal-keepers for Putra Dewata. 'I was raised in Menteng Stadium. Back when I was a teenager playing for a team, setting foot in Mentang Stadium made me proud. The experience of playing in a heritage stadium meant that a player was good enough,' said Dino.

'The city administration has committed a brutal act against the stadium. Many of our trophies that were located in the lobby were damaged by the forceful demolition, and even the computer in the office is missing,' Dino said.

The bitter irony of the tale is the Jakarta governor, under whose watch, Menteng Stadium was consigned to rubble used to sponsor a trophy once year featuring Persija and a number of other teams including some from overseas.

The Gelora Bung Karno Stadium was built back in 1962 for the Asian Games that Indonesia was to host in that same year and since then has been used for a number of events, from religious meetings (including the pope one year), rock concerts, political rallies, civil service examinations, and yes, even the odd football match. It has recently gone under extensive renovation with innovations, like individually numbered seats ahead of the 2018 Asian Games.

Obviously, when the Indonesian national team have games played in Jakarta, they use this stadium and with a capacity of more than 88,000, it is also used by Persija, though they rarely fill the arena.

There was one memorable occasion when they hosted Arema back in 2010. It was the last game of the season and Arema needed to win to confirm their first ever Indonesia Super League title. This was the season when the Singapore players came in numbers and the title clincher featured Noh Alam Shah and M Ridwan wearing the blue of Arema while Mustafic Farhuddin was in the Persija squad at the time.

You could say it was a big game. There was a large Arema following who had converged on the grounds of the stadium over the previous days. Some estimates put the figure at 50,000 travelling fans and that is at the lower end of the scale. Certainly, I flew into Jakarta the day before the match and there were Arema fans on my flight from Batam... look up Malang, Jakarta, and Batam on a map!

We went to the stadium and there were thousands of Arema fans just sitting around, waiting for the gates to open the following day! Come match day, the stadium was a sea of orange and blue, Arema and Persija fans consider themselves brothers so little risk of major disturbances, well over 80,000 crammed inside the stadium. Arema won 5-1, won the title then did their best to get back down the tunnel before the shirts were ripped off their backs!

Typically, Persija attract around 20,000 for their home games at a stadium that costs a small fortune to rent. Obviously, games against the likes of Arema and Persib push the crowd higher.

Persitara are the second team of Jakarta. Based in North Jakarta, they usually play their home games at Tugu Stadium, a ramshackle affair in a hard to get to part of town even with your own vehicle but at least it is in North Jakarta, close to its roots. At other times, Persitara have used Lebak Bulus and Soemantri Brojonegoro in South Jakarta as well as Kamal Muara, which is, politically speaking, at least not even in Jakarta at all but neighbouring Tangerang!

There were a few heady days a few years back when Persitara, average crowd about 3,000, were toying with the idea of using Bung Karno for themselves. Somehow overlooking the small fact, the costs of using that behemoth would far outweigh any revenue at the gate for a club that regularly has problems paying its players on time.

Back in those short-lived days of plenty when Indonesia boasted two national leagues, Batavia Union, who came from North Jakarta and wore Persitara blue and white, played home games at Soemantri Brojonegoro and even the old Patriot Stadium in Bekasi, West Java, while Jakarta 1928 played at Lebak Bulus, in front of crowds that sometimes approached dozens.

In the second season, when the rebel league of 2011 acquired legitimacy in the eyes of FIFA at least, Jakarta 1928 told everyone they would be known as Persija but could never actually play any games in Jakarta! Fans of the other Persija refused to acknowledge them full stop. They were forced to play in places like Solo (Central Java) and Madiun (East Java), all the while stubbornly clinging to the name Persija, defying logic, common sense, and even a court ruling against them. Meanwhile, Batavia Union fell by the wayside, I wonder what happened to their fans, and Persitara carried on regardless at Tugu Stadium.

While Tugu Stadium is relatively difficult to get to, Soemantri Brojonegoro is decidedly easy, along Jl Rasuna Said in Kuningan. It is set behind a kind of shopping area full of places to eat and is also close to a high rise residential development. Considering how easy it is to get to, it is also pretty close to the highway, I was always amused at how the Persitara fans arrived late for their home games!

I got to see a few Persitara games at Soemantri Brojonegoro when they used it as their home ground. It was good for me because it was literally walking distance from a pub! There was one game against Persebaya that was fun. Relations between their supporters and those of Persija have never been particularly cordial. So, on this occasion while the away support was negligible, a few Persija fans had come along to ensure some of the less disciplined followers didn't come along to attack the away support! There was never going to be any trouble between the home and away fans on the day; based on the premise that 'thine enemy is mine enemy.' Persitara and Persebaya fans were united in their loathing of Persija and Arema!

In South Jakarta, again close to a highway, is Lebak Bulus Stadium, a rare purpose built football stadium that has been used by Persija, Persitara, Persiram Raja Ampat (from Papua!), Pelita Jaya, and Persijatim East Jakarta, among others as a home venue. It looks like a stadium and it feels like a stadium and despite a capacity of just 12,5000, a packed house could still send shivers down the spine of the unwary. Alas and alack, no more, for the proposed mass transport system has earmarked Lebak Bulus as its southern terminal and it too followed Menteng Stadium into the history books; a place of myth and legend in the same way Highbury (Arsenal) and Grunwalderstr (Bayern Munchen) have.

Which is a shame. There used to be a small shop at the stadium selling some football stuff. I kept seeing an old PS Krakatau Steel shirt in the window which took my fancy but as a big white guy, there were a couple of pubs nearby that also took my fancy, so I would frequently arrive late for games!

Lebak Bulus was also the scene of one of the strangest crowd disturbances I have ever seen. There was an ASEAN Football Federation Championship for Under 16s going on and featuring Indonesia, Singapore, Malaysia, Bahrain, and Australia. I went to all the games as did this other guy who sat near me. Towards the end of a Bahrain game, there he was in the stand, with his mate, and guy number one was yelling abuse at the Bahrain players in Arabic while his gimpy mate guffawed next to him.

After a while one of the Bahrain lads got fed up and charged down the tunnel, up the stairs, and into the stand where he confronted mister gobshite face to face. Of course, gobshite acted all innocent while his gimpy mate melted away. The lad I was with had coached in Bahrain before and knew some of the lingo. He made soothing noises to the young player while a couple of security types got between the irate Bahrain player and the gobshite who, of course, started playing up again once he was behind a brown wall. It was all great fun for an Under 16 game, of course, and eventually, gobshite was manhandled out of the stadium protesting his innocence, while the Bahrain player returned to the bench. I wonder if it ever appeared in the match commissioner's report?

A few years later I was at Lebak Bulus again for a game between Persiram and Persiba Balikpapan. Again, it is worth putting this into some kind of context. Persiram are based in Raja Ampat, an area in eastern Indonesia famous, nay, world famous for its diving. And Balikpapan come from East Kalimantan. Different provinces, different islands, and yes, different time zones and yet here we all we in deepest South Jakarta waiting for them to go head to head in a top flight game. You couldn't make it up and I certainly couldn't.

I was sitting in the main stand when this young Indonesian lad got talking to me. It turned out he worked in a bank and had taken time off to come and see Persiba because his brother, Eki Nurhakim, was playing for them at the time.

'Ah,' says I, 'he used to play for Persijap Jepara.'

That blew the guy away! How could I, a foreigner, have even heard of his brother, a journeyman pro who had played for the likes of Persikabo, Pelita Jaya, and Sriwijaya during his career? Anyway, to cut a long story short, the kick-off gets delayed and delayed. I contact a friend of mine who should have known what was going on and he just said, 'wait, lah, you know, this is Indonesia.'

The players from both sides were on the pitch warming up and even the match officials were jogging up and down the centre line, but no one seemed in any hurry to start the bloody football match; a game, I might point out, I had taken time off work myself to take in.

Eventually, both teams disappear down the tunnel and yippee, we can get started. Then my new mate comes back. 'The game is cancelled', he said, 'there are no security officers available.' I looked around the ground. There were more people on the pitch than there were in the stand!

Apparently, there were some disturbances in another area of Jakarta and the cops assigned to this match had been shifted there instead. My new mate was happy; his brother had given him his unsweaty match shirt and me? Well, like I said before, there are a couple of pubs near the stadium, so it wasn't a totally wasted day!

Heading east along the highway and you, somehow, get to Ciracas Stadium. Another multi-purpose venue, this arena boasts the usual bog standard stand and, um, little else. The last few times I have seen games there it has been for Persipasi Bekasi who used it while their own Patriot Stadium was being renovated, and some Division One games when the division is split into small, regionally based groups of five or six teams who base themselves at a single stadium for the duration. Persija Under 21s have also used the ground a few times while the current campaign sees Villa 2000, a new team actually based in nearby South Tangerang, playing there.

That leaves Bea Cukai Stadium, tucked away in East Jakarta. By the way, in English, Bea Cukai translates as Customs! In days gone past, Persijatim used to play there which seems appropriate; the stadium, which lies on Customs department land, is in East Jakarta, but in recent years it only really gets an airing for amateur football, read Divisions One and Two, and the odd friendly. In fact, the only time I have been there was for a friendly between Mitra Kukar, from East Kalimantan, and Persikabo in nearby West Java.

Bung Karno, Lebak Bulus, Tugu, Soemantri Brojonegoro, Ciracas and that is pretty much it for a city of several million. Once in a while places like Lapangen Banteng, Ragunan, Halim Air Force base, and a field outside of Bung Karno, get used for unofficial stuff, training, or local stuff, but that is pretty much it for a city of god knows how many teeming millions of sports loving folks. Malls? Yep, plenty of them and more on the way but for a sporting fix there ain't a whole lot. And with nowhere to even get the basics like training, what hope is there for Indonesia producing its own sporting heroes despite the fine words that come from political figures once in a while.

When the news came that Menteng would be demolished, apparently plans were drawn up for Lebak Bulus to be renovated and expanded. When news came that Lebak Bulus would be demolished, apparently plans were drawn up for a new stadium also in South Jakarta, and following a recent gubernatorial election there was much talk this would finally get off the ground.

Going further afield, Bekasi now has a new stadium, Patriot Stadium, but home town club Persipasi have been unable to use it yet. Don't ask me why. Something to do with politics. It often is. The city of Tangerang has Benteng Stadium, Cibinong, in West Java, has Persikabo Stadium which is used by Persikabo and the new Pakansari Stadium. A bit closer to Jakarta is Merpati Stadium in Depok and home to Persikad.

Further afield, there are also stadiums in Karawang (Singaperbangsa Stadium which has been used by local side Persika Karawang, Pelita Jaya and currently Persita), Krakatau Steel Stadium in Cilegon (home to PS Krakatau Steel and Cilegon United among others), Purnawarman Stadium (Purwakarta which has been used by Pelita Jaya), which may or may not be in the process of renovation, and Pajajaran Stadium in Bogor which last hit the news when US president George W Bush came on a visit and used it to land his helicopter. And don't forget Maulana Yusuf Stadium in Serang and home to Persrang. A pretty sparse list for a two hour radius of Jakarta in some of the most crowded real estate not just in South East Asia but the world.

While Jakarta doesn't seem in a rush to build a new stadium, new venues continue to crop up in the most unlikely of places. Sleman, for example, has its very own mini San Siro yet try and find Sleman on a map! Soreang has Si Jaluk Harupat but again, check out the access to Soreang! And Surabaya has the Bung Tomo stadium but again, little consideration has been given to getting people to and from the stadium. I went to see Persebaya at the Bung Tomo, the crowd was given as about 1,200 and it was a pain to get to. Likewise, Si Jalak Harupat. Nice, big stadium but surrounded by rice fields, narrow roads to and from, and little in the way of facilities.

It makes you realise just what a mammoth job lay ahead if Indonesia had won the right to host the World Cup in 2022!

16.
INDONESIAN CLUBS TAKE TO ASIA

It is fair to say that when it comes to Asian club competition, Indonesian clubs have done little to impress the continent with true nadirs being reached in 2010 by Persipura's hapless AFC Champions League campaign and Persibo Bojonegoro's almost comical efforts in the AFC Cup of 2013, when they really gave the impression that they would rather be doing something totally different than travelling around the likes of Hong Kong, Myanmar, and the Maldives representing their country and their town.

However, there have been more recent signs of progress as Arema in 2012 and Semen Padang in 2013 have shown a tactical savvy and willingness to actually go toe to toe with their peers rather than see the games as unnecessary additions to an already crowded fixture list and travel schedule.

Persibo Bojonegoro and Indonesian football would have been better served had they rejected the opportunity to compete in the 2013 AFC Cup. They are playing in Asia's second tier club competition by dint of winning the Indonesia Cup last season, but they do have the feel of a professional football club this season.

They lost their first game in the AFC Cup 3-0 away to Yangon United. Okay fair enough, away games are always tough but more so in this part of the world where a two or three hour flight can take you to a completely different culture and players here are not the most widely travelled people.

Next up was New Radiant at Solo's Manahan Stadium. They couldn't play the game in Bojonegoro because their own ground isn't up to AFC standards. New Radiant come from the Maldives, an island nation, like Indonesia, that boasts a population less than the district of the home team but that amounted to zilch as they returned home with a 7-0 win!

Another home game saw Persibo take on Hong Kong side Sunray Cave and despite leading at one stage had to make do with a 3-3 draw giving them their first point.

Then to Hong Kong. The media there were reporting the Indonesian team as missing, as they had not turned up for a training session at the appointed time amid rumours they had no money and wanted to withdraw.

They eventually turned up. On the day of the match. After flying from Surabaya to Hong Kong, no doubt on the cheapest airline possible.

They handed in their team sheet, which boasted a single substitute, and were set to play.

Everything, of course, went swimmingly for the home team and, with the Indonesian players dropping like flies after their less than perfect preparation, they were 8-0 up after 65 minutes when the ref cancelled the game as Persibo had less than the required number of players to continue the game.

In a damning judgment of Indonesian football delivered after the game, Sunray coach Chiu Chung Man said, 'We didn't expect this situation from Persibo; they don't have any sporting spirit. We have heard many times about the lack of sportsmanship of Indonesian teams but did not expect it to happen with us.'

It would have been cheaper, and easier on their goal difference and bank balance, had they stayed home and taken an automatic 3-0 loss.

So why were Persibo even in the AFC Cup? Rumours in the Hong Kong media suggested the Indonesia Football Association (known as PSSI) were keen for them to continue and the club themselves would rather not bother. To paraphrase the twisted Khmer Rouge who held sway in Cambodia during the 1970s, there is no benefit if Persibo stay in the AFC Cup and there is no loss if they withdraw.

Persipura have had more experience of Asian football than most Indonesian clubs, but they too have their own demons. After winning the

ISL back in 2009, they qualified for the Champions League and were drawn alongside Jeonbuk Hyundai Motors, Kashima Antlers, and Changchun Yatai.

The powers that be deemed Persipura's Mandala Stadium as not up to their standards, so the Black Pearls were forced to play their home games in Jakarta at the Bung Karno Stadium. With crowds in the hundreds, they would have been better off playing at Lebak Bulus as they lost their first two games; 4-1 against Jeonbuk and 3-1 against Kashima. Some respite came with a 2-0 win over Changchun in the final game, but the damage had been done.

On their travels, Persipura were abject. They lost their first away game to Changchun 9-0; the Chinese team only scored one other goal in the group stage. Further heavy defeats followed, 5-0 in Japan against Kashima and 8-0 against Jeonbuk. Six group games saw them score four goals and concede 29!

The idea the club were less than serious about the competition came in local media reports, where journalists who were travelling overseas with them photographed the players wrapped up in winter clothes and frolicking in the snow. Now the players may not have experienced much in the way of chilly weather in their home towns, but the images gave off the wrong impression; it looked more like a group of students on a field trip than a professional football team out to get a result.

Fortunately, in 2012 Arema, the IPL version, acquitted themselves much better in the AFC Cup. But you wouldn't have thought that from the way they started. They were drawn alongside Malaysia's Kelantan, Myanmar's Ayeyawady United, and Navibank Saigon from Vietnam, and they started by dropping points at home to Ayeyawady. The game was played at the Gajayana Stadium in the centre of Malang, but the fans weren't impressed; just 2,000 turned up. The hardcore Arema fans had pledged their allegiance to the other Arema, the one playing in the ISL and as good partners the world over couldn't share their love with another!

Things got worse in their first away game, as a hat trick from one-time Pelita Jaya striker Edison Fonseca gave Saigon a comfortable 3-1 lead despite falling behind in the 5th minute to a goal from Jati.

Next up was a trip to the north east of Malaysia and Kota Bahru, home to Kelantan and this time it was the home team's Lebanese striker Mohammad Ghaddar who did the damage with a hat trick of his own. Halfway through the group stage and things weren't looking good for Arema, who were then being coached by Dejan Antonic. They had just one point from nine and a negative goal difference. Could things get worse? Well, yes, they could. Kelantan travelled to Malang and won 3-1 with that man Ghaddar netting a brace.

With a bloody awful record of one point from 12, Arema were facing certain elimination with two games to go. But Asian football moves in mysterious ways. Their next game saw them travel to Myanmar and defeat Ayeyawady 3-0 before the final game with everything to play for.

Going into the game, Kelantan had already qualified from the group and the table looked like this:

1 - Kelantan 5 3 1 1 9-5 10

2 - Saigon 5 2 1 2 8-6 7

3 - Ayeyawady 5 2 1 2 7-9 7

4 - Arema 5 1 1 3 6-10 4

The fans still stayed away. No doubt feeling the team were as good as out but an early penalty from Chmelo gave the 3,500 that did turn up some hope. Then a flood of four goals in 10 minutes, before half time, turned the tie and the group on its head. TA Musafri hit a couple, Amiruddin and a second penalty for Chmelo shifted Arema into positive goal difference territory and brought them level on points with Saigon and Ayeyawady.

Saigon hit back in the second half with Fonseca scoring their first goal on 54 minutes. Quang Hai scored a second on 70 but the fortunes favoured

Arema. The win in their last game against the team from Myanmar and victory against Saigon ensured they had a better head to head, and though Amiruddin netted on 79 minutes to make it 6-2 on the day. It was job done and they were through to the knockout stage.

The three teams finished on seven points each!

Arema's reward for making it out of the group stage was a one off game away to Kitchee in Hong Kong. It was a homecoming of sorts for coach Antonic, who had played in Hong Kong for seven years including a three year spell at Kitchee.

After hanging up his boots in 2005 he had moved into coaching, spending a further three years at Kitchee then moving to a number of other teams before returning to Indonesia in 2012 with Arema. If any coach was placed to end Indonesian teams poor run away from home, it was surely Antonic.

And so, it proved, Arema winning 2-0 and earning a place in the quarter finals where they were drawn against Saudi Arabia's Al Ettifaq. Arema's luck run out as they were defeated 4-0 on aggregate but they had shown an Indonesian team did have what it takes to make an impression on the continental stage. And a year later, Semen Padang followed in their footsteps.

Persibo may have embarrassed everyone but Semen Padang's efforts sent a warm glow of pride down people's spines.

Semen Padang were joined in Group E by Kitchee, India's Churchill Brothers, and the Warriors from Singapore, formerly known as Singapore Arrmed Forces or SAFFC.

The men from West Sumatra started in fine form, overcoming Warriors 3-1 in their first game with goals from Edward Wilson Junior, Niur Iskander, and Vendry Mofu. That game set the tone; a crowd of more than 9,000 showed that the footballing public were interested in Asian football and Wilson, a prolific striker over the years in Padang, showed he could score at a higher level than the Premier League.

He went on to score eight goals in the group stage out of Semen Padang's 15 as they finished top, winning five and drawing one of their games.

Almost 12,000 turned up for their first group stage game against Danang from Vietnam, but despite the noise in the stadium and the humidity in the atmosphere, it was the visitors who took the lead on 32 minutes through Gaston Merlo after a delightful through ball. Wilson equalised in injury time of the first half with a penalty after former international Elie Aiboy was clattered to the ground. But it wasn't until injury time of the second half that the home team ensured victory when Vendry Mofu got in behind a static Vietnamese defence to slot home the winner.

The quarter final draw saw Semen Padang off to India where they were drawn against East Bengal. Thirty thousand fans saw the home team edge a narrow 1-0 win but as the Indonesian team checked out of their hotel and began their journey home they must have been thinking the tie was still alive.

And it was. Wilson scored halfway through the first half and it was game on. Unfortunately, the Liberian striker took a knock and was replaced at home time. On came his prolific strike partner Iskander and together with Titus Bonai they surely had enough to trouble the visitors.

Alas, it was not to be. Titus did not step up to the plate, being the main man seemed to sit uncomfortably on his shoulders, but Semen Padang lacked penetration up front. At the back David Pagbe was immense as was midfielder Yu Hyun Koo but slowly the Indian side started to exert greater influence on the game and it came as no surprise when James Moga, himself on as a substitute, levelled the scores and so confirmed the end of Semen Padang's Asian adventure.

If an Indonesian team is to win the AFC Cup it is not because the country is due a win. Football isn't that soft. Success will only come because they have earned it on the field. Recent seasons suggest some progress has been made in attitudes and on the field but there are still many factors lined up against a team from these shores tasting continental success anytime soon.

First, there is the travel involved. Like I said earlier, every domestic away game for the likes of Persipura or Semen Padang involves a trip to the airport. Then there is the size of a squad. Indonesian clubs are notoriously tight when it comes to building a squad to compete on multiple fronts, always worrying where the money will come from to pay salaries, etc.

And then there is the Middle East. As the facts show, they dominate this trophy and much of Asian football. A representative from there is likely to win the AFC Asian Cup in 2019 as it is being hosted by United Arab Emirates, but they are still several steps behind the true powers of Asia like Japan and South Korea. They are likely to maintain a significant hold on this particular trophy, especially on home soil where they appear to be near unbeatable for sides visiting from South East Asia.

Still, gently, gently capture trophy as no one has ever said before!

17.
THE WORLD CUP STAR WHO MADE INDONESIA HOME

I must admit, anything east of Jalan Rasuna Said and Jalan Warung Buncit is as much a mystery to me as the charms of Nora Batty were to Compo in Last of the Summer Wine. I don't know East Jakarta and it doesn't know me. I have been there but just about all I can recall from my trips to Kalimalang and Jatinegara is the bloody awful traffic and who needs to drive from my side of town, with all its traffic, to the other side of town with all its traffic?!

So why I am heading to East Jakarta!? I figured the journey from CITOS, a shopping mall in South Jakarta, shouldn't take that long; after all Halim Airport doesn't look that far... as crows fly. Unfortunately, crows weren't asked to develop the roads in Jakarta and for some reason my taxi driver took me on the Antasari flyover, along Jalan Tendean, and into unknown territory. For me at least.

It didn't matter where we were, we were stuck. My timing wasn't the best perhaps as people were leaving work early to get home and break the fast with their family. As we neared Halim the congestion only worsened, and it was only then I found out the taxi driver didn't have a clue where we were going. Neither did I, of course. So, I suggested we pull up in front of a military base and ask them. They didn't know either but helpfully pointed us in a direction they felt might be useful. People rarely say they don't know, out of a desire to be helpful, or just to get rid of these awkward people asking awkward questions, they will say anything!

I wanted to get to my destination before the sunset because I wanted to take some photographs, but I didn't rate my chances. It was like that scene in Dracula where Van Helsing and his mob were racing, by horse, to the Count's castle before the sun set and he turned into something fiendish. Except I wasn't on a horse, I wasn't racing anywhere, and my appointment wasn't with someone who could turn fiendish in the hours after the sun had disappeared over the western horizon.

I was due to meet with the only player in Indonesia who had played in a World Cup. Actually, I am guessing he is the only one; I don't suppose there are too many left from the Dutch East Indies side that played in France in 1938. Jules Denis Onana has been in Indonesia for almost 20 years. He is fluent in French, Indonesia, Spanish, and English yet he struggles with any of the indigenous languages from his home country, Cameroon; Wikipedia says there are 230 languages spoken in the West African country and who am I to argue?

Between me and the taxi driver, we finally find where we want to be just as the sun bids adios. I was told there was a stadium, but it was hardly that... little more than a field with a couple of pitches and a small stand type thing. I had wanted to catch up with Onana to talk academies and preparing the next generation of Indonesian football, but I was too late. The session had finished, I was shattered after my two hour journey and so I decided to talk about Onana's World Cup experiences back in 1990.

That Cameroon team, of course, was famous for the deeds of a certain Roger Milla, the ageless one whose exploits help them defeat holders Argentina in the opening game and led them to a quarter final tie against England. Onana was there from the start to the finish and his recollections recall almost another time in football and provide a fascinating insight behind the scenes of an unfancied World Cup squad far from home and without the handheld gadgets we all take for granted these days.

Back in 1990, Onana was playing for Canon Sportif de Yaounde alongside players like a young Marc-Vivien Foe who went on to play for Lens, West Ham United, Lyon, and Manchester City before tragically collapsing and dying during a FIFA Confederations Cup tie between Cameroon and Colombia in 1993.

Onana must have impressed as he went on to play for his country on 66 occasions but unfortunately has no caps to show for it nor even any of his shirts. 'We had no sponsors so after playing we had to give back the shirts to the team!'

'Even during the World Cup?' I asked.

'During the World Cup we had two jerseys for one game but in Africa we like to share the jerseys with our family, our friends. I gave one shirt to a journalist and one to my idol.'

Onana had first been called up to the national team in 1988, so was a familiar name in the squad. Two months before the World Cup began, 40 players went into a pre-competition training camp in Yugoslavia for a month or so, and when the squad was finally announced they headed to Italy where they were based near Bari.

Their first game, of course, was against Argentina and we know what happened there.

'For us Africans, it was a big stage playing at the opening game of the World Cup against the reigning champion. So, all our preparation was focused on how to deal with Argentina. You cannot even dream to beat Argentina but how to not be ashamed and to see what happened.'

'We were very organised and very strong physically and very, very focussed. Also, at that time it was difficult to know how one team is (sic) getting ready, so no one knew anything about us. We were a surprise element.'

In the dressing room before the game, the coach didn't say too much because everything had already been said before. 'The thing I just remember,' said Onana, 'the Argentine (team) was warming up and then we came we started to train they just left.'

As the teams were lining up in the tunnel one of the Cameroon players started singing and pretty soon the whole team were joining in. 'We sing so loud and every Argentine player, they look at us and they (Argentine team) were chicken!' I guess the script required the plucky African players to quiver in fear of the mighty Argentinians before the slaughter. Seeing the Cameroon players seemingly relaxed enough to sing in the tunnel ahead of such a crucial game must have knocked the World Cup holders off their pedestal for a moment.

'Then we started the game, but we started the game 15 minutes after the Argentinians did!'

What about the goal. Did Onana remember it and what was the view like from the bench?

'Sure. My teammate (Louis Paul) M'Fede came out and then there was a free kick and Emmanuel Kunde took the free kick. Deflection and Omam-Biyke jumped so high and smashed the ball. I don't think he has ever jumped so high.' He chuckles at the memory. It was certainly a powerful header though in this game of ex professionals giving us their wisdom and knowledge. They will no doubt point to the fact that Omam-Biyke was watched by three defenders and with the header downwards, the Argentine keeper, Nery Pumpido, no doubt would be given some of the blame. Oh, that such a moment of romance should be cheapened with the epitaph, 'what were the defenders doing?'

I wanted to know if perhaps Argentina, they were world champions after all, had underestimated the African side but Onana thinks a combination of the pressure on the champions and the roughhouse tactics employed by Cameroon had unsettled them.

Straight after the game, the Argentina team refused to exchange shirts with their victors. Diego Maradono did a swap with Roger Milla, but only him.

'In the dressing room after it was pretty amazing. We couldn't believe we had done it. But we still had the next game against Romania and I started against Romania (following the two expulsions in the first game), who featured players like Gheorge Hagi and Gheorge Popescu.

'I remember that game. Between the training sessions and the game, the coach never said my name as the player who would replace one of those red carded. He would always call me X, X so not to put me under pressure. I knew I was in, he told me I would play but he didn't want people knowing I would be in the line-up. We won the game 2-1, Roger Milla scored both goals. I had an assist in one of them.' He smiled.

But again, after the game the vanquished refused to exchange shirts!

Surely after this stunning start to the World Cup where Cameroon had exceeded all expectations, surely it was party time at the base in Bari?

'It wasn't party time. Two wins after two games, we are doing something, let's just keep focused but we lost the next game 4-0 against the USSR but they still finished top.' At least the Soviets were willing to swap shirts!

For all their success on the field, it was very difficult to keep in touch with family and friends back home. We are talking about the telephone age here kids. When there was no internet, no smart phones, and no mobile phones. What we used to do was take two empty tins of baked beans, remove the beans. Then, using a sharp instrument like a screwdriver, and always with a grown up watching because knives are sharp, we would make a hole in the cans. Then we would take some string, slip it through the holes, tie a knot, and walk as far away from each other as we could. We would then talk to each other. Using an empty baked bean can. And yes, we also knew how to tie knots.

'If we wanted to call our family,' said Onana, taking me from my Blue Peter reverie, 'they had to go to the radio station (in Cameroon) and make an appointment and we would be live on the radio... It was very expensive, and we could only afford it maybe once a week.

They were in Italy for a few weeks. I wondered what they did in their free time. They weren't over endowed with sponsors, so cash was always a problem and they most certainly did not spend their time eating pizza and pasta. In fact, they just went shopping!

'Shopping in Milan, shopping in Napoli, shopping in Bari.' I guess their retail therapy meant they had little left over for calling their families! Anyway, the folks back home could keep in touch by watching TV.

'What came next? We played Colombia. Top of the group meant we played a less strong team. They had Rene Higuita, Carlos Valderama, Freddie Rincon...' So, maybe not a bad team after all!

'We beat them 2-1! I played and got a yellow card, so I couldn't play against England in the next game.'

But were they excited about playing England in the World Cup? You know, we are talking about England here. Paul Gascoigne, Peter Shilton, David Platt, lose on penalties England. Surely Cameroon must have been thrilled at the thought of having their Indomitable Lions come up against the Three Lions?

'Let me tell you about the build-up. We had left Cameroon two months (earlier). We couldn't talk to our families, we could hardly talk to them. We thought we were going to Italy to play three games and go back home. Now we are winning. On the third week in Italy, we were getting bored!' I laughed. 'No, really.' Onana seemed a little put out by my joviality.

'Against Colombia we said we have to win this but against England and we are getting really, really bored. We said even if we lose guys it is against England.'

After England had won 3-2, the English did change shirts and though Onana missed out, the following year Cameroon travelled to England for a friendly at Wembley and Onana got a shirt 'from Gibson (not Colin Gibson) the right back, Dixon, umm... number 2!' I think he means Gary Stevens, the former Everton and Rangers full back!

Onana was sitting on the bench but looking back he feels the game was there for the taking.

'I was talking about getting bored. We wanted to play football and play our best football. If we were best in our heads or a European team we should have won the game because... we start attacking, wanting to play our best football. Leading 2-1 eight minutes to go, we were attacking. Then (Gary) Lineker scored from counter attack. Gascoigne through ball, Lineker ran through the defenders, finish.'

Following the defeat, they could finally return home and to a big party that lasted days. Onana says the whole country was at the airport. Everyone wanted to be seen with the returning heroes with special medals given to mark the occasion. And, of course, in the wake of Cameroon's unexpected triumphs a certain ex-pro named Pele declared to the world an African team would win the World Cup before the end of the 20th century. When a legend makes such a bold prediction, people sit up and listen. Until the same legend later suggested Nick Barmby was on a par with Zinedine Zidane and Ronaldo!

Once the squad returned to earth, a couple players were offered contracts to play in Europe, but most were content to stay home. A few years later, however, Roger Milla was tempted to Indonesia by Pelita Jaya and Onana followed a short time later.

It was dark. The air force base was still fairly busy with incoming and outgoing flights, but I just wanted to get home, in the traffic, of course. We nattered a while about football, Indonesia, academies, Cameroon, then tried to head for home. Taxis were few and far between. We hailed an angkot, a public minivan, squeezed in the back somehow and headed for the nearest main road where we could have better luck in our cab quest.

The football fan in me would have made sure I had kept my shirts from my World Cup appearances and made sure players signed them, but Onana seems so matter-of-fact about the whole thing. I love how he says the squad were bored and just wanted to go home... I guess these days priorities have changed and players will be signing juicy contracts to make sure they don't get 'bored.'

And Onana himself? He played for Persma Manado and Pelita Jaya before becoming an agent for a while. Now it seems his greatest love is coaching kids and he has his own academy, and he still turns out once in a while for the odd game here and there. Proving old players never lose their touch, only their pace!

18.
BANDUNG IS BLUE

On the road from Jakarta to Bandung, at a footballing level, there is a massive, bitter rivalry between the supporters of both sides, Persija Jakarta and Persib Bandung, that transcends distance (approximately 130 kilometers). The hatred on both sides puts this game, known locally as Classico, on a par with the likes of Barcelona and Real Madrid, Liverpool and Manchester United.

Make no mistake, when the two teams go head to head, a massive police operation is put in place to make sure the fans don't go toe to toe. In recent years, there have been fans killed, main highways closed, and team buses attacked. Players from one team have gone into the stands to confront fans from the other team after getting 90 minutes of abuse. The away team typically travels to and from the stadium by armoured personnel carrier and something as innocent as the wrong accent, the wrong letter on a number plate, or not cheer a goal loudly enough can invite trouble.

My first experience of this rivalry came in my first or second season of following Indonesian football. A game at Lebak Bulus in South Jakarta was called off with the stadium already full because police had advised the Persib players they could not guarantee their safety!

Around about the same time, I decided to go with Persija to an away game in Purwakarta, West Java against Pelita Jaya who were based there for that season. At the time their coach was ex Singapore international Fandi Ahmad who this book seems to be stalking having bumped into him earlier in Singapore and Malaysia. There were a few bus loads travelling down for the game and for a romantic old softy like me it was a real throwback to the away days of the 1970s and 1980s... without the beer! There was a friendly atmosphere on the bus I was on and plenty of smoking going on but as we made our way down the highway, the mood changed.

News filtered through a bus of Persija fans, known as *Jakmania*, had been attacked by Persib fans in the town of Karawang, a real border town between the territories of the two sets of fans.

How to explain the phenomena that is Persib? Difficult, but I gave it a go on my blog back in 2008 when Newcastle United reappointed Kevin Keegan as their manager. People were asking why the fuss over Newcastle? Surely, they were a nothing club. They certainly weren't famous in the way Arsenal, Liverpool, Manchester United, and increasingly Chelsea were famous. In south east Asia famous is a synonym for successful! Who cares about Newcastle, they asked?

My response has evolved from just some team oop north to a much clearer, and easier understood answer. Newcastle are just like Persib. It was like flicking a switch. Both towns are steeped in football heritage. Both clubs are an extension of regional identity. Newcastle represent the hopes of the Geordies, north eastern folk with a penchant for funny accents, and going bare chested, 'doon the toon' in the most inclement weather.

They brought us Viz and Jimmy Nail!

Traditional songs fill the Gallowgate every weekend from the Blaydon Races to other stuff. Geordie identity as tough, hard working folk has been cemented in TV shows like Auf Wiedersehen Pet and When The Boat Comes In. A proud people clinging to their working class roots.

Persib represent the Sunda, the original people of that region of Java. Their unofficial tag if you like is Maung Persib or Persib roars. Like Newcastle the people in the city have no time for any other team. Persib Sampai Mati, Persib till death. They hate outsiders but reserve a special enmity to their bitterest foes, Persija Jakarta. Both sets of fans look back proudly on a long tradition of success though most of the fans have never seen a trophy lifted by their heroes.

With fanatical support home and away, both clubs have underachieved over the last several years. The Geordies have won nothing since the 60's. Persib were Liga champions in the mid 90's. Other than that, there was little to celebrate until their local hero, Djadjang Nurdjaman, arrived and guided them to the Indonesia Super League title in 2014, and my comparison became moot.

The province of West Java is Newcastle writ large. Everyone is a Persib fan and everywhere you go, you see the symbols of Persib; their club crest, the Viking logo, 1933, the year of their formation. Clotheslines have blue shirts hanging limply in the still, humid air. West Java is blue, accept it.

As you near Jakarta, there are varying shades of blue. The town of Bekasi, for example, is politically West Java but football speaking it is firmly in the Jakarta orbit. When the new stadium, Patriot Stadium, was opened, the first game was between local heroes Persipasi Bekasi and Persija. Authorities were confident enough to allow the game to go ahead even though they knew there would be a bloody large travelling support.

Funnily enough no games have been played there since. Persipasi were forced to play their home games at a number of other venues as some desk bound guy felt some paperwork was not quite right. Yep, you read that right.

Back to Karawang and my day trip to see Persija in Purwakarta. Fans on the buses started to hear rumours a busload of Persija fans had been attacked in Karawang as they were heading to the highway, the bus had suffered some damage and the driver wasn't keen on continuing on carrying on. The fans from Jakarta waited in a lay by for their stricken comrades to catch up and they made the rest of the journey with the main support.

We made good time and we were soon exiting the highway at Purwakarta, where a police escort was waiting to take us to the stadium. It all seemed pretty well organised with motorcyclists closing side roads to allow the convoy past and all the while the fans were singing out of the open doors and windows and the locals came out to see the dreaded *Jakmania* pass through their town.

The stadium was, it probably still is, in a small village, kampung, with little in the way of facilities. Certainly, there was nothing for the 600 odd visiting fans to do and for me there was no beer!

The game started and soon it was evident while the fans had put in the effort, Persija hadn't bothered. They were awful, and the away support were soon getting fed up. It didn't help that Pelita Jaya had Lopes up front. Let's be polite and say he does go to ground quite easily. I think it is so he can take free kicks, but I don't know for sure. When I saw him playing for Sri Racha against Thai Port four years later, he hadn't changed much! Of course, Lopes scored and, of course, he decided to celebrate right in front of the Persija fans. That didn't go down well. He did though. He continued to go down, once writhing in agony right in front of the away fans who were, by this time, totally fed up. They had come all this way; their team was playing shit and Lopes was taking the piss.

As they goaded Lopes, who miraculously recovered from every little knock, the fans in the main stand started goading the Persija fans and pretty soon there was an exchange of missiles between the two sets of supporters. Come half time and both sets of fans went outside to continue their skirmishes with cars and buses getting windows smashed. It took quite a while for tempers to calm down, but I was left under no illusion the provocateurs were Persib fans. Apart from anything else, Pelita Jaya didn't have enough fans to cause a mini riot!

Two sides to every story, of course, and there are some who would argue the Persija fans were bang out of order and the locals were just protecting their manor. You pay your money and all that.

Given the rivalry that exists between the two sets of fans, it is little wonder away fans don't bother travelling to see their team when they play.

Sometimes, the teams are forced to play behind closed doors, sometimes the game gets switched to other cities. In recent seasons, places like Malang and Sleman have had the dubious honour of hosting Clasico complete with accompanying crowd trouble.

Not too long ago, Persija hosted Persib at the Bung Karno Stadium in Jakarta and a couple of fans were set upon and ended up dying. One, apparently, because he hadn't celebrated a Persija goal wildly enough. Then there was the time in 2013 when Persib left their hotel in central Jakarta to make the short drive to the stadium. As they approached the main road, the bus was attacked by Persija fans, smashing windows, and ending the game as the team just got on that highway and headed home. It is not an excuse, but I don't think it was made clear why they were using a bus and not the usual armoured personnel carrier.

After several failed attempts, a widely publicised peace was declared between the two sets of supporters under the auspices of the police. The big test would come weeks later when Persib were to host Persija at the Si Jalak Harupat Stadium in Soreang, about an hour or so from Bandung.

There were sceptics on either side. Would the peace hold? Who would enforce it? Could the kids, at ground level and at the forefront of many of the clashes, be trusted to hold the peace? Would they even want to? There were many unanswered questions as the match approached.

Come match day itself, an estimated 25 bus loads of Persija fans set off down the highway. They never made it. A massive police operation stopped them on the road and their followed a fairly length stand-off with on-going fighting between the Persija fans, the police, and then some Persib fans determined not to miss out on the fun! The road was effectively closed for a couple hours. A road that takes manufactured products from the industrial estates of West Java to the port at Tanjung Priok for export, while the three sides battled it out in the full glare of the nation's TV crews who had ringside seats.

Eventually, the Persija fans were forced to return home while fans and motorists stuck amid the free for all raced home to upload their images of the fun.

Other occasions have seen Persib fans looking out for cars and motorcyles with a Jakarta number plate. I once made the mistake of driving outside Siliwangi Stadium on match day in my wife's company car, complete with Jakarta plate! We weren't very welcome until we opened the windows and people could see we weren't *Jakmania*, just a couple of dumbass foreign tourists who had taken a wrong turn. It also helped our driver on the day was Sundanese!

Then there was a mate of mine, a nice, twee Batak guy from North Sumatra, who was standing outside the Si Jalak Harupat Stadium after a Classico and was approached by a couple of likely lads who started speaking Sundanese to him. Not understanding a word they were saying and knowing full well if he couldn't answer them he may have some of his body parts rearranged, he tried very hard not to shit his pants. Luckily, his mate returned from the toilet just in time!

Former Persija striker Bambang Pamungkas has his own take on the rivalry between the two clubs. He once related to me the story of a couple new foreign players who had just arrived in Indonesia and they were all down on their knees in the bowels of an armoured personnel carrier while a steady supply of rocks bounced off the vehicle.

He caught the eye of one of the new players, almost a quivering wreck, and said something along the lines of, 'welcome to Indonesian football, this is what makes the game here so special!'

Bandung, like Newcastle, is a football daft city. Sorry, I should modify that. Bandung is Persib daft. Other clubs have tried to make inroads into the football loving community but have failed. Pelita Jaya, them of many home towns, based themselves in Soreang for a while but couldn't attract any supporters beyond a few disinterested neutrals. They have since been taken over by Bandung Raya, now known as Pelita Bandung Raya, and they still have no supporters!

Then there was the case of the very short-lived Bandung FC, part of the very short-lived Indonesia Premier League. They played in the inaugural season, well, there was only half a season as they decided to knock it on the head at the midway point, and they made headlines when they signed a former England international.

Lee Hendrie has been round the football block once or twice. The one time England international has worn the shirts of Aston Villa, Stoke City, Sheffield United, Leicester City, Blackpool, Brighton, Derby County, and most recently Bradford City.

He has played at the finest stadiums in England including an FA Cup Final appearance at Wembley and enjoyed all the luxuries and benefits a top flight football career can offer.

Hendrie's career started just as Sky Sports started pumping serious money into the Premier League, leading to a flurry of stadium redevelopment and higher wages for players. He led the life of a pampered pro brought up on the best surfaces and the best stadiums England could offer at the time.

But nothing from his illustrious past could have prepared him for the Patriot Stadium in sunny downtown Bekasi. It was the second game of his new career with Bandung in the breakaway Liga Primer Indonesia and the team from West Java were lining up against Batavia Union from North Jakarta desperate for a change in fortunes. Their opening four games had brought them four defeats and no goals.

Patriot Stadium would be familiar to any English football fan who recalls the game before it became the slick marketing machine it is now. Metal fences extend all the way round the stadium with the exception of directly in front of the tiny main stand which houses any VIPs who maybe attending, the press area, seemingly open to all, dressing rooms and the match officials' changing room.

The referee and linesmen had already beat a hasty retreat by the time Lee Hendrie slouched on the sofa in the tiny, sweltering room that also doubled as the venue for press conferences. He wasn't happy and only the firm arm of one of the linesmen had stopped the 33-year-old Brummie from running down the tunnel instead of saluting the fans.

'I can't believe it, we're 1-0 up, they have a player sent off and we lose 3-2.'

While the frustration was etched deep in his face, a part of him may have been relieved at the familiarity of the emotion. Because since arriving in Indonesia three weeks earlier he has entered an Alice in Wonderland world that his 15 year career in England had in no way prepared him for.

For a start he had joined a football team, Bandung FC, only three or four months old playing in a league, Liga Primer Indonesia, not much older. For a man brought up in a country where regulations rule every part of life, Hendrie now found himself in a league that wasn't recognized by the local Football Association (PSSI), he ran the risk of being deported and had just played on a pitch that could be used to grow vegetables.

So, how had an England international ended up playing football in front of a couple hundred fans in a ramshackle old stadium in a dormitory suburb of Jakarta on a hot, sunny day in February?

'I'd been approached four, five weeks ago,' he explained, continuously wiping sweat from his brow, 'then nothing seemed to happen for a long time.' With silence from Indonesia he got talking to Mansfield Town but then 'out of the blue' Bandung got back in touch, faxed a copy of the contract and said, 'get a flight over on Monday.'

With little in the way of preparation or research, Hendrie packed his toothbrush and headed south into the great unknown.

'I didn't know what to expect to be honest. I'd heard some good things about the place, some bad things but to be fair the people have been brilliant since I got here.'

Football is still football and despite some trepidation about the dressing room culture Lee is happy with the way things are turning out 'with the lads.'

'After my first training session the players were queuing up to take my photograph, which I'd never had before but they've been great. I've been really surprised and there has been some banter which has been great. I don't understand most of it but some of the lads speak English, so that's okay.'

The city of Bandung is a proud football town. The local heroes, Persib, who play in the official Indonesia Super League, regularly attract crowds in excess of 20,000 and their players are local celebrities from a public thirsty for news of the big names. Things are quieter with Bandung FC as they seek to carve out their own niche in the city and it remains to be seen whether the city can support two teams.

No matter what happens to Lee, he has signed a two year contract with Bandung. He has written his name into the folklore of his new team by scoring their first ever goal. Like the true pro he is, though, he still looks back on the game with disappointment.

In English football, statues have become all the rage as clubs try to convince their supporters they do recognise the efforts of players from a bygone era despite the headlong rush to greed that so defines much of the game there these days.

Ajat Sudrajat is your archetypal football folkhero. Born and bred in Bandung, he spent 10 years playing for Persib and a further seven with Bandung Raya as well as seven years with the national team. The man has Sundanese flowing through his veins and he lives on as a statue in downtown Bandung.

Well, some say the statue represents Ajat. Others suggest the player represented is another Persib legend, Robby Darwis. Then there is another argument, perhaps a middle path, that says the statue represents no one player in particular but the football loving public of Bandung!

Whoever it is, or isn't, every year, members of the Viking supporters club, Persib's main fan group, gather at the statue on their anniversary and clean the statue

You don't need to spend much time in Bandung football circles to realise the people there honour their players past and present in a way missing in many other clubs around the country. Peri Sandria is another. He crossed the great divide and played for both Persib and Bandung Raya back when the latter were a force to be reckoned with. And any conversation with a diehard Bobotoh (a Sundanese word that translates roughly as follower. All Persib fans are Bobotoh, not all are Viking!), you will soon hear talk about a game between Persib and PSMS played in Jakarta in 1985 in front of over 100,000 fans — back in the days before the rivalry between Persija and Persib got out of hand.

That, of course, is another story!

19.
PERSIB, A WAY OF LIFE

'Persib is a culture, a way of life. It starts with our grandfathers, then down to our fathers. There is nothing else but Persib, we are all blue.' I am sat in a hotel lobby in Bandung with a Persib fan and I am keen to know more about the phenomena that is Persib. It's one of the great things about football in Indonesia, that some clubs become more than just a club, they symbolise a culture, a way of life, beyond kicking a ball around.

Consider Germany's Schalke 04, for example or those great anti-heroes of Hamburg, St Pauli and even Newcastle United in England. Then there are the Glasgow giants Celtic and Rangers. History and local culture have combined to elevate those football clubs to another plane beyond the mere passion and devotion of others. They have become an all-encompassing identity, something that perhaps we in England are wary of.

Not in Indonesia. Here, where football remains the game of the underclass (I hesitate to use a term like working class to describe people working in the informal economy), there is little else for many kids to do. All of them shopping malls, hotels, and glitzy high rise you see on TV in the latest news show that is reporting how well the Indonesian economy is doing? They ain't for these kids. Their dress marks them down as unwelcome. Money is circulating round the country but that trickle down effect has yet to have had much of an impact.

Football, at least, remains affordable and it is where these kids can get together and have the Irish would call a crack. Back in their villages, known as kampungs, life is austere and conservative on the whole and revolves around the mosque, motorcycles and kicking a ball around on a dusty bit of wasteland. Money is tight, but they can usually summon up a few rupiah to buy a shirt, which may or may not be the real thing, that shows their favourite football club.

Football, much like it was in other countries, is the high point of their week and they go to any lengths to support their team. And any lengths can mean 'hijacking' lorries in the street for a lift, clubbing together to hire a mini bus with half the fans singing and dancing on the roof, or even walking great distances to get to and from the game, sometimes barefoot. Fare dodging on the train? If it goes near the stadium, then of course!

And often, they don't even watch the game. For some it can be enough to mill around outside the stadium getting high on the roars from inside.

Clubs like Persib, Persija and Arema are among the biggest in the country. Persib as I have said before are a Sundanese brand almost, Persija fans see them as all-inclusive while Arema... well, that is for another day.

My Persib mate is called Z. Actually, he is not really but it will do for this narrative. He is a mad keen Persib fan, in case you hadn't noticed, he earns his money from selling Persib merchandise and he follows them around the country which, in Indonesia, really does mean over land and sea. He tells me he can't remember the last game he missed and was visibly impressed when I told him of Arsenal fans I knew who hadn't missed games for decades.

'I went Selangor to see friendly, I want to go Chonburi but cancelled,' he said. 'Palembang, Sleman, Balikpapan...' He rolls off the names of cities around the country he has seen his beloved Persib. He also told of some batterings he had received along the way, no doubt he had spilled blue blood for his team, but let's not go there.

'Every game Persib play, there is always one enclosure full of *Bobotoh*. From Bandung, from West Java, from all over the country. We took two, three buses to Palembang, others travelled by plane. You know what I mean!' he smiled at me.

'Jakarta,' I prompt?

'Of course,' he says, 'but not wearing *attributes* (the Indonesian word for club colours). I am reminded of another Persib fan I had met a few years earlier who had travelled to Jakarta for the Clasico. Halfway along the highway, he and his mates had pulled over to switch number plates so people wouldn't think they were Persib on tour and set about their motor!

Despite wearing a Stone Island sweater and carrying a jacket, many Indonesians like Bandung because it is cooler than most other cities and they can wear jackets, he says he wears club colours to games. 'I am proud to be Persib.'

There is a group of casuals at Persib called the Flower City Casuals but despite the Stone Island he says he is not part of them. 'Clothes are just clothes,' he says, 'passion not fashion.'

He goes on to say that the Flower City Casuals sometimes get into trouble with the hardcore Persib support, known as Viking who seem to object at the casuals lack of club colours. I tell him there used to be something similar in Scotland back in the day when the Celtic support, all green and white, used to have a pop at the casuals who followed them because they feared they gave the club a bad name!

A number of clubs seem to have casuals following them these days in Indonesia, a fact I most certainly wasn't aware of when I started my blog. Persija, Persis, Persib for sure. I asked Z which club was the first to have a casual element among its support and he was honest enough to say he didn't know.

We talk players and he is unimpressed. 'Just money, players come, players go. I am Persib.' However, he does recall fondly the great names from the past and goes on to talk about the day in 1985 when Persib and PSMS filled Bung Karno Stadium with over 100,000 fans. England has 1966, Singapore has 1994, Persib has 1985.

'I went with my father. We drove, and in those days, there was no highway to Jakarta, so we had to cross the *Puncak* (a range of mountains with a narrow road that links Bandung with Bogor and Jakarta and is notorious for its congestion). It was like a sea, all blue.' He smiles at the memory. He would have been about six-years-old at the time and if your early memories help define your future path, you can see why Persib remains such an important part of Z's life. Even though his real name isn't Z!

We move on to talk about Persija. I wanted to know how the trouble started between the two sets of fans.

'In about 2000 we went there and there was no problem. Then, they came to Bandung. They said they would bring one bus... they brought three. That wasn't what was agreed, we felt they had betrayed us.'

It does seem odd that such a deep and bitter rivalry can rise out of a couple of buses, but I was reminded of a student in a school I used to teach at. This student was bullied all the time and had been for years. One time I built a whole lesson around the pain felt by victims of bullying and I asked some searching questions. You know what had started the whole thing off? The student had left a couple of eggs in a locker several years earlier! More than a couple had tears rolling down their faces at the end of the class and they weren't tears of mirth!

Anyway, the bus story kind of jives with what a Persija fan once told me though he had omitted the bit about the number of fans that had been agreed upon and the number that had travelled. All a far cry from the two dozen odd buses that had tried to make the journey recently only to be turned back after running battles with the police on the highway!

'What about the highly publicised 'peace' deal that was brokered earlier in the year in Bogor?' I asked.

'Pah,' or words to that effect before using words like bullshit with the venom of a Daily Mail reader explaining why he has switched to UKIP.

Does he think there will ever be peace between the two sets of fans?

'No, no way. Go outside and find any five-year-old kid. Ask them what they think about *Jakmania*. They hate them because their brothers hate them and their fathers hate them. In recent seasons, Persib fans have been killed up there (Jakarta), our team bus was attacked.' He was getting quite animated now. 'There can never be peace between us. There is too much bad blood.'

I asked about the movie, *Romeo and Juliet*, made by Andibachtiar Yusuf and his temper rises a notch. 'That wanker!' he spat, describing my mate. He smiled when I told him I knew Yusuf!

He went on to recall a time about two dozen Persib fans had gone up to Jakarta to appear on a TV quiz show which, he proudly announced, they won! As they left the studio, they were attacked by hundreds of *Jakmania*. 'I thought we were going to die,' he says.

'Football is football,' he says 'Any fighting should happen at the football, not far away from the stadium. I know Persija fans, away from football we can talk and drink, there is respect.'

Okay, so we know Persib are a big club and have a large away support. 'But what about teams visiting Bandung, do they bring many away fans?'

'No. Maybe one or two but no, not really.' He was struggling for vocabulary. He had good English, with that and my inadequate Indonesian we were able to understand each other, but he was struggling to find the right word at the moment. He tried racist but the hesitant way he said it, he knew it was the wrong choice. Intimidating?

That was better. Bandung, he said, was a very intimidating place for away fans to come, not without some pride, although Persebaya would come in numbers, they were like brothers.

It was time for him to leave. I had wanted to know more about Persib as a cultural icon but to be honest I already knew most of it. It is kind of like those old Australian National Soccer League clubs Melbourne and Sydney Croatia and their ilk. The football club is a rallying point for a community. Ironic then that I am in Bandung just as Football Federation Australia should see fit to ban all logos and names that hint at ethnicity or race. No more Celtic or

Hibernian for them then!

The ethnic side of Indonesian football is an interesting one. I was in a taxi in Jakarta recently and this lad, who spoke excellent English, was from the eastern island of Timor. I asked him what team he supported. 'In England, I like Liverpool. In Spain, I like Real Madrid. In Italy, I like Juventus...'

Before he could on through the whole European Union, I politely asked him which team in Indonesia he supported. 'Oh, Persipura Jayapura.' Despite living in Jakarta more than 25 years, he still followed the team closest to his home town, though in this case Jayapura to Timor was a fairly lengthy flight away.

Clubs like Persib, Semen Padang, and PSMS Medan have support across the country as people from their provinces have travelled far and wide in search of work or study and like fans around the world, cling to their football team as part of their identity in an alien or distant environment.

It was time to move on. Z had another appointment and so did I.

A few years back I had met with the top ranked guy in Persib's official supporters club, the Viking. I had only been watching the local football for a few months and had been interested in learning about football life in the city, so I arranged to meet with Heru Joko at Siliwangi Stadium. As I was new to the local football scene I wanted to know why so many games were played *tanpa penonton*, behind closed doors.

'Every time kids throw plastic water bottles on the pitch everyone pays. We all get punished for the actions of the minority but when they're doing this stuff, throwing things on the pitch, you know who tries to stop it?' Despite Heru using a language he is really unfamiliar with the words come out in a torrent. English or Indonesian, this is a topic he was feeling strongly about. 'All the police and security want to do is watch the football free, they don't want to get involved with the fans. They are the ones who should be punished! We have hundreds of police at every game, but they do nothing!

The fans are such a vital part of the football experience here. The songs, the movement, the colour on the terraces, are often worth the admission fee alone. There are 60,000 Vikings out there, fan club members, spread all across West Java. For them Persib Bandung is an expression of identity. An outlet of Sundanese emotion and nowhere is this more evident than when Persib play Persija. The animosity felt by Persib fans to their Persija rivals is absolute. Hatred seems so inadequate to describe a rivalry that is certainly up there with Barcelona Real Madrid and Liverpool Manchester United. The Sunda aspect adds an ethnic element that is missing in those aforementioned rivalries, which are more based on politics and success. So, playing the dumb naïve foreigner, why the hatred?

'Where to begin? We are Bandung. We come from Bandung, we live in Bandung, our football club is part of our heritage. Jakarta people have no heritage. They come from all over Indonesia, they have no roots to their city. Instead, they just have arrogance because they live in Jakarta.'

Ten years on from our meeting and Heru is still actively involved with the Persib supporters and has been working hard with security officials and his counterparts aiming the Persija support to bring about a modicum of order in their relationship. Sadly, little progress has been made.

Every weekend and holiday Bandung's streets are clogged with Jakarta registered cars as families from the capital head south in search of cheap shopping and food. For the people who deal with this influx, the car park attendants, shop assistants, the restaurant staff, they are an overbearing, overwhelming, and unwanted guest. Getting round Bandung for Bandung folk becomes a slow moving chore as Jakartans get lost in the confusing one way system looking for their favourite factory outlet and think nothing of parking where they want. The money they spend ensures a passive, if sullen, service but the feelings are real and are released on the terraces.

Hard to believe but there was another team in Bandung. At least they played in the city. I have known Rawindra for a few years now. Our paths first crossed when he was the head of the Arsenal Supporters Club in Indonesia, about 7,000 members and climbing. We kept bumping into each other over the years, and at one stage he was manager of Pelita Bandung Raya. PBR came about when Bandung Raya, a one-time great of Indonesian football fallen on hard times, effectively took over Pelita Jaya, one of football's great nomads, a couple years back. It was the perfect job for the Arsenal daft Rawindra.

Ah, Arsenal. When Rawindra got married in 2014 he took his newly betrothed on honeymoon to London, taking in a couple games, of course. He also had a wedding picture featured in the match day programme! I bet he never told anyone in London that his wedding coincided with the start of the Indonesian season and by rights he should have been on assignment with Pelita Bandung Raya, not living it large at the Arsenal!

What to say about Pelita Jaya? They have played all over the shop but never managed to attract a lasting fan base. After starting in Jakarta and bringing big names over like World Cup legends like Mario Kempes (Argentina) and Roger Milla (Cameroon) as well as the latter's teammate Jules Denis Onana, their frequent moves have given them an image of nomads.

In the early days they were known as Pelita Mastrans and then Pelita Bakrie before relocating to the football daft city of Solo where they became known as Pelita Solo. In 2002, they moved to Cilegon after teaming up with a large industrial concern there and were known as Pelita Krakatau Steel.

In 2006, they moved to Purwakarta in West Java where they enjoyed a couple years, including a game against Persija I referred to a couple days ago. From Purwakarta they were off to Soreang, south west of Bandung then Karawang where they seemed to have finally found a niche for themselves and indeed some supporters.

But nothing lasts forever in the whacky world of football and they were taken over by Bandung Raya on condition they kept the name Pelita whatever that means.

Trying to keep loyal to their supposed roots PBR played in Soreang but in front of no supporters. It is after all staunch Persib turf. Rawindra told me that after a game against Persija where the Jakarta team had had the temerity to bring down a couple hundred supporters, angry locals, pissed at this invasion from the enemy, had blocked the road back to the highway and were searching vehicles for the unwanted visitors, including stopping and searching the PBR team bus!

Despite their lack of a fan base PBR managed to attract some big-name players including former Indonesian international Bambang Pamungkas, Argentine striker Gaston Castano, former Latvian international goalkeeper Denis Romanv, and naturalised Indonesian Kim Jeffery Kurniawan. And it was for the latter I jumped in Rawindra's car and headed off to see the team training.

PBR were training at Lembang. So, we wound our way up the narrow lanes to the mountain resort town, famous for being chilly and rabbits sold on the side of the road; to end up as fluffy wuffy pets or impaled on sticks as rabbit sate, a popular (not for the rabbits) local dish served with a spicy peanut sauce.

The training session took place at a military base and was a pretty casual affair. Being the fasting month, many of the squad hadn't eaten or drunk anything for more than 12 hours. The coaching staff went easy on them. Plus, of course, we were still some four weeks or so from the next competitive game though the club were hoping to squeeze in a couple friendlies just to keep fitness levels where they needed to be.

The question of naturalised players donning shirts and playing for the national team has been controversial ever since Singapore used its Foreign Talent Scheme to fast track citizenship for players like Aleksander Duric, Agu Casmir, and Mustafic Fahruddin in their quest for success.

Somewhat surprisingly, Indonesia decided to go down that track back in 2010. Primarily, as it sought to attract players with Indonesian descent overseas but also foreigners who had stayed in the country for long period of time. In the latter category, some players like Greg Nwokolo, who had worked with Singapore's R Sasikumar several years back when he had first arrived in Asia, Christian Gonzales (Uruguay), Victor Igbenefo (Nigeria).

Back when Irfan Bachdim mania spread across Indonesia in 2010, Kim was the lesser known support act on the card. When Persema signed Irfan after other clubs had a look and decided no, they also signed Kim with their coach at the time. Timo Scheuneuman was impressed by the midfielder's tenaciousness.

Early 2011 and Persema were the unlikely glamour boys of the short lived Premier League, attracting big crowds and screaming girls. They tore Solo Ksatria apart 5-1 in the first game of the league and went from strength to strength until the league stopped. I went to a game away to Bogor Raya and there were girls outside the hotel waiting for a chance to see their heroes; their heroes were Irfan and Kim. Indonesian football had its first ever glamour team!

Later at the game, there were more screaming girls with their homemade, 'I love Irfan/Kim' posters, while the players were mobbed by security details. Heady stuff.

Kim had been brought up in Germany by an Indonesian father and a German mother but when he was offered the opportunity of representing his father's nation he jumped at the opportunity and found himself at the spearhead of a new trend in Indonesian football alongside the likes of Cristian Gonzales. Naturalised players.

It is, of course, a familiar path in Singapore where players like Aleksander Duric (Bosnia), Mustafic Fahrudin (Serbia), Qiu Li (China), and Agu Casmir (Nigeria) have gone on to play for the Lions on a regular basis, coinciding with the country's most successful footballing era.

But Singapore with its small population is one thing. Indonesia boasts a population of 250 something million. Attempts to bring in a few players from overseas were initially treated with cynicism but the success of the national team at the 2010 ASEAN Cup, with Gonzales leading from the front in more ways than one, changed a few minds. While the idea seems to have gone off the boil lately, players like Raphael Maitimo, Diego Michiels, and Sergio van Dijk have become familiar names in various national team squads in recent years.

Despite being one of the first to take on Indonesian citizenship, Kim has struggled to make an impression on the national team. I saw him come up against Montegrian striker Ilija Spasojevic in a Premier League game between Persema and PSM and was impressed by Kim's determination and reluctance to be awed by a much larger, much more powerful player. Indeed, Kim did so well, you could see Spasojevic getting more and more wound up, though I understand there is a healthy respect between the two players as I found out when I interviewed Kim.

With the players heading straight for the changing room to break the fast, Kim, being a Christian, headed straight for me. He was dripping in sweat, so much for a light training session, but happy enough to talk football and comfortable in English. And German. And Indonesian! I wonder whether an English-born guy with a similar background to Kim would be able to switch between languages so effortlessly?

Growing up in Germany, Kim didn't know much about Indonesia despite having a grandfather who had played for the national team in the 1950s. He had visited a couple times to catch up with family members and no doubt he was as exotic to them as they were to him.

Kim was attached with Karslruhe SC when he was young before he moved to a local side playing in the fifth tier of German football and the next thing he knew he was being contacted by Timo Scheunemann, the Indonesian born German coach whose parents actually lived pretty close to Kim!

Timo visited Kim's house and asked if he would be interested in moving to Germany to play for Persema, and the diminutive midfielder was immediately attracted to the idea. He knew nothing about Malang for football in Indonesia but what the heck! Soon after the Indonesian football association began its policy of tracking down players in foreign countries with some Indonesian blood in them and Kim's name turned up. So, within a few short months his whole career path changed!

Timo didn't even like what he saw because he actually saw nothing!

'I recruited him without even having looked at him once. Such is my faith in the German academy and impressive stats that he had. He is a European type of player; smart, plays fast, prefers teamwork over individual flash. Great person on and off the pitch,' said Timo, when I asked he how he came about to bring Kim to Indonesia.

'At some point others are bound to see in him the great qualities I've long seen in him. I checked him out over Facebook, that's how I heard about him and then done my research and looked for stats over the past 3 years.'

'I began the naturalisation process after coach Timo brought me to Indonesia. I trained there (Persema) and coach Timo said okay I like you,' continued Kim, as the call to prayer echoed around the valley.

But how difficult was it for Kim to renounce his citizenship and become Indonesian? As things stand, the country doesn't allow dual citizenship for its citizens. Kim was forced to revoke his German passport if he wanted to play for his father's country.

'No, not really because I already knew I didn't have a career in Germany or the German national team. Why not? I saw my chance to become a professional player.'

He certainly came into Indonesian football at a thrilling time. The split was just taking place and while he joined Persema as an Indonesia Super League team, they would withdraw from that league and join the rebel breakaway Premier League. Kim was caught in the middle without really knowing too much about what was going on and why.

On the one hand the guy processing his naturalisation papers was pushing for him to join an ISL side, on the other was Timo who had brought him to Indonesia and offered him a new career. As a league that was not recognised by the PSSI, and by extension FIFA, there was a lot of talk about players and coaches involved in the IPL being sanctioned or banned from playing professional football; indeed that was just about the only tool the PSSI had as they were faced with massive unrest at the way they were perceived to be running the game and in those early days, the IPL seemed to have the image of the white knight charging on to the field and change the game as their slogan said.

Kim was clear though. 'I owed Timo much and I was really in a twist. I decided to go with Timo at Persema and the naturalisation was also okay.'

Unfortunately, his dream of playing for his new country was damaged by an injury just before the ASEAN Cup in December of 2010, so he was forced to watch the games on TV as his new Persema teammate Irfan Bachdim wooed fans, celebrities, and liggers alike with a series of stunning performances on the way to Indonesia's loss in the final to Malaysia.

'Okay, before my career in Germany stopped because of injury and now I get another injury before (my career in Indonesia can) start. I already had bad thoughts,' he said ruefully.

Once he did recover he became an integral part of the Persema road show. 'It was only Persema, Persema. That was a good time.' He smiled. 'For me it was always a dream you know to have fans and it was the first time to have something like this (the screaming girl hysteria!)'

When the IPL went tits up despite all the hype, Kim decided to stick around rather than return to Germany and after spending a season out of the game, he was proving himself with Pelita Bandung Raya.

Just before I arrived at training ground, Kim's brother-in-law, Irfan, had tweeted he had been recalled to the Indonesian national team. With the military blowing a bugle and the flag being lowered, I asked Kim what he felt his chances were for a recall.

'I don't know, I don't know,' his voice dropped. 'It's also not my decision, of course, every player wants to play in the national team, but it is the decision of the coach and, of course, that is why I changed my passport to become Indonesian and I want to become international.'

Despite the ups and downs, though, Kim is happy he made the move and has no regrets. 'Not a single minute I regret it,' he said, as he headed off to the changing room and no doubt to congratulate his brother-in-law on his good news.

During the interview I likened Kim to former Leeds and Scottish midfielder Billy Bremner. Of course, they weren't on the same level talent wise and Bremner had the kind of red hair you just don't see anymore. They were both small but tenacious players blessed with no small level of skill. Anyway, the comparison was wasted; Kim had never heard of him!

Growing up in Germany, Kim was used to being around bigger players, but his attitude was always, 'you're not going to take me for granted you lump (or words to that effect),' and like Spasojevic in the game, I saw you could tell there was a measure of respect between the two.

Meanwhile, the debate about naturalised players will no doubt rumble on but they seem to have become an accepted part of the fabric of the game here with Australian born Brendan Gan looking to become a Malaysian international after his spells with Sabah and Kelantan.

I guess the question is do these players have any responsibilities to their adopted countries once their career is over? For example, in Singapore. Should the offspring of a naturalised international have to do national service in the same way other Singaporeans have to? Or can they just come over, bask in the glory of international football then return home when their legs say enough is enough?

Kim, at least, seems to be in it for the long haul. He has settled in well and with a brother-in-law like Irfan he knows family is never far away.

I was driven back into Bandung by the club's assistant secretary. He had first worked with Rawindra at Pelita Jaya up in Karawang, where he had possibly been the league's youngest match commissioner and had followed his old boss down the highway when the merger took place. He certainly loved what he was doing, telling me it, 'wasn't a job.' He never felt bored! I asked why he didn't get involved in coaching or some such activity, but he said he was more attracted to the administration side of the game. So, there we have it. When he takes over at the PSSI, I wonder if he will remember the slightly overweight Englishman he once gave a lift to all those years ago!

20.
GIVE YOUTH A CHANCE

One evening Indonesia's Under 19 team defeated Arema Malang's Under 21 under the floodlights at Kanjuruhan Stadium. I had planned to go to the game. In fact, I plan to go to quite a few games but often back out at the last moment blaming family commitments or happy hour. Do David Conn or Martin Tyler have that kind of problem I wonder?

Back in 2013, football fans were suddenly taking notice of the Under 19s and for a very good reason. They were winning! Indonesia is so unused to a team winning anything on the international stage, they took the kids to their hearts and the kids responded by travelling all round the country playing friendlies on the scale of a Rolling Stones tour-de-force.

But I am getting ahead of myself here. The tale began back in September 2013, when the East Java cities of Gresik and Sidoarjo, both almost satellite cities of the provincial capital Surabaya, hosted the ASEAN Football Federation Under 19 championships. Coming to town were teams from Vietnam, Malaysia, Myanmar, Thailand, and Brunei for a week of football.

Incidentally, the other group featured Singapore, Laos, Philippines, Timor Leste, and Cambodia.

Indonesia's first game came against minnows Brunei in Sidoarjo and no heads were turned when the hosts won 5-0. That was to be expected. Next up was Myanmar, traditionally a tough fish to fry in regional competition and they proved no exception this time round, Indonesia edging it 2-1 with the name of Evan Dimas getting on the score sheet for the first time.

Next up was Vietnam, and despite Evan giving the home team the lead in the first minute it was the Vietnamese who went on to win the game 2-1. So, after three games the hosts had started in less than spectacular style. Even the Brunei thrashing needs to be put into perspective; the Thais beat the oil rich state 8-0 while Malaysia also rammed in five! It was a competent start but little else.

Games against the Thais are always seen as the bench mark in the region. Their national teams in all age groups are considered to be, at least, as strong and if not better than any other nation. While they may have been struggling of late, they would be no pushover. Except no one told Evan Dimas and his mates. The 18-year-old hit a hat trick as Indonesia beat the Thais 3-1.

A draw in the final game against Malaysia, Ilham Udin equalising Jafri's 16 minute opener, meant Indonesia finished second in the group, five points behind Vietnam who had won all their five group games. In the semi-finals, Indonesia met Timor Leste while Vietnam came up against Laos.

Ilham opened the scoring for the merah putih on nine minutes and Hargianto made it safe on the hour mark, setting up a final against Vietnam at Delta Stadium, Sidoarjo.

By now, of course, interest had risen in this crop of unknown youngsters coached by unknown coach Indra Sjafri, formerly of PS Padang in the late 1980s, and there was even talk of moving the final to cash in on the interest. In the end it stayed in Sidoarjo, and a full house saw Indonesia win on penalties after extra time ended 0-0. There was, however, some crowd trouble reported as fans arriving for the game were told the tickets had all been sold, only for plenty of touts to appear on the scene carrying wads of them. I wonder how that happened?

It was a strange feeling for Indonesians, success on the international stage. Well, strange for me 'cos I am English, and we can't even win the toss to decide which end we kick in.

The AFF Championship was but the first step on the road to the finals in Myanmar some 12 months later though I don't think many who celebrated the triumph were aware of that. For them, they had seen Indonesia win something and, in their eyes, earn some respect on the international stage.

The next stage was the AFC U19 Championship qualifying round and again, Indonesia were hosting it. This time the event was moved to Jakarta in the hope of bigger crowds but with prices ranging from Rp 50,000 to Rp 1 million ($5 – $100 very approximately at exchange rates then) greed got in the way of a full house.

Indonesia opened the competition by crushing Laos 4-0 at the Bung Karno with two goals from Muchlis and one each from Sitanggang and Evan Dimas setting the tone, but it needed two in the last few minutes to settle the nerves. The crowd, by the way, was reported as 15,000. Good for an Under 19 game but perhaps not what the organisers were hoping for.

Next up were the Philippines but goals from Hargianto and Yabes allowed the home team to go into their final game against South Korea feeling confident. They were unbeaten and had a positive goal difference of plus six while the Koreans had plus eight promising a tension-filled evening when they went head to head at the Bung Karno Stadium.

This time 50,000 turned up knowing Indonesia just had to win. A draw was not enough, they needed to overturn that goal difference. Cometh the hour, cometh the man. Evan Dimas gave the hosts the lead on the half hour mark but immediately the Koreans pegged them back from the penalty spot. It was pressure on now for the youngsters in front of a demanding public. Had they the balls to overcome that setback?

Of course, they bloody well did, or I wouldn't be devoting this here entry to them. Evan Dimas scored again early in the second half and completed his hat trick four minutes from the end to send the crowd potty. The nerves were cranked up even higher when the Koreans scored a second to ensure the final minutes were played out with everyone present suffering from squeaky bum syndrome. It was heart wrenching stuff, but Indonesia held on for a famous victory and in Evan Dimas they had surely found a star in the making? He had scored nine goals in the qualifying stages in East Java and Jakarta and had surely laid the ground work for passage to Myanmar?

But football around the world is littered with tales of promising young players who struggle to adapt to the big time. Just google the likes of Peter Coyne, John Bostock, or the sadly deceased Wayne Harrison.

With a place alongside the likes of Australia and Japan assured in Myanmar, the nation waited for the draw to be announced and it wasn't long, of course, before some decided Indonesia's was the group of death as they joined Uzbekistan, Australia, and United Arab Emirates in Group B. Indonesia kick off the tournament against Uzbekistan on 10 October and play their opening two games in the early afternoon, which may well be another big obstacle they face.

Before then of course, there is the small matter of the Under 19 roadshow which travels the length and breadth of Indonesia by plane, bus, and boat as well as overseas stints in the Middle East and Spain.

In February, they criss-crossed Central Java, playing six friendlies in a fortnight, winning four and drawing two.

Next up was East Java. Four games in 10 days with three wins and a draw.

Then one week in East Kalimantan, which produced two wins and the now obligatory draw. From early February until 21 March, the Under 19s had 13 games and spent uncountable hours cooped up on uncomfortable buses on bumpy roads.

Time for some air miles lads, they were off to the middle east where they played five games in 10 days, winning three, drawing one and losing 2-1 against Oman.

The merry month of May was fairly quiet by their standards. Just five games, against Myanmar twice (one draw, one loss) in Jakarta, Yemen (one win, one draw), in Sleman and a 0-0 against Lebanon in Solo.

There followed five games in just under three weeks on Sumatra, which were all comfortably won before returning to Java with one in Bandung against Pre-Provincial Games West Java ending in a 1-1 draw.

After a two week rest they were off to the distant is land of Ternate for another friendly before heading to Spain in early August where they competed in the L'Alcudia International Football Tournament, an annual Under 20 event hosted by the city of Valencia. Some guy called Raul played in it for Spain 20 years ago, you may have heard of him.

The COTIF, as it is apparently better known, kicked off for Indonesia in August when they played Mauritania. Three days later they played Saudi Arabia and then faced Argentina two days after that. The following day Indonesia came up against Barcelona's youth team. You know, the place that spawned Messi, Fabregas, Guardiola, that lot. So, not much to worry about there! As long as the Indonesians concentrated on their job and didn't worry too much about who they would exchange shirts with at the end of the game.

In theory, there is a two month break between when they return from Spain and when they head to Myanmar, but I can't help feeling the powers that be will be keeping the kids busy. But is it all too much? Is there a risk of burn out ahead of such an important competition?

The problem facing young players in Indonesia is not talent. It is having other people, and not least the clubs, interested in them. Too often they go for what is perceived to be the tried and trusted path of recruiting older, more experienced, especially strikers and especially foreigners.

The longevity of the likes of Bambang Pamungkas and the presence of so many foreign strikers or middling ability has surely hindered the careers of players like Rahmat Affandi. Over the years he has played for PSMS, Persib, Arema, and Persija, among others yet nowhere has he really had someone sit him down and say, 'listen son, you are my number one striker, get out there and show me what you can do.' He is now 30 and despite representing

Indonesia at various age group levels, he has never gone on to play for the national team and seems to spend his career hoping someone gets injured or his team don't opt for a big, burly foreign striker.

Rahmat is not alone. Samsul Arif first came to my attention when he was playing for Persibo Bojonegoro in the Indonesia Cup a few years back. Short in stature, he looked like an intelligent player but for some reason the big clubs stayed away. He had a short stint with nearby Persela Lamongan before returning to his home town and it wasn't until he made the move to Arema that he got his big break. Even then, he was often overshadowed by the likes of Cristian Gonzales and Alberto Goncalves, both in their mid-thirties.

Or what about the exciting talent that was Jajang Maulyana who first broke through at Pelita Jaya back when Singaporean Fandi Ahmad was the coach. Jajang was so highly thought of he had a spell with Boavista in Brazil back in 2008-2009. No one, it seemed, in Indonesia was impressed by the samba on his resume. He returned to Pelita Jaya and after stints with Sriwijaya and Mitra Kukar started to flourish under Simon McMenemy at Bhayangkara.

Back in 2013 when they hype around the Under 19s team was at its height I wrote this:

While Indonesia may still be dining out on the glory of that night in Sidoarjo, it is in the past. Today sees a new competition kicking off. And ultimately, success for Evan Dimas and his teammates comes not in East Java or the AFC U19s. It comes five or six years down the road when they have become established players in their own right and they are able to dine out on their performances of the last game as men, not a little known pot they won as teenagers.

Well, in 2017, Evan Dimas and Ilham Udin, along with Jajang Maulyana, were part of the Bhayangkara side that surprised everyone by winning the title. Coached by Scotsman Simon McMenemy, Bhayangkara were short of supporters but McMenemy had gathered together a team built around a core of youth and experience with Evan, Ilham, and Jajang at its core.

I enjoyed watching Bhayangkara during that season and while you had to recognise the impact of experienced old pros like Ilija Spasojevic, Firman Utina, and Paolo Sergio, I was impressed by Evan and especially Ilham who created a buzz of excitement every time he got on the ball. The two Under 19 veterans, now full internationals of course, were rewarded with moves to Malaysia where their partnership continued at a Selangor side trying to keep up with the cash rich Johor Darul Ta'zim.

21.
THE GOOD, THE BAD, & THE UGLY

Back in early 2008, Arema played Persiwa Wamena in a play-off. The game was played at the neutral Brawijaya Stadium, Kediri and ended up being called off after a pitch invasion by Arema fans furious at referee decisions they claimed did not go their way.

Arema's Patricio Morales had already seen one goal disallowed for handball after 10 minutes and Arema, roared on by some 15,000 travelling fans had fallen behind when a defensive mix up had allowed Oscar Mariano a free header.

A second Arema goal was disallowed, this time for offside but while the replays showed the officials had made the correct call some Arema fans didn't see it that way. Objects were thrown on the pitch and one oaf attacked a linesman, decking him before getting caught. Play was held up for 15 minutes while the official received treatment and order was restored on the terraces.

Persiwa, from the Papuan Highlands had started aggressively, attempting to intimidate both their opponents and the fans but Arema soon got in their stride. Emile Mbanda was soon wound up and was haraunging the ref at every opportunity, but some football was being played, notably by Elie Aiboy for the Malang side and Foday for Persiwa who looked somewhat incongruous for a team bidding for their first championship. What's the matter lads, couldn't find a shop with a complete set of socks?

Second half was more of the same. And worse.

On 52 minutes Mbamba had a goal disallowed, Arema's 3rd of the night. It takes very brave officials indeed to do that in this country. Moments later Jaenal hit the post with his first touch after coming on as substitute.

Just on the hour Persiwa were two up. Arema were commited up front and the Papuans broke at pace. Foday crossed and Pieter had a free header. Straight down the other end and Mbamba this time had a goal allowed but tensions were brewing off the pitch. The Kediri stadium has fences round the running track and there was a lot of movement as fans prepared to make their own move, incensed at the referring that had cost them three goals.

On 70 minutes a linesman was felled for the second time in the match and it all went off. Some moron carrying a fluffy lion charged the pitch and slapped one of the officials and he was followed by others. The ref and his linesmen were led off the pitch surrounded by security officials as fans vented their fury.

The TV cameras returned to the studio for about 15 minutes. When they returned to the stadium the terraces were empty. One goal was ablaze, another fire was raging on the far touch line. The other goal had been trashed. Litter was scattered all over the pitch while security personnel scratched their gonads and wondered what to do.

The game was over. The officials were evacuated from the stadium, somehow, while Arema fans ran riot outside. The morons had won.

In the wake of the disturbances that night, I got to speak to some Arema fans about the riot and how they perceived it. ** was one of an estimated 15,000 fans who made the journey to Kediri last night.

I asked him if he had been in a good position to see the first two goals the referee disallowed.

I hadn't been in a good position to see any of the disallowed goals. There was no problem with the goals disallowed, rather when Persiwa scored their second which didn't cross the line.

When the linesman was knocked over in the first half what was the reaction of the fans near you and how did the police react?

Fans jumped onto the pitch and the police ran away.

How easy was it to get from the stands to the pitch?

It's a small stadium and with only a small number of police what did you expect?

Did any Aremania stewards try and stop fans getting on the pitch?

There were no Aremania stewards. It's in Kediri and we don't have organization, they don't have controlling system. It's like in Britain 15/20 years ago. (Some fan clubs, like Persija, have a more organised set up including their own stewards who are meant to intervene when things look like they are getting out of hand.)

How many fans invaded the pitch and who cleared the pitch?

The police finally cleared the pitch.

How much damage was done in the town and how did you get home?

Kediri was dead last night, no electricity. We walked to Blitar and got back to Malang at 4 am.

How do fans feel about being banned from games for 3 years?

We feel very strongly we are being set up. We believe there is a conspiracy against us and that people don't want us to win the Liga.

Will Arema fans still go to the remaining play off games?

Don't know yet.

Have the fans heard anything from the club or the players?

Not yet.

Can they appeal the ban?

We hope so. We want to arrange a meeting with BLI/FA.

What did they hope to achieve by rioting and trashing the stadium?

It was impulsive. Come on, we were angry, who'd think of an impact.

In closing they apologized to the people of Kediri and said less nice things about the Indonesian FA who he and many other Arema fans believe have an agenda against them.

This interview was carried out by text message with an Arema Malang fan who was at the game and got caught up in some of the incidents. The responses are his as translated by movie maker Andibachtiar Yusuf. The only censorship I have done is regarding his remarks about the FA but I'm sure you can guess.

There is a fine line between a football fan and a football thug at times. Many fans I have spoken to admit they would consider themselves to be a hooligan but shy away at anything that I would call 'hooligan activity.' They are happy to throw stones at targets several yards away but then that's just mindless vandalism. They are happy to join in with a mob and kicking a guy lying on the ground but then that's mindless bullying.

As Danang Ismartani, former leader of the Persija supporters club the *Jakmania*, once told me, 'there is opportunity and there is reality.' Many people would take part in the aforementioned activities if they saw it going on around them, they were not alone and there was little chance of getting hurt. Throwing rocks and bottles is easy because the chances of being hit by one are slight. Throwing punches is harder because they can be returned. And they can hurt.

I talked with a couple of fans about hooliganism a few years back. Rather than identify them by name I'll call one J and the other M.

I asked what they thought about the riot at Kediri and M gave it the thumbs up, a big grin breaking out on his face. Okay, let's try another tactic. What about when someone ran on the pitch and assaulted a linesman. That was 'very good.' The reaction was less enthusiastic when I rephrased and asked what they thought about one guy with 15,000 mates attacking a guy on his own from behind.

Interestingly, on the night of mayhem in Kediri apparently only one arrest was made and that was the guy who first attacked an official in the first half. Then he was arrested less for his actions and more to save his skin. After decking the linesman, he ran straight back into the crowd where some of the Arema support were less than enamoured by his actions and proceeded to beat the crap out of him, in the end he was saved by the police!

J lived far from his team. I asked him when the last time was he had been caught up in a brawl and he replied, 'ages. Too far to go.' Come on, I teased him, Solo or Yogyakarta aren't that far, just jump on a train. 'No, I must be in the office most Saturdays.' J had too much to lose by getting caught up in a football brawl even if the chances of getting arrested were small.

M had less to lose. I wanted to know who his teams' biggest rivals were and unhesitatingly he said Persik and Persebaya. Did he travel to the Persebaya game last season I wondered? He nodded. Anything happen? 'No, there was too many of them.' I wasn't having that! I told him in England and Germany you earn more brownie points when you have a go outnumbered. 'Police escorted us from Pasuruan (a district in East Java), we couldn't get out, they (Persebaya fans) couldn't get us.'

I'm reminded of something Danang told me. In the wake of the riot at Bung Karno that left one young fan dead after the game, he said that had police escorted the Persipura fans to their transport that lad would still be alive.

Being a hooligan gives M a kind of status in his community, a community that generally lacks any kind of status from society. But being a known 'face' at his club has also given him opportunities that many would not receive. He was invited to Wamena by Persiwa fans interested in developing a 'fan culture' of their own. The drumming, the songs, the movement on the terraces was what they wanted to know about, and M is first and foremost a fan. He also is one of the drummers at the stadium, keeping up an incessant tempo throughout the game but ever willing to down sticks should he be needed elsewhere.

J and M were an interesting couple of case studies and perhaps deserved more time than we could allow. J, perhaps the older hand, just about given it up because of the effort and the cost. And too much to lose. M, still involved, delighting in the recognition he gets on and off the terraces of his home town.

For Indonesian football matches to become a safer place to be it needs more M's to become J's. For people to have a stake in the society they live in. But I hope the game here keeps the M's for they are the ones who provide the colour and the passion that make football here so alive.

Another incident of football disorder that has gone down in folklore here is the time when Persebaya's fans, known as Bonek, travelled by train to Bandung; about a 14 hour trek at the best of times along the mostly 656 kilometers of single track. Some beautiful scenery for sure as the train traversed the spine of Java but I don't think many of those who travelled that day will be recalling the rice fields or the majestic volcanoes rising up above the early mist.

The problem was that hundreds, nay thousands some would say, Persebaya fans on that train had no tickets. Instead, they just swarmed around the train at Surabaya's Gubeng station and despite the warning signs saying passengers must be in possession of a valid ticket in order to travel, these kids just got on the train. When the carriages were full, they sat on the roof. When the roof was full, they clung to the sides. And in this patently dangerous condition, the train slowly pulled out of Indonesia's second largest city and into infamy.

Quite why the train was allowed to depart is a question worth considering, just check out the videos on line. Of course, it shouldn't. At best, it should have been delayed until the fans cleared but then that is easy to take a viewpoint from a comfy sofa. For the officials on the ground, they probably knew what would happen if they even tried telling hundreds of kids to get down off the roof and queue orderly for a ticket, there's good lads. Nope, that wasn't going to happen and the few officials at a railway station would have been in no position to have enforced any regulations.

Police reinforcements could have been called in but how many would it have needed to clear the train and then the station while at the same time securing the streets around the station?

Many people like to say they don't give a fuck. Sit in a railway carriage on a commuter train going into London and hear the suits say it. Sit in a fast food restaurant and listen to school kids try to outdo each other with how they just don't give a fuck. But they still bought tickets and they paid for their burgers. If they didn't, they knew, for all their Billy Bullshit Bravado, there would be consequences far more painful than not buying a season ticket into Waterloo.

But a bunch of kids pretty much left behind by society? Brought up in slums alongside the railway tracks with little prospect of escape and a diet of instant noodles and meatballs? Where money comes, or doesn't come, from parking cars or stopping traffic to allow other cars to u-turn or selling newspapers at busy junctions, they don't really see themselves as having too much to lose.

As the train passed through the city of Solo, Central Java, there were reports of fans alighting and going on a big thieving operation to replenish supplies for the still long journey ahead. A fight broke out between local residents and the Persebaya fans and it took some time before the train could proceed.

And that pretty much was how the whole journey panned out. Clips on YouTube tell the story of how residents of track-side kampungs turned out in force to attack the train with rocks and bottles while a few hardy policemen stood on the engine waving their shields in an impotent gesture of 'please don't' while others stood on bridges to add their only arsenal to the onslaught.

The way back was even worse with everyone pre-warned by the rolling news coverage that had reporters stationed at strategic stations to catch the disturbances in all their fury. At Solo, things got pretty tasty as the Persebaya fans cowered on the ground of their special train and thousands of local residents used the plentiful supply of rocks to let them know precisely how they were viewed in those parts.

A number of fans died on the journey, falling from the roof of the train, while dozens needed hospital treatment. Once they returned to the city of Surabaya after their time in the limelight, the local authorities arranged food for them and transport home, not wanting thousands of pissed off and hungry young lads short of cash wondering what to do next.

One city that has suffered more than its fair share of football violence is Tangerang, just a few kilometers west of the capital, Jakarta.

Known for its factories as much as anything, Tangerang boasts two football clubs; Persita Tangerang and Persikota Tangerang Kota (City) and in the fine tradition of mid-sized cities with two teams (Sheffield springs to mind), the different sets of supporters loathe each other.

Most football clubs, actually they are more like associations than clubs as we know them in Europe for example, are a part of the local government and until recently their name gave a clue as to which government they were under. Persita, for example, come under the Tangerang district government while Persikota is the city government. On paper, I guess, the Persita fans are more spread out while the Persikota fans are more local.

Until recently, both teams shared the city's Benteng Stadium, a crumbling edifice with a track that I guess people used to run on in the past, and a single, covered stand. The rest of the stadium is a mixture of terracing and grassy banks.

The two teams have not played in the same division for several seasons now; the risk of trouble is too great. Hell, these two don't need to play each other to kick off, they are quite happily having a pop at any time and their frequent offs have also extended to the local kampungs who also get involved. Put it this way. The half dozen times I have been to the Benteng

Stadium to catch either Persita or Persikota, there has been evidence of crowd trouble, if not inside the ground then outside, each time.

One time, I went to see a Persita game. Getting on the main road at nearby Serpong, just a few kilometers from the stadium, and there were plenty of violet clad home fans on buses and trucks they had 'persuaded' to offer them a ride. Every so often, people from small alleyways leading off the main road, would dart out into the traffic and throw rocks and wood at the Persita fans then dashing back to the safety of their warren before the mobile fans could ponder their next move. And this carried on pretty well all the way towards the stadium, stopping only when a police checkpoint forced the fans down from their vehicles.

Inside the stadium and during the games, you would often see fans roaming from one end to the other, looking at the land behind the open terrace. Occasionally they would be joined by large numbers and there was obviously something happening down below, if not with rival fans, then with local residents.

The funny thing is, the one time I saw a reasonable away following at the Benteng Stadium, when Persikota hosted Persiba Bantul, a half-hearted attempt to get near the visitors was easily halted by a handful of cops just going for a walk along the terrace.

But the tripartite disturbances between Persita and Persikota fans and the local residents were getting out of hand and it seemed neither the clubs, the supporters' clubs nor the security officials could do anything about it.

A local religious organisation stepped in and ended the trouble overnight by the simple expedient of declaring the playing of football at Benteng Stadium *haram* or forbidden in 2012. With Persita and Persikota forced to play elsewhere, the people who lived near the stadium could now enjoy their weekends in peace and the fans from the respective teams had to find their own way to row with each other.

Persita celebrated their return to the Indonesia Super League by playing their home games in Kuningan, West Java, before moving to Karawang, also in West Java for the current campaign while Persikota went all studenty and took a year off from football in 2013, returning in Division One in 2014.

Of course, when it comes to football violence in Indonesia, two sets of supporters have become synonymous with it for whatever reason. Persebaya's *Bonek* and Persija's *Jakmania*; is it a coincidence they happen to come from the country's largest cities where much of the media tends to concentrate? Whatever the reason, *Jakmania* and *Bonek* have come to be synonyms for hooligans and the names, and stigma, have stuck.

Thing is, of course, things are not so simple. Not all Persija fans are fully paid up members of the *Jakmania*, and likewise with Persebaya. It is just lazy stereotyping. One time on the way to Lebak Bulus I crossed the road with some friends and someone who hadn't been to an Indonesian game before despite being brought up a goal kick away from the stadium.

The traffic lights were up but so slowly does Jakarta traffic move we crossed regardless, weaving in and out of the foul smoke emitting cars, buses, and motorcycles. My newbie friend, struggling to keep up, giggled and said we were 'like *Bonek*.' No, we weren't. We were doing what people across the capital do on a daily basis but because there was a football element added it added some mystique, some bravado, and it deserved a name. We were crossing a road on the way to football... we were *Bonek*!

Of course, fans of both Persija and Persebaya have been involved in high profile disturbances over the years. Persib fans were killed at Bung Karno Stadium in recent seasons because they had the wrong accent or didn't cheer loudly enough when Persija scored. And while Persija have struggled to play games in Jakarta over the years as the police have been often reluctant to give permission, their fans have exported the trouble to places like Sleman, Malang, and Yogyakarta.

There are a number of reasons for this. As one of the best supported clubs in the country, Persija draw their support from all over the country. This means when they are forced to go on one of their frequent road trips for a home game, they are nearly always assured of a healthy following even before we include those that travel from Jakarta.

For those with long memories in England, many will recall the time Manchester United were relegated to the old Division Two back in 1974. I was 10-years-old, and every week saw a parade of destruction as United fans rampaged around smaller towns and cities trying to prove at least one Red Army was invincible. And, of course, as the so-called top dogs came to town, the locals who fancied themselves were keen to get among them and have a pop. It's similar in a way to Persija and their travelling support.

Of course, not everyone who dons the team's orange colours on match day is full of virtue, peace, and love. Some of them do fancy a tear up themselves, especially when the opportunity arises against their most bitter foe, Persib. But the vast majority of the Persija support are not interested and the few who do try and lob a few rocks back have people trying to stop them. Of course, if something does kick off and they are in the ascendency then everyone is a top boy!

Back to those who like it! Persija's support is a mixed bag of *Jakmania*, Ultras, Garis Keras (Hardline), and Casuals. Yep, Casuals. All Fila, Tacchini, and Stone Island out here in tropical Jakarta. These guys take their inspiration from the casual movement that sprung up in England some 30 years ago. Thanks to ebay and the rise in thug lit, these guys look the part and have learnt to use English pretty damned well thanks to the literary output from the likes of Cass Pennant and Andy Nicholls!

I arranged to meet a couple of Jakarta's casual firm in a bar in Jakarta after they had broken the fast. Needless to say, they arrived wearing adidas retro plus clobber from their own clothing range and were looking forward to a couple of beers after a long day. As with the Persib lad last week, no names,

I shall call them X and Y!

Like many lads, X's family come from outside Jakarta, in North Sumatra, and came to the capital city looking for work and opportunity. He grew up in West Jakarta, where he was surrounded my many people who saw themselves as true Jakartans and he and his mates, who also came from other parts of the country, grew up playing football and fighting the local lads who wouldn't accept them.

'We were outsiders! Me and my mates grew up together, we loved punk music, we loved football.'

Ironically, X's first involvement in fighting at football came against PSMS Medan, a team he grew up watching on TV and having a soft spot as that was where his parents came from.

'PSMS already had a reputation for being flash when they won. In the early days, nobody supported Persija. PSMS lost and, you know, natural thing.' He laughed.

Y took up the story. 'After the game in 1998, PSMS supporters hurled abuse at the Persija fans. They were bigger and older than us, but we surprised them!'

In those days, football was the cheapest form of entertainment for these leads. 'It was only about 80 cents. We could go together and have fun. Shopping malls weren't as much fun!' Ain't that the truth?

X started going to away games back in 2000, at that infamous game when the trouble started. He also went to see Persikabo Bogor District which he described as 'fun!' Truth be told, he was not an easy interview. He seemed to be uneasy talking about himself and what he had done, even the fun bits, and I don't think it was a language thing. X just comes across as the kind of guy who doesn't feel the need to big himself up and certainly supporters from other teams I had spoken with had plenty of respect for him. Despite the team he supported!

He was a member of the *Jakmania* back in the early days as was Y even though they never really ran together as such, round about the time the financial crisis hit Indonesia at the end of the 20th century.

'I only went with *Jakmania* once but they...' Y struggled to find the right vocabulary. He eventually opted for opening and closing his index finger and thumb. They were all talk.' They only wanted to defend and I wanted to attack,' he said, unwittingly highlighting the difference between George Graham's Arsenal and Arsene Wenger's Arsenal!

'We are not a casual firm. So, we don't claim to be the first casual firm in the country. We all have the same interests, the same music. We used to be skinheads, it doesn't matter. We are all together,' said X, talking about the introduction of the casual scene in Indonesia.

'We took about 30 boys to Malang for a Persib game a few years back and that was the first time I felt we were developing into a proper firm. We now usually take about 50 or so to away games,' X explained.

We went on to talk about Persija's recent trip to Bandung which was interrupted by the police. Fights broke out on the highway and it was a couple of hours before things got under control and the Persija fans' coaches returned to Jakarta.

X is no longer an active figure on the terraces as his business is thriving. Okay, maybe not thriving but he decided to do something with his creative skills and started his own clothing range back in 2003. 'Five years ago I decided to focus the business on the merchandising of Persija and selling on the floor outside the stadium on match day. Now, I have a shop and the people who work for me are friends from the firm.'

Again, X is proving to be very understated. His father was a civil servant, here was X growing up, listening to punk, getting in fights, becoming a football hooligan then starting his own business. This undoubtedly caused some friction on the home front, with two vastly different cultures colliding. And X's struggle is the struggle of Indonesian football. On the one hand, the rules and regulations of a bloated, stagnant bureaucracy; on the other a creative youth who saw a changing economy as an opportunity to make money.

X was blowing stereotypes out of the water and he didn't know! I had taught in a school for some eight years in Indonesia and those with a creative bent and with the balls to do something with it were very few and far between. Nearly everyone, not all, was content to follow a career path set out by their parents. Why, I wondered, was X different? Why was he rubbing against the grain? I could guess the answer but I wanted to hear him say it himself.

'I think punk music was an influence. You know, do it yourself, anyone can do anything. I have a dream to make my own way and while I haven't reached my dream, basically I am a lousy business man. I don't even have a car!'

'But I feel a responsibility to my friends. They are my brothers, they are my family,' said X. 'If one of our friends came to X,' said Y, 'he would help for sure.'

I had sensed the respect people held for X on earlier meetings and I wanted to explore it more, so I told him to fuck off while I spoke with Y. But I have since decided I don't want this entry to end up like some sappy soap episode. So, I knocked it on the head. Suffice to say, X is held in high esteem as a guy they can trust and rely on.

X returned with the beers, I told you he was a nice guy, and we carried on chatting. We touched upon hooligan firms who had contacted him online, we touched about undercover cops visiting his shop trying to blend in as casuals, we talked about much. As with his namesake in Bandung, it was a fascinating conversation and while much of it would have been familiar to anyone who watched football in England back in the 1980s, it was fascinating to see how much he had in common with lads back home on many levels.

Then there was Y. Sitting silently for the most part, I soon learnt when he did jump in with something to say, it was worth listening to, hence telling X to do one for a bit. While he would be considered a 'lad' in the truest thug lit sense of the word, there was enough to differentiate him from his English peers.

He stopped drinking quite early in the evening because he didn't want to get home to his wife smelling of too much beer for example. This from a guy who had gone to a recent trade convention held in Jakarta and tried to have a fight with people up from Bandung!

Despite their propensity for the odd tear up and a beer or 10, these lads remain, at heart, pretty conservative. They were unequivocal in who they had voted for in the presidential election the previous day and they took their religious obligations pretty seriously, fasting and praying as best they can. They are not perfect and then they admit they are not but they try their best in that regard.

It was time for them to leave. I was feeling sorry for Y who had gone a couple of hours without a beer and I hoped his wife wouldn't give him too much grief when he got home! But, as X says, Y is a smart guy, he could handle it. They, along with Bandung X, are all smart guys, hard-working, and pretty bloody honest, at least with me in our conversations.

If a lad like Cass Pennant can go on to be a prolific writer, documentary and film maker in England then who knows what these lads can do in the future. One of the things I love about this part of the world is the can do attitude everywhere. Not everything is strangled by rules and regulations, and if ambitious lads like Jakarta X and Bandung X get the entrepreneurial bug, they are not weighed by down volumes of petty restrictions imposed by high ups. They just did it and fair play to them both.

I went up to the bar to find a way of not paying my bill and got talking to one of the waitresses. She was as passionate about her preferred presidential candidate as the lads were about theirs and was angry at her friends' apathy.

As they sat their playing with their smart phones and checking their make up before going home, she waxed lyrical about her candidate, not the same as the hooligans' preferred choice, and why he would be good for Indonesia and what did I think. I left the bar with the kind of fluffy wuffy feeling that comes from heaps of good cold beer and good conversation with good people!

22.
MAY THE GREEN FORCE BE WITH YOU

'You are my Bajul Ijo

My only Bajul Ijo

You'll never know

How much I love you

Please don't take

My Bajul Ijo away.'

Okay, so, it is highly unlikely fans of Persebaya Surabaya will be bellowing out that particular chant anytime soon coming as it does from the 1970s and 1980s terraces of English football, but the sentiment transcends miles and years. What would it be like if someone did take a football club away? How would the fans react? Would it be the end of the world as the above chant seems to be suggesting? For the fans of Persebaya their football club was taken away from them towards the end of 2013, but they haven't shrugged their shoulders and got on with their lives. Their lives were, sorry, are so wrapped up in their football club they manned the barricades and, as befitting folks from Indonesia's second largest city, they took the fight to the highest corridors of power in the land. Name, power, nor reputation means nothing to these fans without a football club. They want it back and they will struggle until their club is returned to them. And for those who know the history of Surabaya, we should expect little else.

After a 12 month stint in Jakarta I had managed to upset enough people at my workplace to be forced to look elsewhere for a paying gig. After a fruitless couple of interviews locally I was given a job in Surabaya. Yeah, new city and all that but I had met the lady who would later tell me we were getting married, so I was forced into a long distance relationship kept going thanks to the myriad of cheap airlines that ply the Surabaya to Jakarta route, one of the busiest domestic routes in the world.

I was still a few years off launching Jakarta Casual on an unsuspecting world but who needed Indonesian football when the Arsenal were going through their invincible season, unbeaten in the Premier League defeating all before them. The local football was a closed book though I do recall saying the other half at the time it might be a good idea to catch a game while I was living there. Her vehemence knew no bounds as she educated me tersely on the notorious *bonek*, as the fans of the local side were known. I wasn't massively interested anyway but I pooh poohed her cautions. 'Ever been to Millwall or Middlesbrough?' I asked with what I thought were my own football experience Top Trumps.

As it happens Persebaya went on to win the Liga Indonesia that year for the second time in their history with the likes of Dwi Yulianto Kurniawan, Danilo Fernando, and Cristian Carrasco rippling the old onion bag in front of manic crowds at 10 November Stadium. For my 12 months in the capital of East Java I only recall the local football team entering my consciousness on a couple occasions. Some of the girls at work used to talk about the Latin American footballers they would meet in various bars way past my bedtime. It meant nothing to me, of course. My beer fund was spent on plane tickets.

The other time I did get to see the notorious bonek up close and personal, I was at Gubeng Station sitting patiently on my train to Yogyakarta waiting for some movement when a local chuffer pulled in disgorging what seemed like hundreds of teenagers united only by flip flops, green tickets, and the lack of tickets. These were the bonek and they sprawled across the railway tracks and through the carriages on my train as they sought to evade any kind of officialdom who may have crazy ideas of checking their tickets.

As this green tidal wave swept through the station I became aware of air horns and klaxons outside. Initially I put that noise down to the normal stop start traffic common in most Indonesian cities but boy was I mistaken.

As I looked aghast from the relative security of my airconditioned carriage I saw pick-ups and mini buses decked in green scarves, green flags, and green t-shirted youths. It was obviously match day and I was totally oblivious and ignorant of what was going on around me. Even as the train finally pulled out I was looking forward to visiting Yogyakarta, travelling through Java's green rice fields, and enjoying the vista of the island's mountainous spine. Oh, how things would change within 24 months!

While the city dates its provence back to 1293, it hasn't always been a place of great importance. Indeed, Dutch sources at the end of the 18th century, early 19th century described it as 'a small town not mentioned in any geography although it is an establishment of some importance and very healthy.' The colonial masters from the Netherlands did intend to transform Surabaya with its fine port into a trading hub for the east of Java and beyond but the pesky English arrived in 1811 and kicked them out for a few years at least. However, one of their number, a Major William Thorn, was impressed enough by what he saw. Comparing Surabaya favourably nearby Gresik he wrote, 'the new town of Sourabaya (sic) has risen rapidly in population and prosperity; and the improvement which it has experienced within these few years is astonishing.'

Thorn goes on to describe a city where the different communities lived lives apart with the Europeans on one side of the Kalimas and the Indonesians on the other side. He also described the area around the city as being particularly 'delightful' while he was less than impressed with the cost of land in the area, a fine attention to detail this military man possessed.

While colonials and invaders waxed lyrical about the city and its charms within a century praise was less than fulsome. A tourist guide from 1903 has this to say, 'we would advise travellers to stay no longer at Soerabaja than necessary, the more so as a single day is amply sufficient to reach several attractive spots in the highlands.' What to do when even those charged with promotion advise visitors to pass right through! A business directory later suggested Jakarta was home while Surabaya, 'is a mart and a factory. No more hardworking place can be found east of Suez.' People worked all day bringing gridlock to the streets and they sought pleasure all night, meaning solace in the city was hard to find. It was a place of trade connecting distant ports like Hong Kong and Manila with those closer to home like Semarang and Jakarta. The pursuit of cash doesn't permit time for much merriment. So, when merriment is to be had it is to be grabbed with both hands and held on to.

Football started to create an impression across Indonesia, or what the Dutch, who returned after a brief British interregnum, knew as Dutch East Indies and it does seem so appropriate that as clubs started to be established in major cities like Medan, Jakarta, Bandung, Semarang, and Surabaya, there would be rival football associations to cater for the different ethnic groups.

At one stage there was a football association that catered to the Europeans; one for the local people, and one for the Chinese which became known as Comite Kampionswedstrijden Tiong Hoa or, mercifully, CKTH but later called Hwa Nan Voetbal Bond. Three associations at the same time! Records indicate the first club in Surabaya was formed in 1896, by British schoolboy named John Edgar and was called Victory later to be followed by Tionghoa, a club catering for the Chinese community. I must say I have never seen any of their shirts or programmes on Ebay but will keep looking. Persebaya were themselves formed in 1927.

Against a burgeoning nationalist sentiment with some tension between the Chinese and the local population in March 1932, the European football body was known as Nederlands Indische Voetbalbond and their Surabayan arm, if you like, was known as the Soerabajasche Voetbalbond and as befitting their colonial master status they had grabbed the best playing surfaces. With the SVB looking to organise some games, there was dissent from the local Asian media aggrieved at what they felt was unfairness from the Dutch. With NIVB organising a game in Surabaya, the local media called for a boycott of the game, instead promoting a clash between Indonesia Marine and a Chinese Arab selection. The boycott worked, hurting the Dutch where it hurt them most, in their pockets.

Tensions later cooled, and the Chinese-backed club was later allowed to enter competitions organised by the NIVB and on the eve of World War Two they further humiliated the colonial masters by winning the SVB Cup, being crowned Java Club champions as well as lifting their own HNVB Cup. With war and uncertainty beckoning, the city of Surabaya was already providing a model of unity and a talent for upsetting those in authority.

This is not a history book but we all know how the war ended. Indonesia declared its independence, but the Dutch were reluctant to let go of their valuable eastern possession. So, fighting continued as the new nation struggled to kick them out once and for all. Suffering huge losses and a shattered homeland, the Dutch lacked the firepower to carry on the fight themselves and relied on their trusty friends from across the North Sea, the British, to do their fighting for them. On their part the British thought they would just have to seize weapons from both the Japanese and the local militias, process prisoners of war, and oversee the repatriation of the Japanese soldiers. It didn't quite go to plan.

Tensions were high in Surabaya and when a group of Dutch prisoners raised their red, white, and blue flag over the Oranje Hotel, now known as the Majapahit Hotel, the local people responded with anger, tearing down the flag and ripping off the blue stripe, leaving the *merah-putih* we have today. The outgoing Japanese supported the Indonesians in their goal for independence and freely provided them with arms for the struggle ahead and by the time he surrendered to the Dutch early in October 1945, local militias were well-armed and well-prepared for a battle ahead.

With Islamic clerics saying the fight for an independent Indonesia was a holy war, thousands of students from the religious schools of East Java flocked to the city to take on the better armed but war weary European soldiers. The heavy fighting, whipped up by Bung Tomo and his inspirational speeches on local radio, took its toll and by the end of October a ceasefire arranged which with the East Java governor which the British thought included the Indonesian militias handing over their weapons.

To publicise the ceasefire, and in the absence of social media, the British dropped leaflets across the city from aircraft. This annoyed the local militia and they responded by killing 200 allied soldiers on 28 October. Two days later the president of the new republic of Indonesia, Soeharto, flew in to Surabaya to negotiate a new ceasefire but again this floundered on a lack of trust and poor communications. The Battle of Surabaya was underway. As the commander of the British forces, Brigader Mallaby, moved around the city telling his troops of the latest ceasefire his car was surrounded by a mob of angry nationalists by Jembatan Merah and he was shot dead. The British military responded in the only way they knew how.

With support from tanks and a naval, air bombardment on 10 November the British sought their revenge on the city that had slain their officer. In the fierce fighting that followed the British had occupied half of the city within three days. When the last bullet was fired three weeks later an estimated 200,000 Indonesians had fled the city and up to 15,000 had lost their lives defending it from the invaders. The British may have won the battle, but they were stuck. They didn't want to get involved in a bloody war on behalf of the Dutch while they had their own problems to deal with. At the newly formed United Nations, they openly supported the formation of an independent Indonesian nation. Twelve months later the British were gone from the city. Today 10 November is known as Heroes' Day, Surabaya is known as *Kota Pahlawan,* Heroes' City and Persebaya's old stadium is known as 10 November Stadium. Their new venue is Bung Tomo Stadium.

If the city of Surabaya wasn't going to bow its knee to the might of the British Empire there is no way it was going to allow anyone to take its football club away.

As Surabayans set about rebuilding their city from the war that had caused so much damage and destruction their football club was to enter a golden age. In the absence of a national league, Persebaya won the *Perserikatan*, a national amateur competition, in 1951 and 1952. In the early 1980s, Surabaya again had a football club they could be proud of, but it wasn't Persebaya. At that time, they were still competing in the Perserikatan but one step higher, in what was called the Galatama, a semi-professional league. There existed another side that was doing the city proud on the field. Their name was NIAC Mitra and way back then they were that powerful they encouraged one young player from Singapore to spurn the advances of Ajax Amsterdam for the opportunity of playing in East Java.

His name was Fandi Ahmad, a Singaporean legend and perhaps the best player the island state has ever produced. At the time, 1982, he was about 20-years-old, and NIAC Mitra were Galatama champions having won the title in the 1980/82 season finishing five points clear of runners up Jayakarta. Fandi joined up with fellow Singaporean David Lee and together they helped NIAC Mitra to win the Galatama for a second successive season. Joining the foreign contingent were the likes of Rudy Keltjes, Budi Aswin and Syamsul Arifin.

Sadly, at the end of the season the Galatama announced there would be no more foreign players in the upcoming campaign and despite their successes Fandi and Lee would be on their way out. Their farewell came in a friendly against no less a team than Arsenal on touring in Indonesia following a difficult season at home. They still brought a strong team and after defeating PSMS Plus and PSSI Select quite comfortably, would have fancied their chances in the final game of their tour at 10 November Stadium in Surabaya. The Gunners lined up as follows:

Arsenal: Jennings, Hill (Robson), Sansom, Talbot, O'Leary, Whyte (Lee), McDermott, Sunderland, Meade (Chapman), Davis, Rix.

Niac Mitra: David Lee, Budi Aswin, Wayan Diana, Tommy Latuperissa,

Yudi Suryata, Rudy Keltjes, Rae Bawa/Yusul Male, Joko Malis, Hamid Asnan/ Syamsul Arifin, Fandi Ahmad, Dullah Rahim/Yance Lilipaly.

Seven full internationals started the game, but Arsenal's tour attracted little of the razamattaz that accompany such events these days. They had finished the previous season in a disappointing 10th position in the old Division One, this was in the days before the Premier League and Sky invented football, and attendances were way down as disillusioned fans, including me, stayed away. Even when Manchester United came to town at the beginning of May the crowd was only 23,000. The programme for the final home game of the season makes no mention of the upcoming visit to Indonesia and the season petered out with a win away to West Ham United and a loss at Aston Villa.

Within a month of the domestic season ending a small Arsenal party were heading to Indonesia for their first ever visit but the headlines were elsewhere. The media was in a frenzy. Celtic prodigy Charlie Nicholas was being chased by the big 3, Arsenal, Liverpool, and Manchester United. Liverpool, then the biggest club in the world, were favourites. After all they had Charlie's hero, Kenny Dalglish. Terry Neill, our manager at the time and the man who got Spurs relegated, was quietly confident Charlie would come to London but for a couple weeks the hunter and the huntee would be half a world apart with Charlie on tour with Scotland in Canada. Ken Friar stayed in London to deal with the Celtic board, Charlie and Neill.

On 8th of June Arsenal played Medan and won comfortably, despite the conditions. Coach Terry Burton and Terry Neill both had run outs and, apparently, even Don Howe was impressed.

A couple of days later Arsenal flew to Jakarta with Nicholas still undecided. On the 13th he announced in The Sun he had decided to join Arsenal and Ken Friar was soon on the phone to Neill at the Arsenal hotel in Jakarta with the good news. Naturally he was delighted, so he joined the directors in the hotel bar and ordered champagne. Initially he told them Nicholas had decided on Liverpool, he was sorry but hey let's get wasted but he soon relented. It cannot be understated just what this signing meant to Arsenal and the fans. This was a lad of immense ability, a glamour figure, and his arrival lifted everyone at Arsenal after years of stagnation and signing players of average ability. It was a shot in the arm for the club and proof that we were still a big club, though admittedly one in the doldrums.

The directors set about the champagne with gusto. Partly because they had secured the services of this talented player but also partly because it may have been a rare sight to see their manager dig deep at the bar! They had an official do at another hotel with the Indonesian FA, at which they arrived late and a little bit the worse for wear before continuing the party later on.

Arsenal moved on to Surabaya for the final game of the tour and perhaps the excesses of champers lingered. Someone, who was at the game, posted their memories on Jakarta Casual.

I watched the Arsenal — Niac Mitra game in Surabaya. It was the farewell match for Fandi Ahmad and David Lee, the striker and goalkeeper from Singapore. The stadium was packed. Niac Mitra, Galatama champion at the time played well. I still remember Fandi made a backheel pass to Djoko Malis in an attack to Arsenal's goal. Other Mitra players were Rudy Keltjes and Syamsul Arifin. Niac Mitra fans were no hooligans, unlike the current sorry state of Persebaya fans.

NIAC Mitra took the lead through Fandi on 37 minutes and Joko Malis made it 2-0 with a goal five minutes from the end to secure a famous victory but it is a tour that Arsenal don't seem to remember too fondly. With the new season, we were all excited about the arrival of Nicholas and the programme for the first home game against Luton Town has much about the arrival of the Scottish superstar.

There is one letter from a fan who travelled to Indonesia but was unable to see any of the games. He did, however, meet the players on a flight and was interested to know that soon after arriving at the hotel the players were stripped and ready for a training session. The witty reply from the programme editor was along the lines of '(we) thought it was a holiday trip!' The only other reference to the trip was Kenny Sansom saying he had grown a beard in Jakarta!

In their memoirs published several years later neither David O'Leary or Sansom seem to have fond memories of the trip. O'Leary, expressing a rare strong opinion, says, 'We were on one of those end of season tours, this time to Indonesia, which was pretty awful. We finished with a rather pleasant few days break in Bali…' before going on to talk about the signing of Nicholas. To be fair to O'Leary, I think he was bemoaning the tour rather than the destination. Clubs these days just don't do lengthy tours so soon after the end of a long season. As for Sansom, he describes Indonesia as being an experience and half before retelling an experience where a young lad tries selling him his young sister for sex. It was, he says, his first encounter with the effects of poverty and it hit him hard. As an Arsenal fan it is a bit disappointing that players' recollection of their visit here were so negative, but I am pretty sure when the club returned 30 years later, a wholly different impression was made.

Anyway, I digress. Shorn of their import players NIAC Mitra struggled to make headway for a few years and it wasn't until 1987/88, were they to taste success one more time when they lifted the Galatama one more time. Their reward this time was a place in the Asian Champions League for the first time the following season. Continental club competition still wasn't particularly well-established and struggled for interest among fans who had little knowledge of the game beyond their shores.

NIAC Mitra were drawn alongside Royal Thai Air Force, Malaysia's Pahang, Geylang International, and Bandaran from Brunei. The games took place at the end of July 1988 and as I type this up I realise I was in the manor not too long before the games kicked off. In fact, I had seen Geylang International at

Jalan Besar in Singapore just a few weeks before they headed to Bangkok, my first game in Asia, and I flew out of Bangkok not too long before the group stage games kicked off!

NIAC Mitra opened their bid for continental supremacy by defeating Banderan 3-1 on 21st July. Two days later, as I was hitching to Yeovil to see Arsenal play in Alan Skirton's testimonial, they were held to a 0-0 draw with the Malaysian team Pahang. No drama. After two games they had three points and were in second place. One point behind the hosts RTAF (two points for a win at the time). The Surabayan side lost 2-1 against the home team, but infortunately a draw against Geylang International wasn't enough to secure a spot in the next round of the competition and NIAC Mitra returned home to Surabaya proud but ultimately beaten. As it happens RTAF withdrew from the competition, but it seemed no one thought about asking the Indonesian side to join the semi-finals which were played in Guangzhou, China.

In 1994, football finally went professional in Indonesia with three teams from Surabaya, competing in that debut campaign; Mitra, Persebaya, and Assyabaab, with the latter side taking honours in the battle for Surabaya bragging rights, finishing third in the eastern conference. Persebaya won the Liga Indonesia for the first time in 1997, with a team featuring the likes of Jacksen F Tiago and Aji Santoso. Both scored in the final against Bandung Raya. They would also, both, later coach the football club. Jacksen was leading the side when they won the Liga Indonesia for a second time in 2004. In fact, 1997 was a special year for the city of heores with Mitra also reaching the semi-finals before losing to Bandung Raya.

Since then, with the exception of that triumph in 2004, pickings have been slim for football fans in Surabaya. Nineteen ninety-eight saw the season halted as the country descended into financial crisis and when football did return for the 1998/99 season Mitra were gone. Money problems ending the privately owned club. Their license was bought, and they moved to South Kalimantan where they were known as Mitra Kalteng Putra. They struggled to make an impact and in 2001, they were playing in Division Two. So far down the pyramid to be all but forgotten and a mere shell of the side who had defeated the mighty Arsenal nearly 20 years earlier. Today, of course, the Mitra name lives on in Mitra Kukar, now playing in East Kalimantan and boasting a tidy stadium close to the mighty Mahakam River.

As we entered the 21st century Persebaya became better known for a different type of struggle as elements of their support, known as *bonek*, acquired a reputation for misbehaviour. Indeed, *bonek* almost became a synonym for naughty boy, rule breaker that transcended football. *Bonek*, which comes from Javanese and is an acronym of *Bondho Nekat* which approximately translates as naughty lads or wild ones. It became part of the national vernacular when an estimated 25,000 Persebaya fans travelled to Jakarta to see their side play Persija in the late 1980s. At the time, a headline making event as fans travelling to see their team play way in a country where distances were vast were pretty rare.

In January 2010, the *bonek* put on a show and this time the whole nation watched, enthralled and terrified at the same time. Persebaya were playing away to Persib Bandung and with the relationship between these two sets of fans pretty close, thousands were expected to travel from Surabaya and oh boy did they travel. A nation watched aghast as a slow moving train wound its way across Java with thousands of Persebaya fans sat in the humid carriages or perilously on the roof. At various stops along the way fans of teams, which looked less kindly on their Surabaya brethren, welcomed them with a symphony of rocks and bottles with news camera crews there to catch the carnage for the armchair millions. Around the country feelings were mixed, tut tuts were accompanied by the old refrain, 'this is Indonesia' as the train made its slow journey.

Twenty-two years after *bonek* had descended upon Jakarta, a second generation was going through its own rite of passage only this time they shared it with a nation. When we talk about great away followings in

Indonesian football we recall that Persib trip to Jakarta to see them play PSM in the early 1990s. Arema invading Jakarta when they won the ISL in 2010, and now Persebaya fans were heading to Bandung. On many levels the tut tuts are fully deserved. How could so many young lads be allowed to board a train, to climb on the roof? How was the train allowed to leave? How was it allowed to carry on its journey? I guess the truth is once it had started it had to finish. There were too many stations along the way that were bandit country, where the *bonek* would not have been welcomed.

The game itself passed off fairly peacefully despite the large numbers of penniless away fans, and the focus was on how the fans would be ferried home. While in Bandung, they were provided with refreshments and a special train was provided to take them back home, with the usual rocks and bottles greeting them as they passed through towns and cities alerted to the threat of the *bonek* by the rolling news coverage.

It was to be the last away day for a while. They finished the season 17th in the 18 team ISL and were looking forward to life in Divisi Utama when Indonesian football split in two and Persebaya joined the 'rebel' Liga Primer Indonesia at the start of 2011. A decision with ramifications that continue to this day. With ex-player Aji Santoso in charge, Persebaya 1927, as they became known, finished the first half of the season top of the 19 team LPI and were no doubt looking forward to lifting the title when the season was ended despite FIFA recognising it as the official league in April 2011.

The following season, 2011/2012 saw the dualism kick in big time. With Persebaya 1927 continuing in the much reduced LPI, now with 12 teams, another Persebaya took the original club's rightful place in Divisi Utama where they finished second but ultimately missing out on a promotion play-off spot. But Persebaya fans were not happy. They saw the rightful club as being the team playing in the LPI and more than 50,000 saw them play Arema in one game. The club playing in Divisi Utama they saw as an imposter, claiming they were in fact Persikubar from East Kalimantan masquerading as their great club. *Bonek* voted with their feet but no one was listening.

In 2013, Persebaya 1927 continued in the LPI finishing fifth when the campaign was annulled for a second time in its short-lived life. Three clubs, Persema, Jakarta FC, and Persibo never returned after the mid-season break as the PSSI reached an agreement to merge the two leagues for the 2014 season. Persebaya 1927 were banned from entering the new competition as doubts continued over their ownership against the backdrop of two clubs sharing the same name.

Brazilian Fabio Oliveira was coach for the final games of the 2013 IPL campaign. 'It is not a normal thing to have two teams with the same name in a single city,' he said. 'Imagine… if that happened in London! But this we all took in our focus, so we knew we were on the right side.'

The clubs were suffering from a lack of money and Oliveria recalls this could affect performances on the pitch. 'Every time the coaching staff and directors tried to pass a message of support to the players about late salaries we knew at some point this problem would disturb us on the field.'

It is telling though that amid the off-field concerns there was one area he and the team never worried about. '*Bonek* never disappointed us. They were always walking with us… was an amazing atmosphere.'

Persebaya's last home game came against Pro Duta and they lost 3-1. At the half way point they sat 3rd on 30 points behind leaders Semen Padang and second placed Perseman Manokwari. Their final five games, played against a backdrop of uncertainty, saw them pick up just five points and slide down the table to fifth. Persebaya played their last games on a road trip to Aceh, never the easiest place to go at the best of times. Coach Oliveira takes up the story.

'In the last games, I spoke with all the players to enjoy their football. We had nothing to lose! Forget all the problems and try to do what we love… play football. We knew Aceh trip would be the last games for us.' Persebaya

1927 drew 1-1 with PSLS at the end of September and a few days later were held 2-2 by Persiraja in Banda Aceh. And that was it. More than three years later and Persebaya haven't played a competitive game since but the fans have carried on keeping the name out there. Persebaya hadn't died. It was just resting.

Meanwhile Persebaya/Persikubar continued their merry way in Divisi Utama with a small band of hardy fans. They finished top of their group, unbeaten in 14 games and 12 points clear of second placed Perseba Bangkalan. They fought their way through the play-offs to reach the final where they triumphed 2-0 over Perseru. Triumphant but still unloved, they were in the ISL for the 2014 campaign finishing top of the Eastern Conference, the ISL that season was split into Eastern and Western groups. I travelled down to Bung Tomo to see them play Perseru and while they did have a good team coached by Rahmad Darmawan the fans were still staying away, adamant the club masquerading as Persebaya were imposters. Unfortunately, they were unable to progress beyond the play offs, finishing bottom of their group without a win.

Come 2015 and Persebaya continued with the myth they were the true inheritors of the title, but finally people at the top table werent listening. The ISL started in April but was soon halted when the sports ministry refused to give clearance for games to go ahead. They were unhappy at the presence of two clubs, Persebaya and Arema, who they felt were not the rightful owners of the club names. It was a moral victory for the bonek. Vindicated for their long struggle but still a long way from achieving their goal of seeing Persebaya on the pitch one more time. As football entered a kind of twilight zone Persebaya changed their name to Persebaya United in a bid to show themselves as a unifying force in the city but it was never going to work. During the President's Cup in 2015, one of the competitions introduced to fill the void left by the ISL suspension, they defeated Sriwijaya 1-0 at home. For the second leg they changed their name to Bonek United, stayed in the dressing room and saw the game awarded to the home team 3-0. The whole Persebaya/Surabaya saga had descended into a farce.

Ahead of the unofficial Indonesia Soccer Championship, the club rebranded itself Bhayangkara Surabaya United as they became embraced by the national police force, ending the campaign in a credible 6th place but now known as Bhayangkara and drawing on the constabulary for many of their players. Based in Sidoarjo, a city just to the south of Surabaya they struggled for support and their future remains unclear as rumours swirl about a possible move to Central Java.

As for Persebaya surely the future is brighter. In May 2016, a Persebaya Legends team took to the field at 10 November Stadium, also known as Tambaksari Stadium, to play a friendly against a PSSI All Stars. Now I don't have a scooby about who played for the PSSI side but then I am not sure this game was about football.

With Persebaya existing in name only this was a chance for the legions of loyal fans to flock to the hallowed turf of the Tambaksari one more time to roar on the badge and more than 25,000 did precisely that.

To put in context only Persija boasted a bigger crowd in Indonesia and it is unlikely many other clubs in South East Asia attracted more over the weekend in their respective leagues.

Fans came from all over Surabaya, of course, as well as Malang, Sidoarjo, and Lamongan including some who had travelled from as far as Jakarta. They had to really, didn't they? Who knows when Persebaya will make a return to the top flight of Indonesian football.

As for the game? Like I said earlier this wasn't really about the football. It was about the badge and when the fans invaded the pitch at home time to take pictures with their heroes that was it. The game was over, and the event turned into a retro afternoon. A photo fest for Persebaya and their long suffering Bonek supporters.

When PSSI held elections in Jakarta towards the end of 2016, thousands of bonek headed to the capital city to state their case. Camped out at Persitara's Tugu Stadium, they attracted plenty of TV camera crews who made sure the issue of Persebaya was going nowhere anytime soon. No decision was taken about Persebaya, but positive noises were made and it does look like the bonek's struggle is coming to an end along with this whole sorry saga.

Just like Indonesia in 1945, football needs Surabaya. Football needs Persebaya. Football clubs in Indonesia become more than just a badge. They become part of a person's identity. Come from Medan, you are PSMS. Makassar? You have PSM in your veins. Surabaya is no different. Persebaya is part of the identity of the city. Surabaya is Persebaya and vice versa.

Indonesian football is changing and if Persebaya do reenter the national arena in 2017, they are likely to be back in the second tier. Newer clubs like Pusamania, Madura United, Bali United have joined the top flight and brought a new professionalism to the game. Lacking the depth of support Persebaya enjoy, they have been slick in their marketing and their social media presence. A 'new' Persebaya would need to match their ambitions and their talents. Indonesian football is at the stage where having a big name is no longer enough. Look at the likes of Persija, PSIS, PSMS. Clubs with proud histories struggling to stay relevant in the second decade of the 21st century. But given the way their fans have struggled to keep the name of Persebaya alive while others tried to wish it away, who is to say a new look Persebaya won't arise and become a major power once again in Indonesian football. For that is the way of Surabaya folk. They don't roll over and die. They fight for what they feel is theirs. They did in 1945 for their city and they have been doing so in the last few years for their football club!

23.
CHOIRUL HUDA – 100% LAMONGAN

So, I went to Lamongan. To meet a man. If it wasn't for football I think it's fair to say the East Java town of Lamongan would never have appeared on my radar. I'm no foodie but if the town is famous for anything it is food, especially Soto Lamongan. That's about it. I stayed a year in Surabaya, about an 80 minute drive to the east, and I don't think the town ever came up in conversation. It's just there, one more town on the road that connects Surabaya with the west of Java. One more anonymous town on a busy highway where drivers are focused more on avoiding the bloody great lorries that race along at stupid miles per hour than the towns they pass through.

The first time I think I wrote anything more than a couple of lines about Persela was in 2008, when I described them as a bit like Middlesbrough. Not the most glamourous of football clubs, difficult to find on a map but possessing a very passionate home support. As I write this, 11 weeks into the Liga 1 2017 season, little Persela are averaging better crowds than mighty Arema. They may never win a trophy but at the same time I have never heard a bad word said about them. Foreign players have praised the club's management and said they were always well looked after at the club. In return, some stayed for two, three years, or more. Unheard of loyalty in Indonesian football but testament to the town and its football club.

My plan was to stay in Lamongan for a couple of days to get a feel for the place, but I couldn't find a decent enough hotel online with the facilities I felt I needed. Jeez, what a wuss. Back in the day I would just turn up in a town and find budget lodgings myself. Now I can't do a thing without the internet. Plan B was to stay in nearby Surabaya and travel out by train. Surely there had to be a reasonable service connecting the two places? Surely there were people who lived in Lamongan but worked in the bigger city? Well, no actually. There wasn't much of a service. Less than a dozen a day.

I ended up hiring a car and driver from my hotel in Surabaya and cursing my reliance on the internet. I should have just fronted up in Lamongan and made do with what I found. But I didn't. I'm a useless snowflake who feels uncomfortable without a luxury or two to ease my burden. Bollocks isn't it but that's the way it is now, and I am using middle age to defend myself.

The drive itself wasn't much of a hardship. Just not fun. Whizzing along the main road out of Surabaya you escape the ugly industrial buildings and soon race past flat rice fields. To my left, looming large like a spaceship which had taken the wrong turning, was the Gelora Bung Tomo or Bung Tomo Stadium, Persebaya's new 55,000 seater stadium in the middle of nowhere. Not much further on, this time on the right-hand side, was Joko Samudro Stadium in Gresik, under construction for local heroes Gresik United. Living in Jakarta I marvel at these new stadiums so close together going up amid so much open land.

We exit the Jalan Tol Surabaya Gresik and head straight west. The land here is not what I am used to in and around Jakarta. It looks flat and arid, more like what I have seen to the east of Surabaya on the island of Madura. Most definitely non tropical. The road is flat and straight but not dull. The bloody lorries make sure of that. I don't know what, if any, road etiquette exists for drivers of large vehicles in the country but out here there appeared to be none. They would quite happily drive two abreast, the inside lorry putting the pedal to the metal at a staggering 30 miles per hour while another large vehicle would be overlapping the central reservation, hogging the road and pissing off all other road users as he attempted to overtake at a majestic 33 miles per hour. I was in a car. We were small, so we were nothing. Yes, we had speed that counted for little as the big truckers vied for road supremacy.

The scenery might have been quite pleasant had I had the chance to enjoy it, but I was too scared to draw my eyes away from the road in front. My driver didn't seem too worried, he was probably used to having his life flash before his eyes on these roads, but it was okay. I was shitting enough bricks for the both of us, especially when one 40 foot monster came raring down the middle of the road leaning too far to his right for my liking.

The white knuckle ride ended as we entered Lamongan. We passed the football stadium, Surajaya Stadium, on the right-hand side, crossed the railway tracks and entered the town proper. I had arranged to meet Persela's legendary goalkeeper Choirul Huda by the Lamongan Sports Centre and I was early. We parked outside the centre in a quiet lane opposite a small warung. All was peaceful and quiet which I enjoyed. I sent Choirul a message and waited for his reply. The occasional motorcycle broke the silence, but they were quiet and respectful, not like those big city buggers who get a hard-on from the mufflers from the exhaust and revving the engines just to piss the neighbours off.

I checked the phone but Choirul hadn't replied. I wasn't too worried even though the meter was ticking over. I was being seduced by the somnolent surroundings. The sun was high, the sky was blue, and there was plenty of green stuff even though I was in the heart of the city. Town. The driver got out to stretch his legs. Still no reply from Choirul. The driver returned, and we nattered a little, a good chance to practise my bahasa Indonesia. 'What about your friend?' Oh, yeah. I checked again. Nothing. In fact, he hadn't even seen my message. Bloody hell. Okay, this was getting naff. I had been sitting here for 45 minutes and still was no nearer to meeting this guy. I contacted my mate Gabriel Budi, an agent who had put me in touch with Choirul. 'Wait, I will try.' And the phones went silent again.

Finally, after slightly over an hour of unproductive nothingness I got a message from Choirul. 'Sorry, I was asleep.' I could believe that. I was half way there myself. I asked him whether we could meet at the sports centre or the stadium. His answer? Okay. I switched to the old fashioned way. SMS. 'Meet dimana?' Fifteen minutes later he said we could meet at the mess, the clubhouse which was shared by many of the local players. Great. We found the house on Google Maps and were there in five minutes. I walked in through the open doorway. *'Choirul dimana?'* *'Uh?'* The one person I found saw the big white guy and disappeared into a room. I honestly had no idea if he was running away from me or had gone to find someone to translate. It was the latter as he reemerged with one of the coaching staff. I sent Choirul another SMS.

'Choirul dimana?' They looked at me with suscpicion. What the hell was this white guy doing here they were probably thinking. *'Kamu ada meeting?'* *'Yep.'* *'Kita ada latihan jam 3, mungkin dia langsung ke stadion.'* *'Okay, bisa ikut?'* He smiled. *'Kamu tau Mas Choiru?!'* he asked. *Tau tapi belum bertemu.'* *'Kamu pelatih?'* I smiled at that. You seen my beer gut? *'Saya penulis,'* I said, reaching into my bag for a copy of my first book which it just so happened I was carrying with me. He seemed unimpressed and passed it round to his pals who had gathered in the front room of the mess. They seemed to share his apathy and it was returned to me with not even a page turned. My phone beeped. *'Nanti di stadion saya berlatih jam 3.'* It was Choirul.

So, two hours after I was due to meet Choirul I finally got to see him as he jogged down the tunnel to join his teammates in their training session ahead of their home game with Persija 24 hours later. He turned to look at the main stand, saw this big white guy, assumed it was me and waved. I waved back and let him get on with it. I wasn't angry that I had been waiting so long to meet him. In fact, if I'm honest I half expected it. Choirul Huda, born in Lamongan, raised in Lamongan, educated in Lamongan, day job in Lamongan, plays for local side Persela Lamongan. His town, his rules, and I liked that. I wasn't expecting a brash Billy Big Balls who had been changed by the fame and fortune of professional football.

John Terry played for Chelsea for 19 years. Steven Gerrard played for Liverpool for 17 years. Tony Adams played for Arsenal for 19 years. Francesco Totti played for AS Roma for 25 years. One club men. Legends. Icons. Choirul Huda, in my book, deserves to be mentioned in such august company. He has played for Persela for 17 years and, if he has his way, has a few more years in the tank. But while Terry, Gerrard, and Adams were lauded and feted by the media and their club and, truth be told, embraced the celebrity culture football brought them, Choirul is a more humble man with a full-time job outside of football. He doesn't seek the limelight and would not have cared one jot had I written about Lamongan and not mentioned him. Quiet, understated, quietly spoken, humble. He may not have the qualities needed to be a hero in other countries who prefer their superstars to be bad ass boys, Choirul is a legend in Lamongan and is a legend in Indonesian football. He deserves a few lines to be written about him to celebrate his career but then he deserves to be allowed to slip quietly back into the anonymity afforded by his quiet home town.

I'm not really one for watching professional footballers train. It looks just like people doing a job and I like footballers to have an element of mystique about them. Still, I was here for Choirul and it was interesting to see how he did his job in his work place. The 37-year-old goalkeeper, he was to turn 38 just a few weeks later, was in his element. Not one for bawling, he led by example, coming for every cross, every shot while offering words of encouragement to his younger teammates. The consummate professional footballer, one most coaches would be grateful to have in the dressing room.

At the end of the session he posed for some photographs from fans who had been sat by me watching before making his way t o me. He was drenched in sweat and his training shirt was covered in dirt. We shook hands and smiled at each other. 'Sorry,' he said in halting English, 'I was sleeping.' Forget about it I told him. I asked if he wanted to get showered and freshened up before we chatted but he said, no, let's do it so we headed for the Persela dug out, I took out my note book, refreshed myself, and pressed the record button on my phone.

After driving for 90 minutes, waiting two hours, watching him train for a further 90 minutes, our chat lasted all of five minutes. Again, I expected that.

Any information I wanted, I knew I would have to really dig for. But the truth is I didn't really want to dig. This is a guy who loves football, loves Lamongan, and is happy in his world. I decided I wanted to focus on Choirul and his love affair with Lamongan. I'm sure he has juicy tales to tell from years in the dressing room but that's not what I want. I want his town, his rules.

I guess we sat there for about 10 minutes in the home dugout of the Surajaya Stadium, me asking my questions in my bumbling Indonesian and Choirul answering politely but not really saying much. He stayed in Lamongan because he loved the city and the people. The management of the football club were good people and basically he was comfortable in his skin. How could anyone really be interested in his story. I got his view point, I really did.

I'd grown up with one club men like Bob Wilson and Pat Rice at the Arsenal and what stood out, for me at least, was their normalcy. They were just ordinary people doing a job they loved at a place of work they loved. They weren't heavily tattoed, neatly coiffured pretty boys more interested in developing themselves as a brand with a PR team promoting their paid endorsements, driven by a manic greed to add more zeroes to their bank account, they were doing very well thank you and who was it who said if you're doing something you love you're not really working anyway.

There were no sweeping mission statements, no management buzz speak from Choirul. Just that humbleness that I anticipated mixed with a tint of bemusement. Why was this guy asking me questions he was probably too polite to say, I'm nothing special. And he's right, he isn't anything special; except that he had been with his home town club for so damned long and his wish, he said to me, was to coach the next generation of goalkeepers at the football club...'if they want me.' No irony, no bitterness, no sense of entitlement but a deadpan delivery and the fear that perhaps he may one day be cast aside. An anti-hero if you like, a genuine counter weight to the growing number of professionals who are becoming more famous for their social media following than their exploits on the pitch.

Despite saying nothing that would warrant a three page exclusive in a sleazy red top Sunday paper I was moved by my time with him. Have I mentioned the humility, the lack of airs, and graces, the politeness, the bemusement? I drove back to Surabaya deep in thought. I had got confirmation of my presuppositions but no story or maybe that was the story? Maybe if I wanted more I would have to talk to his teammates past and present, but wouldn't they just confirm what I already knew? Legends are supposed to be, well, legendary with a long list of achievements to fill out their resume but that is just what we have been led to believe by a media who see the legendary status as an opportunity to sell extra copies or garner extra clicks or by governments who seek legitimacy by selecting heroes for us who, through their selfless acts, have made the world a better place for us and future generations.

Young people have always sought rebellion in their heroes, at least we did when I was growing up. Bored with our dull old lives we turned to rock stars and sports stars who lived life to the full. Waking up next to glamorous models or throwing furniture out of hotel rooms seems quite fun when you contemplate the mysteries of logarithms or cosines. But now, in the internet age, when we are told things are in a constant state of flux perhaps it's good to have a Choirul Huda to anchor ourselves to, to remind ourselves everything will turn out all right in the end. In the face of all this change there is one man who, if he doesn't quite stick his middle finger up to the world, just carries on in his own sweet way, living his life the way he wants to live his life.

I hadn't arranged to meet Choirul again, but I had his number and with Persela due to play PS TNI and Bhayangkara later in the season I felt confident we would meet up again. With my son a budding goalkeeper I would have liked him to chat with Choirul about the game. And football boots. And shin pads. And gloves. I made a mental note to contact Choirul next time his team were in the Jakarta area. Then I moved to Egypt for a couple months.

On Sunday 15th October I was lazily scrolling through my Instagram account when I suddenly felt like I had been punched in the stomach. Words were leaping out at me from my small screen smart phone. Words like pray, Choirul, RIP, rest in pride. What the fuck? I became fully focused on my phone as I searched for more news. I went to Twitter. 'What happened to Choirul Huda?' I asked the internet. The answers came back in a rush. He's injured, he's in hospital, he's died. Oh my god, how did this happen? Why Choirul. All the questions families and friends of the bereaved rush to ask.

Choirul Huda had made his debut for Persela in 1999, I thought he would last forever. Instead he breathed his last following a freak collision on the field with a teammate which seems to have caused a heart attack. He was rushed to hospital where the medical staff frantically worked to restore life to the fading goalkeeper. Meanwhile, inside the stadium the game carried on and at the final whistle his teammates rushed to the hospital to be by his bedside. He died soon after.

In the days following his death, football united to share their grief at the loss of a legend. Even Arsenal's Petr Cech tweeted a message of condolence. I was contacted by the BBC and asked to say a few words on the World Service as word spread. English and Spanish language newspapers picked up on the news. For the first time ever, this unassuming man from East Java was headline news around the world; tragically it wasn't for his unstinting loyalty but his untimely end.

Games went ahead with a minute silence before kick-off and players across the country wore yellow shirts with the number one and Huda's name printed on them and supporters have been holding up banners remembering the legendary keeper. But showing incredible insensitivity the Liga 1 authorities refused to allow the shell-shocked Persela players time to come to terms with their loss and forced them to travel to East Kalimantan to fulfill their fixture with Borneo in Samarinda.

The timeline would have been very traumatic for the team. Following their 2-0 victory over Semen Padang on Sunday afternoon when Choirul was initially injured in a collision with teammate Ramon Rodrigues, the team gathered at the hospital where they were greeted with the news their inspirational teammate had died. By Tuesday, they would have been on their way to Juanda International Airport in Surabaya to catch a flight to Balikpapan and then north for the three hour drive to Samarinda all the way coming to terms with their grief and the knowledge there was one glaring omission to their travelling party.

On Thursday they lined up against Borneo as they had done in recent games with Ferdiansyah in goal but the memory of Huda, a player who had spent 18 years with the club, would have been everywhere. In the dressing room, geeing up the players, leading by example. And Ramon, sadly perceived the villain in some dark quarters of social media, started the game. One cannot imagine what he was going through.

Borneo were 2-0 up at halftime and doubled their lead in the second half before Persela scored two late penalties through Samsul Arif and Ivan Carlos Coelho but surely they should never have been put through this rigmarole. Common decency should have suggested the Persela football club be allowed a few days to contemplate recent events and a polite few days been permitted to allow them to come to terms with their grief.

But no, not here, not in Indonesia. The game goes ahead as it always does after every tragedy. A few words are offered saying more will be done to stop this happening and we carry on as normal. But a death of a player on a football pitch or coming from injuries that occurred on the pitch is not normal. In fact, Huda's death is the fourth in the last 17 years!

03/04/00 Eri Irianto (Persebaya)

07/03/09 Jumadi Abdi (PKT Bontang)

10/05/14 Akli Fairuz (Persiraja)

15/10/17 Choirul Huda (Persela)

A week later and Persib were in Lamongan to play Persela. The football world and Lamongan were gathering around Choirul's family while the PSSI were forcing his teammates to travel to Samarinda. Fans were waving banners to honour the keeper; ex teammates were dedicating goals to him. The Lamongan local government assured Choirul's family they would fund his children's education. Netizens debated how the goalkeeper should be remembered? A road named after him perhaps? A statue? Rename the stadium? The Persib game would be a sell out as the Lamongan public would gather one last time to remember their favourite son and the Persib players visited the grieving family to offer support.

Perhaps the best memorial we can erect in Choirul's name is that there are improved medical facilities at each and every football match played under the auspices of the PSSI to ensure this kind of tragedy is never repeated. Indonesian football lost a very special person on that fateful Sunday. Please, let's learn something from it.

ACKNOWLEDGEMENTS

And thanks to...

My ever patient wife May and MyLittleGooner Dominic. When I first told my wife I wanted to go to Bangkok for a weekend to watch football, let's say she was a little suspicious! Now though, she has gotten used to the idea her husband is a football nut.

This book is dedicated to the memories of Choirul Huda and Darren Stewart

In no particular order thanks to; Fabio Oliveria, Fandi Ahmad, Simon McMenemy, Jacksen F Thiago, Dez Corkhill, Steve Darby, Andibachtiar Yusuf, Dale Farrington, Visakan Subramanian, Ko Poh Hui, Devinder Singh, Scott O'Donell, Budi Limanto, Nabil Husein and everyone at Borneo FC, Kurniawan Dwi Yulianto, Achsanul Qosasi, Richard Offiong, Oryza A. Wirawan, Dimas Maulana and the Bawah Skor Crew, Paul Freelend, Sven Beyrich, Dimas, Fajar Junaedi, Bojan Hodak, Zesh Rehman, Rawindra Ditya, Mustafic Fahrudin, Aleksander Duric, Andie Peci, Pak T Shirt, Andhika Suksmana, Robert Rene Alberts, Danang Ismartani, Ferry Indrasjarief, Kim Jeffrey Kurniawan, Nenad Bacina, Dave Roberts, Haresh Deol, Scott McIntyre, Baihakki Khaizan, Mijo Dadic, Sandy Pramuji, Taff Rahman, Dale Mulholland, Matias Ibo, Jules Denis Onana, R Sasikumar, Pangeran Siahaan, Koh Mui Tee, Willy Schanz, Don Parkes, Robbie Gaspar, Wimbo Satwiko, Bambang Pamungkas, Miljan Radovic, Timo Scheunemann, John Duerden plus all the supporters from Jakarta, Bandung, Surabaya, Malang, Lamongan, Yogyakarta, Sleman, Semerang, Balikpapan, and others who helped out anonymously and apologies to anyone I may have omitted from this list... as is always the case, any errors are my responsibility.

ABOUT ME

I don't remember a time when football wasn't part of my life. I just don't know how it all started. My earliest memories are of being given Arsenal books and programmes in the early 1970s and when we moved to Belgium I would listen to the BBC World Service commentary on a Saturday afternoon, mentally kicking every ball as I sat on the floor of our bungalow listening to the probably large radio. Every Monday I would read my father's English newspaper to catch up on the results. I would talk football non-stop at school to anyone who would listen and I was so chuffed when I got my first Arsenal shirt one Christmas I was told to shut up and stop boasting by a classmate; I had to ask my mother what boasting meant!

We returned to England in December 1973. I remember it well. The sea crossing from Ostend was awful as befits that time of year, and I wasn't feeling good when we checked into our bed and breakfast in Dover. In fact,

I felt so bad I threw up the sausage sandwich that was our evening meal. Something else happened on that day. It was a Tuesday and Arsenal were playing Wolverhampton Wanderers in the afternoon. An odd time to play football I'm sure you'll agree but this was the time of the National Emergency when Britain was beset by striking unions and an energy crisis. Sorry lads, no floodlights decreed the authorities.

I went to my first ever football match a few weeks later, travelling on a double-decker Southdown bus to Brighton to watch them play Plymouth Argyle with my father and perhaps my older brother. This was the Brighton of Brian Clough though I was unaware of that fact at the time. My abiding memory was of not being able to get a programme! It took more than 20 years to finally track down but I was soon learning. Football was about memories. For years after every December 4th I would remind my parents this was the anniversary of our return to England… and make sure you buy a bloody programme!

As we lived near Aldershot I started going to see some of their home games whenever I could nag my father or brother to take me and in April 1974, I finally made it to an Arsenal game when my old man took me to see us play West Ham United. April 6th in case you're wondering! It was a 0-0 draw and the highlights were on the Big Match the next day prompting my mother to suggest it was all a waste of time if I can stay home and watch it on TV. As if, Mum!

Those first few years saw me flitting between Aldershot and Arsenal games before heading up to Wembley to see England on school trips. Do kids still do that? The buzz of meeting your classmates after school, jumping on the bus and fighting the traffic along the busy roads of a London rush hour before getting inside Wembley, the only stadium we could ever see live on TV in those days but still a magic moment for us 12-year-olds.

Life was good except for school. I would save my pocket money and the money I earned from delivering newspapers and would go and see either Aldershot or Arsenal depending on how much I had. Then in 1979 I did something different. We had gone to Exeter on a family holiday and our guest house was close to Exeter City's home ground. And what do you know? They were playing Hereford United in a League Cup tie during our stay. My parents weren't ones for hitting the town when on holiday but they were only too pleased to be spared of my whining for a couple of hours while I went along to the game and I found myself a new hobby. Watching football for the sake of watching football. Arsenal? They were a passion, a duty. Aldershot? They were my local side. But watching Exeter gave me a freedom to watch the game with a detachment that had hitherto been missing and I loved it. So much so that later in the seasons I was to visit Leeds United, Hartlepool United, and Queens Park Rangers before going to see Portsmouth play Huddersfield Town in a crunch top of the table Division 4 clash on my mother's 50th birthday!

The next logical step was, of course, to see some football overseas and this happened in 1984, when I planned my return to Europe just over 10 years after I had left. Arsenal were playing a couple of friendlies in Germany and the Netherlands and, of course, they would be the pivot of my trip. The rest of the holiday was teaching myself to read local sports papers so I could find some games to see and I managed to catch a league game between FC Basel and SC Zug in Switzerland before catching a night train south to Italy to catch Sampdoria v Inter Milan in a pre-season friendly!

I repeated the exercise a year later when I caught more games in Germany and Switzerland before hitting a dilemma. I was working in an insurance company in Guildford but they were relocating to Gloucester and did I want to go with them. I was 22-years-old and while I was tempted by the idea of new surroundings it was a long way from London and besides the thought of committing myself to a mortgage at such a young age scared the bejesus out of me. Commitments? No thanks.

So I went to Australia via Thailand and Indonesia for 12 months. And what is the first thing you do when you arrive in Sydney? In my case it was to visit a newsagent and track down some local football magazines. With the Australian Soccer Weekly in my back pocket, the next destination on my first full day in town was to visit the tourist office just off Martin Place, I think it was, and ask them how to get to the Croatioan Sports Centre. They weren't much help. So I asked about St George Stadium. Once they found out I actually wanted the round ball game we soon figured out how to get there and my first game down under was sorted. St George v Marconi in the National Soccer League with a certain Frank Farina playing for the visitors.

St George became my adopted Australian side and I was to follow them quite a bit home and away over the years with games at APIA and Wollongong providing heaps of laughs. Of course, any game would do and I thought nothing of catching Sydney Olympic home games if their, and my, schedules allowed and over the next few years I must have seen about 50 games across Sydney, Brisbane, Wollongong, Melbourne, Canberra, and Adelaide with most of them being St George. I would go to NSL games, international, state league, Olympic qualifiers, Under 20s, I didn't care, football was football. Whether it was Coalstars defeating Olympic United 5-3 at Perry Park in the 1987 Ampol Cup Final or Australia hosting England in 1991, I wanted to be there if I could to savour the match day experience.

Obviously I didn't get to as many games as I would have liked. I was living in King's Cross most of the time and, well, there were plenty of other distractions going on for a young English lad out for a good time. In addition I never really had a full-time job and though I was well looked after by a couple of outfits I worked for there was never any job security and what with rent and beer tabs, football often came a lowly third when it came to pay day priorities meaning I missed out on some cracking days out including a St George game at Marconi and the 1991 Grand Final just weeks before I left the country for the last time.

After a short spell back in England I decided what I really needed to do was follow in the footsteps of one of the best TV shows of all time and head to Germany. Auf Wiedersehen Pet was about a bunch of Englishmen who went to Germany in search of labouring work and having heard from people in Australia how art was imitating real life I decided I needed to give it a go. Never mind I had never worked on a building site before I was precocious enough to know I could wing it somehow and anyway it was the season the Arsenal were developing the North Bank at Highbury and I convinced myself I didn't want to see the famous old stadium with a gaping wound behind one goal.

I flew to Cologne on the day we were playing Blackburn Rovers and made my way from the station to an Irish pub in the heart of the city while thousands of Borussia Dortmund fans were heading to the Mungersdorf Stadion for a Bundesliga game against 1FC Koln. I started on the beer that lunchtime and woke up the next morning on the floor of another Irish pub in a different part of town. 1FC Koln played Celtic a few days later in the UEFA Cup and some 4,000 Celts were descending on the city for a good time and the Irish pub was the centre of that good time. I pretty much stayed there the next three or four days donating my meagre resources to the bar manager's pension fund and local brewery Maximillian Kolsch before deciding what I really needed to do was get my act in to gear and get a job.

Eventually I got a job and found an apartment and life settled down to a routine of work and beer and football in that order. The problem was, of course, I wasn't skilled for a building site and I couldn't do the jobs like brick-laying or being an electrician. I ended up pulling cables under the tuteledge of two green-teethed Russian Germans who had returned to the land of their ancestors after the Berlin Wall had come down. This hard-drinking duo had hands like frying pans, fingers like sausages, and no time for sky-larking young English lads. We would enter the caravan that doubled as our work base in the morning nursing our hangovers only to get pissed all over again on the fumes of our emigre chums intake from the night before.

With looney drunks and work and looney drunks at the weekend I was getting nowhere slowly. In my naivety I really thought I could save some money working on the site but it wasn't working out, so when someone mentioned hotel work in the Alps I was all ears and boarded the next train south. I was gutted to leave Cologne, a wonderfully vibrant city with a great night life and, of course, loads of football in the neighbourhood. I saw a few games of course and visited a few games but unfortunately never made it to Schalke 04 or pre-Yellow Wall Borussia Dortmund.

Anyway, after a couple of false dawns in the Alps I got a job on top of Germany's highest mountain and stayed in a hotel on the slopes, commuting to work by cable car in the middle of the ski season. It could be minus 35 degrees at night but we'd leave the windows open leaving our beers wonderfully chilled. And this being Bavaria meant we were entitled to a couple of free beers a day while at work and indeed encouraged to do so. I must admit I had problem counting in those days! On my rare free Saturdays,

I would descend the mountain into the picture postcard town of Garmisch-Partenkirchen and catch a train to Munich to see FC Bayern Munchen before returning to spend the night in the Rose and Crown. I was still struggling with money, of course, and my Christmas meal in 1992 was McDonald's. I was loving Germany, still do, but man cannot live on beer alone. I had spurned a mortgage but seven years into my expat life I wasn't even treading water. I needed something new. So not for the first time, my old man bailed me out by paying for me to do an English teaching course back in England. I think he was just relieved I was thinking sensibly and trying to put my O levels to good news. I moved to Bangkok in 1994 with brand spanking new teaching certificate in hand but no job and no money. I found a cheap guest house with a fan doing its best to keep the humidity manageable and went out to network.

The 90s are a blur to me. Tony Blair and his Cool Britannia totally passed me by as I was a Blur Brit in Bangkok doing my best to juggle a drinking habit with a day job. I discovered places to stay where I could pay in arrears and smoky, dimly lit bars where I could postpone bar bills to the end of the month. Sensible people move on. Smart people get out. I was sucked in and for five or six years my life was a drunken haze. I worked Saturdays and Sundays, they were the busiest days of the week for the private language schools. I couldn't go to any local football had I wanted to. I'm not sure I really wanted to. Most of the time I worked in downtown Bangkok just a few minutes walk from the bars of the infamous Patpong Road. I convinced myself by living locally I was saving money on transport costs. The reality, of course, was bed and beer were on the never never; come pay day I would go round and pay off my debts and start all over again. Every day was hand to mouth, planning for tomorrow was a luxury.

England became further and further away. It was all I could do to afford the dreaded visa trip every few weeks by train to Malaysia. I wanted to live overseas to see the world but here I was in Bangkok and I was seeing nothing.

The world had become small, very small indeed, extending to a handful of streets and bars with the odd trip out of the country to renew my visa.

It took a trip to England in 2002. My first visit back in five years to shake me out of my torpor. I looked at England and didn't like what I saw but I liked what I saw in the mirror even less. Fifteen years into my expat life, and what had I to show for it beyond a few exotic passport stamps and enough drunken tales of stupidity to bore anyone to tears?

These were the days of an imperious Arsenal but I made no effort to catch a game during that trip. Indeed, I even sold off all my memorabilia, not just Arsenal but from Germany and Australia. I needed the cash. I needed to start anew. Australia had been fun. Germany had been fun. Thailand had been fun. But here I was, 38-years-old and still drifting like I had been in 1987.

Thanks to that new fangled invention called the internet I got a job. I decided I was done with Thailand. I loved the place, loved the food but couldn't go back to that lifestyle. I was offered a job in Jakarta, Indonesia, so packed my toothbrush and headed there. Another crowded Asian mega-city, Jakarta took some time to get used to. It's not as immediate as Bangkok, none of those saffron-clad monks or brightly coloured tuk-tuks but once it sucks you in it is difficult to leave. I flitted around from job to job for a while, had stints in Surabaya as well as Malaysia and Pakistan then was told by my girlfriend we were getting married, she demanded to know when. I was in a familiar position of having no money and no job, now I was in an unfamiliar position of planning for a wedding!

'Next year,' I mumbled. This was in January, 2005.

'When next year?' she demanded.

I don't know. I had no idea but I knew I had to say something. 'June.'

A year later and I started Jakarta Casual as much to keep me out of the pub as anything but also to reignite my love in football which had floundered over the previous 15 years.

Jakarta Casual and marriage gave a meaning to my life that had been missing the previous decade and a half.

I found a new job, where I stayed eight years, found somewhere decent to live for the first time since moving overseas and found every day was an adventure as I taught myself everything I could about Indonesian and later South East Asian football.

Want some more really good football books from Fair Play Publishing?

Encyclopedia of Socceroos - Every National Team Player
by Andrew Howe

The World Cup Chronicles - 31 Days that Rocked Brazil
By Jorge Knijnik

Coming Soon:

Encyclopedia of Matildas - Every National Team Player
by Andrew Howe and Greg Werner

Jarrod Black - Hospital Pass (published by Popcorn Press)

From our US partners, Powderhouse Press of Wyoming:

Whatever It Takes - the Inside Story of the FIFA Way
by Bonita Mersiades

Find them all at www.fairplaypublishing.com.au

www.ingramcontent.com/pod-product-compliance
Lightning Source LLC
Chambersburg PA
CBHW051939290426
44110CB00015B/2033